1931-2014
THE MANY LIVES OF APARTMENT-STUDIO LE CORBUSIER

This publication is the result of a research project entitled
"L'appartement-atelier de Le Corbusier, 24 NC.
Étude patrimoniale et recommandations. 1931-2014",
conducted by Franz Graf and Giulia Marino in 2013-2014,
and commissioned by the Fondation Le Corbusier.
The work was supported by the Getty Foundation's
grant program *Keeping It Modern,*
Architectural Conservation Grants.

Devised by
FRANZ GRAF AND GIULIA MARINO

Project Editor and Scientific Coordinator
GIULIA MARINO

Text and images
GIULIA MARINO

Graphic design
JENNIFER CESA, L-ARTICHAUT

Layout
GIULIA MARINO

English Translation
DAVID MASON

Printing
LEGO S.P.A

Cover Photos
PAUL ALMASY, 1938

The authors and editor thank the École Polytechnique Fédérale de Lausanne for its support and encouragement in publishing this volume.

Published with the support of the Institut d'architecture, ENAC-EPFL and the Fondation Le Corbusier.

EPFL PRESS is an imprint owned by the Presses polytechniques et universitaires romandes, a Swiss academic publishing company whose main purpose is to publish the teaching and research works of the École polytechnique fédérale de Lausanne (EPFL).

PPUR, EPFL – Rolex Learning Center, CM Station 10, CH-1015 Lausanne
info@epflpress.org

www.epflpress.org

© 2022, First edition in french (2017), EPFL Press
ISBN 978-2-88915-484-5

Printed in Italy
All rights reserved.
Reproduction, in whole or part, in any form or by any means, is prohibited except with the written permission of the publisher.

1931-2014
THE MANY LIVES OF APARTMENT-STUDIO LE CORBUSIER

FRANZ GRAF AND GIULIA MARINO

6 **PREFACE**
ANTOINE PICON

8 **FOREWORD**
FRANZ GRAF AND GIULIA MARINO

HISTORY

12 **1931-1934: CONSTRUCTION**
"They are asking us for a mansion block to lease in Boulogne.
If it happens I'll have a roof over my head"

76 **1934-1965: THE LE CORBUSIER PERIOD**
"It was risky for me to go and live in my own architecture.
But it's actually wonderful"

108 **1965-2014: LE CORBUSIER'S LEGACY**
Apartment-studio as 'historical monument'

PROJECT

130 **RECOMMENDATIONS FOR PREPARATORY INVESTIGATIONS**
Analysis and diagnostic assessment

166 **GUIDELINES FOR RESTORATION**
Conservation of a palimpsest

182 **Sources
and Bibliography**

184 **Acknowledgments
and Photograph credits**

ANTOINE PICON
Chairman of the Fondation Le Corbusier

PREFACE

One cannot restore a complex work of architecture without first trying to understand it. This rule of thumb applies particularly to the apartment-studio of Le Corbusier, which can be read as a "palimpsest" of interventions, as Franz Graf and Giulia Marino usefully reveal in the opening words of this study, the result of a project commissioned by the Fondation Le Corbusier. Over and above the initial complexity of the design there are the complications arising from the alterations made by the architect himself and later by those responsible for maintaining the apartment-studio after him. The facades and interior colours varied considerably from one period to another. There were five different versions of the pavilion leading to the roof terrace. The apartment-studio continues to give a remarkable impression of coherence and harmony, but there is no hiding the challenges posed by its restoration, beginning with the thorny issue of the preferred 'reference state' and whether one architectural phase has greater merit than another: the original 1934 design, the "brutalist" inspired manifestation from 1945-50, the status quo at the time of the architect's death in 1965, not to mention the many other intermediate variants and works undertaken after Le Corbusier died.

The research objective for Franz Graf and Giulia Marino of the École Polytechnique Fédérale de Lausanne was to analyse in detail an apparent trajectory, a succession of moments, each with its own identity, rather than an object fixed in space and time. The apartment-studio appears in this sense to be the perfect antidote to the temptation to search for an ideal state of architecture that alone will have meaning, an approach associated with Viollet-le-Duc that is sadly all too widespread even today.

As the reader will readily observe, this study has fulfilled its objectives. Through the palimpsest or skein of alterations and transformations analysed with great precision and finesse by the authors, we can more generally consider the fate of one of Le Corbusier's most astonishing creations prior to restoration. This restoration, we must remind ourselves, is all the more sensitive in that the Immeuble de la Porte Molitor is one of the 19 works of Le Corbusier inscribed on UNESCO World Heritage List.

It's never easy for an architect to build a house for him or herself. To that we add the rather banal facts of the apartment-studio and the residential building on which it sits. The apartment-studio does in fact appear to do exactly that, perched atop the Immeuble de la Porte Molitor, like a "townhouse on the rooftop" to use the authors' neat expression. Conceived as an architectural experiment, it also reflects Le Corbusier's very distinctive concept of the couple, a concept summed up by Charlotte Perriand: "Monsieur and Madame in different spaces, separate but communicating, with a meeting point in the centre." The separation is reflected in the apartment-studio in a way not common with modern architecture. Not least among its paradoxes, this very unusual work yet in some way presents a universal value, as the assessors for the World Heritage Committee have recognised. This value is fully apparent throughout the study Franz Graf and Giulia Marino have produced.

Like the works themselves, conservation-restoration is a trajectory. In the case of the apartment-studio, it is a trajectory that begins in advance, through reading this study and following through on some of its recommendations. The Fondation Le Corbusier is delighted that this document will be accessible to a broad readership. Restoring is not just understanding. It is also about comparing points of view, managing the conversation. The publication of this study is part of that approach.

FRANZ GRAF AND GIULIA MARINO

FOREWORD

In this one iconic object, "24 NC"—as Le Corbusier's Paris apartment-studio in rue Nungesser-et-Coli is known—many of the grand themes of conservation of twentieth-century heritage are concentrated. Far removed from the cold, bare image conveyed in the *Œuvre Complète*, the architect's home appears as a real "palimpsest", the product of a complex stratification, layer upon layer of alterations made by Le Corbusier, like a construction project in perpetual evolution. In the approach to artificial lighting, in the colour design, we see constant change over the years. In the envelopes—the dining room's glass wall was rebuilt three times during Le Corbusier's own lifetime: the first iteration was in pressed steel, the second in timber in accordance with the Modulor scheme, the third in anodised aluminium. It is part of a transfiguration during which the apartment-studio gradually sheds its character as a "purist" interior and acquires a more "brutalist" feel.

So which "version" should we be aiming for in conserving this emblematic, and now heritage-listed building? Should we recover the 1934 original, although it had already been considerably reworked by 1939? Should we try and restore it as it was during Le Corbusier's final years in residence, the version of 1965, the year of his death, including the many "poetically-charged" personal objects that also dwelled within the home? Or should we conserve it as it is, with the remains of the renovations—some more successful than others—carried out after he died?

In this study, commissioned by the Fondation Le Corbusier as part of its research phase prior to commencing conservation works at "24 NC", we tried to respond to these crucial ethical questions. The guidelines arising from the heritage study described in this book, which are intrinsically linked to the broad and successful work done to identify the museographical options, have been developed to orient the process of conserving and enhancing the values of this apartment-studio. The vast amount of documentation in the FLC archives, and fruitful engagement with the Fondation's then Research former Director, Michel Richard, and architect, Bénédicte Gandini, provided much of the substance for our research. We thank them sincerely for their support.

The heritage study contained in this book demonstrates our commitment to the field of conservation of modern and contemporary built heritage both in terms of methods and results. By dividing this study into two parts we effectively bring together our primary disciplinary themes—"history" and "project"—as a rigorous process, whereby through an exhaustive material understanding of the built object one arrives at the most appropriate solutions to adopt during its conservation.

The first edition of this book appeared in 2017, published by Presses Polytechniques et Universitaires Romandes. This English edition responds to the demand for dissemination of the study to the global research community. The content of the French-language edition, presenting the research team's conservation guidelines for the apartment-studio, is scrupulously reproduced. Since the volume was first published, Le Corbusier's apartment-studio has undergone a complete restoration, jointly steered by François Chatillon Architects and the Fondation Le Corbusier. The apartment-studio reopened to the public in 2018.

HISTORY

Le Corbusier wrote as follows to Yvonne, his wife, in 1949, with reference to the apartment-studio at 24, Rue Nungesser-et-Coli: "My life often transports me to glories I am indifferent to and in the midst of boorishness that infuriates me and injures me. When I return to 24 NC, I return to my home, our home". This was a place where he was both builder and co-owner, designer of his dwelling and inhabitant of his architecture; the architect's theories coexisted side by side with everyday life "at home": here, like a manifesto, the intimate dimension of "24 NC" was laid bare.

The apartment-studio is indeed a striking biographical testimony, but it is much more than this. 24 NC was a crucial moment in Le Corbusier's output, an "adventure" in both his life and his work, an opportunity for near-constant, and fertile, experimentation. Le Corbusier adored this "gorgeous" and "wonderful" home—his own home, his own idea. During the heroic days of the early changes he threw himself at it, with equal excitement masterminding the apartment's "new direction" after 1945. Moreover, rueing some of the construction defects, he tried to rectify them using all manner of architectural devices, each of which clearly reveals the fundamental precepts of his poetry. As if the major changes during his lifetime did not already have a huge impact, they were followed by a series of lesser interventions after his death, at the time when the work was itself coming to be recognised as a heritage place and a work of iconic significance.

This study seeks to retrace the "many lives" of the apartment-studio at Rue Nungesser-et-Coli, a revelatory story, lush, tumultuous at times, a tale as rich in meaning as it is complex to piece together. The three chapters that form the first part of the study correspond to the grand phases of development at 24 NC: its initial conception—inseparable from that of the Immeuble Molitor where "the conditions of the *ville radieuse* are assembled"; its

endless evolution during the architect's lifetime; and its recent history, as an heritage-listed building (Monument historique), to be restored and restored again.

Le Corbusier himself gives us much of the insight to make sense of this rare object. There is correspondance with close friends, his personal archives, part of a very full body of documentary records kept by the Foundation. There is also the spectacular collection of artwork and objects. The architect himself shows us the underlying reasons behind certain spatial, plastic and technical decisions. Some of the century's great photographers—René Burri, Lucien Hervé, Robert Doisneau, Felix H. Man , Yousuf Karsh and many others—passed through its doors, producing portraits of the architect in the spaces where he lived, and, even more so, in his painting studio, a bedrock of Corbusian mythology. From these images, together with the archives and accounts of his former colleagues—from André Wogenscky to Robert Rebutato—and the impressions of historians, fascinated by the architect's inner sanctum once the apartment-studio was opened to the public in 1965, we can piece together so much about its evolution.

This documentary resource—largely untapped and of a significance equal to the building itself— enables us to reconstruct the "many lives of 24 NC", to differentiate the "strata" that have built up over time. It is a painstaking enterprise of organisation and interpretation of the source material, intersecting with minute observation, *in situ* analysis down to the finest details, of the surviving physical traces, components, materials, textures. The material history of the apartment-studio thereby reveals qualities intrinsic to the object. It becomes part of the process by which the importance of the built object can be defined, the heritage significance of 24 NC going well beyond "inexpressible space", acquiring new meaning through its material evolution over the long term as a veritable "palimpsest".

1931-1934: CONSTRUCTION

"THEY ARE ASKING US FOR A MANSION BLOCK TO LEASE IN BOULOGNE. IF IT HAPPENS I'LL HAVE A ROOF OVER MY HEAD"

The apartment-studio at 24, Rue Nungesser-et-Coli occupies the top two floors of the Immeuble Molitor, designed and built between 1931 and 1934 by Pierre Jeanneret and Le Corbusier for the real estate agency Société Immobilière Paris-Parc des Princes. Le Corbusier, who "seems to have been interested in the site much earlier"[1], recognised the potential of this parcel of land on the edge of Paris, a product of the 1924 development plan for the city fortifications in a subdivision allocated for private development. With its "ideal situation in which, by happy coincidence, the characteristic conditions of the *ville radieuse* are assembled"[2], the Molitor rapidly acquired "prototypical" or "experimental" status. As plainly stated in *L'Œuvre complète*: "The architects were keenly interested in the construction of this building because the block met the conditions of the *ville radieuse* and building it might substantiate the ideas Le Corbusier was —and is—developing in this regard"[3].

1 Marie-Jeanne Dumont, *L'immeuble de la porte Molitor. L'appartement de Le Corbusier*, in *Le Corbusier Plans en DVD*, Paris, Editions Echelle-1, 2005, no page numbers.
2 Jean P. Sabatou, 'Immeuble à Paris. MM. Le Corbusier et Pierre Jeanneret architectes', in *L'Architecture d'aujourd'hui*, n° 7, 1934, pp. 41-46: 41.
3 *Immeuble locatif à la Porte Molitor, Paris, 1933*, in *Le Corbusier et Pierre Jeanneret. Œuvre complète. 1929-1934*, published by Willy Boesiger, vol. 2, Birkhäuser, Basel-Boston-Berlin, 7th edition, 1967, [Les éditions d'architecture, Zurich, 1935], pp. 144-153: 144.
4 *Ibidem*.
5 Jean P. Sabatou, 'Immeuble à Paris. MM. Le Corbusier et Pierre Jeanneret architectes, *op. cit.*, pp. 41-46: 41.
6 Stade Jean Bouin, J. Lambert, G. Saacké, P. A. Bailly, P. Remaury, architects, 1925.
7 Piscine Molitor, L. Pollet architect, 1929.
8 Le Corbusier, handwritten note, Vézelay, 14 April 1941, Fondation Le Corbusier Archives, Paris (FLC, H2-7-210).
9 Letter from Le Corbusier to his mother and Yvonne, early April 1931, in Rémi Baudoui, Arnaud Dercelles (ed.), *Le Corbusier. Correspondance*, vol. II, Lettres à la famille 1926-1946, Infolio, Gollion, 2013, p. 327.

Fulfilling the conditions for the *ville radieuse*: "Immeuble Molitor is the witness"

"The building is partly situated on the sports fields covering the former fortifications, 200 meters across, and partly on the gardens of Boulogne, where the hills of Saint-Cloud and Suresnes loom in the background. At the Fourth International Congress of Modern Architecture, in Athens, Le Corbusier affirmed the elements of urbanism: sky, trees, steel and cement, in that order and hierarchy. He claimed that the inhabitants of a city classified accordingly would find enjoyment of what he called 'the essential joys'. This building is the witness"[4]. The situation was therefore seen as exceptional: "east-west facing for sunlight, [...] greenery and vast horizon, [...] sports fields below the houses"[5], concentrating the paradigms of urbanistic theory developed in the 1920s. "Straddling the Commune of Boulogne-sur-Seine (now Boulogne-Billancourt, Rue de la Tourelle, to the west), and the City of Paris (Rue Nungesser-et-Coli, to the east), opposite the Jean Bouin Stadium[6] and close to the Piscine Molitor[7]. Le Corbusier felt this was the ideal site for an ambitious undertaking, with the added value—or so at least was the intention—of becoming a true "demonstration piece".

From apartment living...

The Commune of Boulogne was in the throes of transformation under the auspices of socialist mayor André Morizet. After the Lipchitz-Miestchaninoff residential block (1923-25) and the villas for the musician Paul Ternisien (1923-27) and American journalist William Cook (1926-27), the area offered particularly favourable conditions; in the mind of Le Corbusier, it was the venue for a new, emblematic work. "In this period of overload"[8] as he wrote to his mother—with work "coming from all sides: it's a crescendo. We're getting closer to creating some real buildings!"[9]—the architect saw in the realisation of his "immeuble-villas" townhouse concept the culmination of a phase of exceptional productivity following his theoretical projects of the 1920s, signposted by major architectural works from Cité de Refuge (1929-33) to the Pavillon Suisse (1930-33).

His Geneva housing projects served as a model. In July 1931, in a letter to the metal construction entrepreneur Edmond Wanner, with whom he devised the (unbuilt) Projet Wanner (1928) and the Immeuble Clarté (1930-32), Le Corbusier imagined in fact the Immeuble Molitor as the first stage of a much grander work: "Dear Monsieur, we are going to build an apartment building at the location marked red on the plan. They are asking us to combine it with a second (in yellow). This is one of the best pieces of land in Paris. The first part is already agreed in principle. Would you like to build it using some of your processes?

1

10 Letter from Le Corbusier to Edmond Wanner, Geneva, 21 July 1931 (FLC, H2-2-513).
11 Handwritten note, unsigned [LC], 28 June 1933 (FLC, H2-1-182). See also: FLC, H2-7-141.

See the large cross section drawing: we are going for high quality luxury apartments on levels 8, 9, 10, 11, with gardens (I have clients for some already). Below we will have batches of urban villas (without suspended gardens) with large corridors. [...] If you would like to come in on it, it will have a whole new appeal once B is combined with A, you can execute the larger part of them. The demonstration will be in an admirable part of the district. My letter is very disjointed. Just tell me if you are interested at all (by return mail). I'll give you all the details then"[10].

Le Corbusier's key role in the search for funds for the real estate business no doubt explains the contact with Wanner, the developer behind the Immeuble Clarté; in addition the section drawings the architect attached to his letter to the Geneva industrialist—double aspect apartments nested into duplexes and served by internal thoroughfares—clearly show the ambitiousness of the project. After the vicissitudes of Projet Wanner (the Immeuble Clarté remains the only finished element) the Molitor development would be the model for an "apartment living" concept while also being ideally sited in the fabric of the *ville radieuse*.

...to investment home

Le Corbusier's grand aims would nevertheless (yet again!) be considerably downsized by the Paris-Parc des Princes agency, who ended up being the buyer for just one parcel, 24, Rue Nungesser-et-Coli—the 'B' mentioned in the letter to Wanner. The architect, of course, would later work up several new schemes for the island block—number 18 in 1933, for instance, with the architect Jean Fidler, a corner building in Nevada bricks that was never built[11]. For the Molitor development, though, Le Corbusier was forced to concentrate on one lot of approximately 300 m² (12 m wide × 26 m deep), sandwiched between

Previous Page Portrait of Le Corbusier on the guest-room balcony, shortly after the war, by Robert Doisneau.
1 "Essential joys": birds' eye view of the area with infrastructure and residences on Rue Nungesser-et-Coli (sketch FLC, H2-7-141).
2 Concept for the Porte Molitor residences; note in connection with letters to Edmond Wanner, July 1931 (FLC, L2-10-93).
3 Study for residential block between Nungesser-et-Coli and Rue de la Tourelle: transverse section of *maisonnettes* with separate villas on the upper floors (plan FLC 13606).

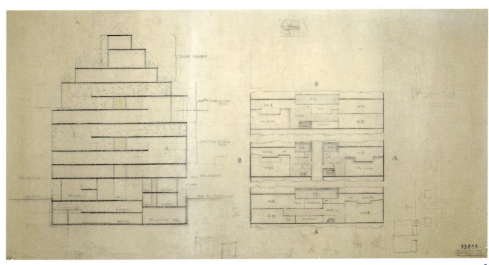

15   1931-1934: CONSTRUCTION

12 Published in *L'Architecture d'aujourd'hui* in June 1933, the Henri Bodet building illustrates the Chapter "modernité conventionnelle" by Eric Lapierre (ed.), *Identification d'une ville, architecture de Paris*, exhibition catalogue (Paris, 2002), Éditions du Pavillon de l'Arsenal-Picard, Paris, 2002, pp. 114-115, 123.

13 "Calculation of share costs for the apartments have been made on the assumption that our building will be 7 ½ storeys high, and with stone facades on the two sides"; Letter from Marc Kouznetzoff and Guy Noble, Société immobilière de Paris-Parc des Princes to Le Corbusier, 5 August 1931 (FLC, H2-1-517).

two buildings under construction in Rue Nungesser-et-Coli: no. 26, (by Léon Schneider) and no. 22 (by Henri Bodet), completed in 1933.

The first proposals illustrated in the fine bird's-eye view show an independent volume, largely glazed, taking up the greater part of the block. Thereafter the context evolved slightly. Not only did Le Corbusier have to work between two regular apartment buildings displaying a certain "conventional modernity"[12] typical of the 1930s, but he also seems to have been subject to instructions from the agency as to the distribution of apartments intended to be offered for subscription or rental. In effect, the typical floor plan conserved in the architect's archives (probably used for costing of the building "in freestone"[13] initially proposed) shows already the layout of apartments around the courtyard. This undated plate, the drawing style of which seems far removed from that of the Atelier LC, indicates the disposition very precisely. Dwellings in duplex form as he had suggested to Wanner have been abandoned, along with the distribution principle used for the early sketches, with a central hall created between two stairwells face to face. The shaft for vertical services, clustered together in the small yard, now supplies two (levels 1, 2, 3 and 6) or three (levels 4 and 5) single aspect apartments. A landing leads to the walkways giving access to the apartments, whilst a separate passage gives access to the kitchens via the small courtyard. The position and orientation of the stairwell and lifts is quite laboriously defined—in the countless variations there is no direct opening onto the main courtyard—and the principle of distribution follows strictly the one imposed by the agency, at least for the service rooms, grouped in the building's central core. The living and bedrooms meanwhile have a glazed wall facing the street and freely arranged vertical supports to retain maximum flexibility for the apartments, to be fitted out "in accordance with the lessee's wishes".

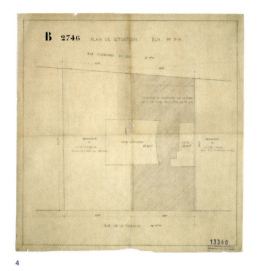

4

5 6

4 Location plan of the lot (FLC, 13340).
5 Context: apartment block by Jean Fidler and Alexandre Poliakoff, at 28, Rue Nungesser-et-Coli, 1934.
6 Henri Bodet architect, apartment block at 22, Rue Nungesser-et-Coli, 1933.
7 Le Corbusier and Pierre Jeanneret, architects, apartment block at 24, Rue Nungesser-et-Coli; exterior view published in *Encyclopédie Morancé*, 1937.
8 Immeuble Molitor after completion, captured by the photo agency Gamma Rapho.

THE MANY LIVES OF STUDIO-APARTMENT LE CORBUSIER   16

17   1931-1934: CONSTRUCTION

14 Negotiations for the "sale of party wall rights" were creating controversy from February to April 1932. Léon Schneider and Henri Bodet claimed that "possession of the separating wall" should be regulated appropriately. There was also lively exchange between the architects on the method of construction, which risked damage to the existing structure. The idea of getting rid of linings to party walls seems to have come from Établissements Quillery who tendered for the structural component; letters from Établissements Quillery to Le Corbusier and Pierre Jeanneret, 19 December 1931 (FLC, H2-2-46).
15 Edmond Wanner had sent to Pierre Jeanneret "a brief schematic study for structural frame with the encumbrance of piers" on 21 September 1931 (FLC, H2-4-257).

"Independent frame, open plan, free facade". From manifesto to sales pitch

In spring 1931, the general layout was defined (or perhaps imposed by the agency). Adjustments followed aimed at tightening up the structural frame. From the sheaf of plans dated March 1931 to the version submitted for the construction permit in October of that year, there was significant development.

It was assumed the building would literally tie in to the adjoining walls, so the matter of party wall negotiation had never come up, which led the architects into a terse exchange with Léon Schneider and Henri Bodet who accused them of simply "forgetting" to negotiate an agreement![14] The arrangement of central supports, meanwhile, had to be studied more seriously and various iterations drawn up. In an early version of the plan—somewhat rigid—it is a double row of uprights at specific intervals. But it became a more "organic" arrangement, although the infill walls conform to a regular grid timidly sketched on the plan. Such nuances aside, the solution for the floor plan, with double-flight staircase perpendicular to the facade, serving the walkways to the apartments and more or less curved in profile, seems to have been retained. In September 1931, Edmond Wanner, once again solicited by Le Corbusier and Pierre Jeanneret, overlaid a regular metal structure of twin piers—U-sections stabilised by a welded plate—traversed by longitudinal beams, similar to the steel frame for the Immeuble Clarté (apart from cantilevers to the facade, which are absent in Geneva)[15].

In the plan's genesis, once the main stair disappears (separate circulations for masters and servants is still an issue) and the service stair retreats, turning away from the walkways, the structural evolution appears at last to come to a halt. Compared to interim versions of the Immeuble Molitor, this solution has a certain radical quality, and dates probably from September 1931 (it corresponds, except in a few minor details, to the built version). Integration of the structure into the walls has been rejected. Apart from the corner of the main courtyard, the posts are now effectively disconnected from the partitions; points of support, enhanced by a circular section, have become part and parcel of the '*plan libre*', or open-plan concept.

9 Leasehold units between two courtyards: 'typical plan' probably sent to the architects by the real estate agency Paris-Parc des Princes (FLC, 13881).
10-14 Genesis of the plan, variations devised in 1931 (in numerical order: FLC, 13586, 13478, 13471, 13319B, 13612).

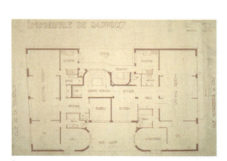
9

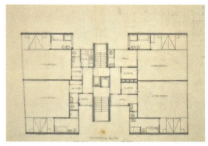
10

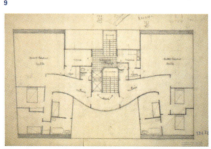
11

12

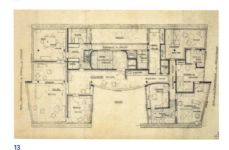
13

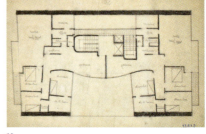
14

16 Jean P. Sabatou, 'Immeuble à Paris. MM. Le Corbusier et Pierre Jeanneret architectes, *op. cit.*, pp. 41-46: 45. In reality, as shown in the execution drawings by the firm of Cornet, it was seven piers, two of them being integrated into the envelopes of the walkways, at the ends.
17 Werner Oechslin, *5 points d'une architecture nouvelle*, in Jacques Lucan (ed.), *Le Corbusier une encyclopédie*, Centre Georges Pompidou, Paris, 1987, pp. 92-94: 92.

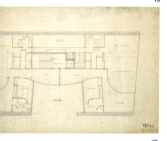
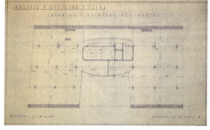
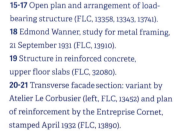

15
16
17
18

15-17 Open plan and arrangement of load-bearing structure (FLC, 13358, 13343, 13741).
18 Edmond Wanner, study for metal framing, 21 September 1931 (FLC, 13910).
19 Structure in reinforced concrete, upper floor slabs (FLC, 32080).
20-21 Transverse facade section: variant by Atelier Le Corbusier (left, FLC, 13452) and plan of reinforcement by the Entreprise Cornet, stamped April 1932 (FLC, 13890).

In addition, the "structural grid" is more open and the transverse supports increase at the facade. The three rows of metal piers suggested by Wanner (too expensive?), reduced to two as sketched by Le Corbusier's office, are reduced again to a single line of posts, placed in the centre of the lot and paired only at the central core (10 supports in total).

The reinforced concrete structure, consisting, in the architects' words, "in depth, of five posts linked by a frame carrying the floors tied into the party walls"[16], means to be seen. A pier is placed in the very centre of the building: slightly offset from the longitudinal line of the structure, it detaches from the curved facade open onto the main courtyard. Equally the two uprights in the living room are independent of the walls, including in the levels where there are two apartments on the facade, strategically joined in bayonet fashion. The vertical frame in other words is quite plainly independent, whereas exposed beams on the underside are firmly proscribed in the tender schedules so as not to impinge on the reading of the '*plan libre*'.

"With this radical choice Le Corbusier was re-invoking one of the 'Five Points of a New Architecture' that gathered together experiences and reflections going back to the Maisons Domino and constructions of the early 1920s"[17]. The intent was demonstrative and the description he gave it, completely doing away with rectangular piles built into the envelopes of the central core, is further proof. However, the "plan libre" concept, which became stronger as the detail design progressed through minute control of internal perspectives (most of them drawn by Charlotte Perriand), was also a response to utilitarian considerations brought into the equation by the client. Already tried out in

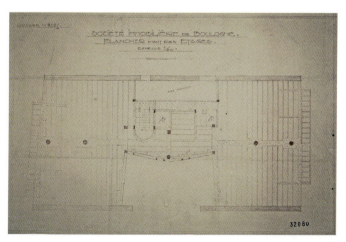
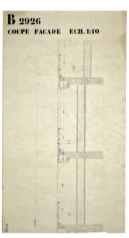
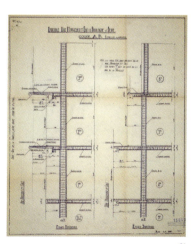

19
20
21

1931-1934: CONSTRUCTION

18 P. Morton Shand, 'A First Instalment of the Immediate Future', in *The Architectural Review*, vol. 77, 1935, pp. 73-76: 73.
19 Jean P. Sabatou, 'Immeuble à Paris. MM. Le Corbusier et Pierre Jeanneret architectes, *op. cit.*, pp. 41-46: 41.
20 *Ibidem*, p. 44.
21 *Ibid*.

22 Henri Bresler, *L'immeuble parisien: la théorie mise à l'épreuve*, in *Le Corbusier et Paris. Rencontres de la Fondation Le Corbusier*, Fondation Le Corbusier, March 2001, pp. 113-125: 118.
23 Jacques Sbriglio, *Immeuble 24 N.C. et appartement Le Corbusier*, Birkhäuser, Basel, 1996, p. 21.

several late-1920s projects (such as the Maisons La Roche-Jeanneret in 1923-25), this architectural solution was also an effective sales strategy. *The Architectural Review*, in 1935, noted that the only "solid blocks" were those of the wet areas[18]; the resultant, very open spatial form signified flexibility, allowing a multitude of different combinations to be presented to potential subscribers. "The idea of 'new', apartments, different from the classic layout"[19], an aspect "no less attractive to the financier who saw it as reducing potential competition with neighbouring offers in a district already very well endowed with modern apartment blocks and the draw of 'new' development"[20], was pursued with real purpose.

On the ground, however, the 'new' open layout had a more mixed reception. The architects noted as much, somewhat bitterly, in their review of the process: "Once the main frame and standard internal walls—kitchens and bathrooms—were complete the clients came to see the apartments. Their reactions are worth recording. The architects had designed several variants which they showed the visitor, or potential lessee, so that each might choose a layout to his taste. Nobody wanted to discuss it, all declaring that they knew nothing, even pointing out that what they were visiting there was not an 'apartment' at all. Wearily one had to resolve to add partitions to some of the rooms in several apartments, with several variants. But to sign the lease, not one of the tenants would accept to retain the existing layout, and they all had the partition walls demolished to go back to some of the plans that had been offered to them before. Even better, once the first tenant accepted the principle of an open plan apartment, where life is very much simplified, the others, on seeing that apartment, wanted that layout too. Diverse, facile, peremptory or paradoxical—one can take one's pick. But the first conclusion is indisputable, namely how sad it is to observe that the educated classes are incapable of understanding a plan"[21].

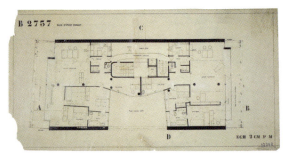
22

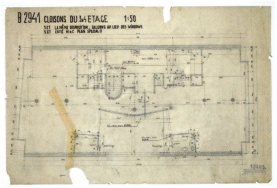
23

Despite an internal layout that remains, ultimately, "relatively traditional"[22], the open plan used at the Immeuble Molitor is one of the essential characteristics of the Paris-Boulogne building. The treatment of the ground floor, where "projecting and receding volumes are linked together around a load centre marking the axis of the facade's symmetry"[23] is in this sense emblematic. The general ground floor layout is modified further in this direction by a central entry point (from Rue Nungesser-et-Coli) between two volumes serving as the concierge's flat (on the left) and office (on the right), with servants bedrooms and basement garage access behind.

The plan dated August 1931 is an essential milestone in the early history of the entry level: the somewhat rigid scheme for the spatial arrangement softens thanks to a curved entry hall animated by a number of very effective architectural devices. Profiting from the projecting line of the rear of the stairwell and the presence of

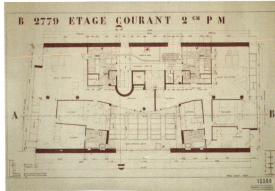
24

24 Quote from Maison Désagnat for painting and decorating, addressed to Arsène Cornet, 30 May 1933 (FLC, H2-4-447).
25 André Wogenscky, *Les mains de Le Corbusier*, Éditions du Moniteur, Paris, 2006, p. 62.

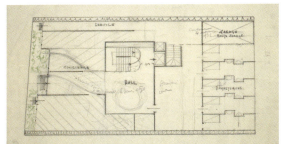

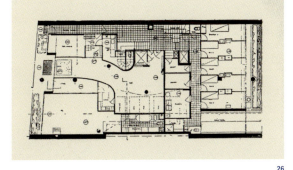

unrestrained columns—which would have stood out from the pale wall surface by virtue of their darker colour—the entry is spatially sober yet sophisticated, chiming perfectly with the treatment of the external envelopes.

It is without doubt one of the key spaces of the Immeuble Molitor. Additionally, there is a particularly pronounced contrast between the bright, double-height hall, which is top-lit, and the relatively low-ceilinged vestibule. In the early stages it was intended to line the latter with "verre-mural Désagnat", a "flexible layer of glass glued to a special fabric" in light blue and green[24]. The stair, turned towards the splendid reinforced concrete walkways, demurs from the rules of "functionalism"—a word Le Corbusier rejected in strong terms. Where Brinkmann and van der Vlugt, in their Bergpolder housing block in Rotterdam (1930-35), were careful to provide vertical circulations built to allow the passage of a casket (the surest of all modules!), "Le Corbusier tells us of the unease he felt when the first death occurred in one of the apartments. They could not get the coffin down the stairs. They had to lift it up on a hoist and lower it down into the service courtyard. The family was scandalised and Le Corbusier much distressed. Both he and Pierre Jeanneret had no idea!"[25]

22 Standard floor, undated variant (FLC, 13348).
23 3rd and 4th floor partitions (FLC, 13405A).
24 Standard floor, 12 October 1931 (FLC, 13369).
25 Base plan showing development of the ground floors (FLC, 13646).
26 Final version of the ground floor plan, published in *Encyclopédie Morancé*.
27-28 Ground floor on Rue Nungesser-et-Coli: a disengaged, form-finished concrete column marks the entry. On the left: plan and elevation at 1:20 scale (FLC, 13462); on the right, an image from the 1930s.

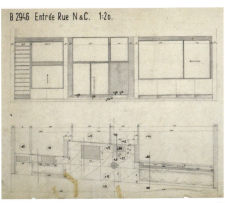

21 1931-1934: CONSTRUCTION

26 Plan FLC, 13477.
27 Jean P. Sabatou, 'Immeuble à Paris. MM. Le Corbusier et Pierre Jeanneret architectes', *op. cit.*, pp. 41-46: 46.
28 Éric Lapierre (ed.), *op. cit.*, p. 100.
29 'Les briques Nevada', in *Glaces et verres*, 3rd année, n° 14, February 1930, pp. 16-21: 16.

"The glass wall, a superior architectural resource… alone can make an apartment"

Within the open-plan idea so critical to the Immeuble Molitor, glazed facades—"surfaces of light" as they are referred to in the sketches[26]—were always seen as an opportunity. "The glass wall, a superior architectural resource, which alone can 'make an apartment'"[27], was a constant theme throughout the project's evolution. Equally, rolled steel joinery and glazed infill—transparent or translucent—were literally presented as paradigmatic of modernity in architecture, an aesthetic derived from industrial materials.

29

The facades evolved somewhat independently of the plan for the apartments. This was driven more by regulations than by the room layout—by definition a 'free' arrangement—or by the structural posts which, set back slightly towards the interior, have no mechanical connection to the envelopes. The early versions have a fairly sleek, regular grid, enlivened only by alternating glazing at higher level (through the double-height spaces of the duplexes) with smaller spandrel sections in the manner of the Immeuble Clarté. When the idea of double-storey apartments was abandoned, the facade design retained its slightly ethereal appearance, ordered by the variable width of the modules, sometimes in symmetrical sequence—a narrower vertical strip aligned with the disengaged post of the ground floor or the smaller modules at the ends—and sometimes more freely aligned. These options, sketched in countless variations, evolved towards a facade of increasing "thickness", enriched by projecting bow-windows or balconies. This solution "would mark a key moment in the evolution of the modern facade in general, and the Parisian facade in particular"[28].

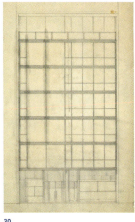
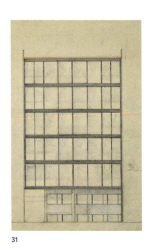

30   31   32   33   34

THE MANY LIVES OF STUDIO-APARTMENT LE CORBUSIER   22

38 39 40

It was during this phase of work within the thickness of the envelopes that a key element in the reading of the Immeuble Molitor—and, as we shall see, the apartment-studio—appeared. Translucent Nevada glass bricks[29] had been developed by Saint-Gobain in 1928. Pierre Chareau had made a feature of them in his Maison de Verre (1928-31) and Le Corbusier and Pierre Jeanneret had used them on several occasions in their recent projects. They would become a leitmotif at the Molitor. Le Corbusier's spell working for Perret left its mark: among his "poetically charged personal objects", can be found one of the glass brick's most famous antecedents, a "brique Falconnier"…

The architects made use of the contrast between a tight grid-pattern of Nevada brick and smooth glazed modules, the alternating of clear and 'cathedral' glass effects rendering greater richness to the envelopes. It goes beyond merely inserting slabs of "translucent concrete" into the spaces between volumes like in the stairwell of the Pavillon Suisse, or, as Le Corbusier proposed in 1933 in early sketches for the Immeuble Grand Boulogne, of replacing masonry walling with fully translucent facades where the traditional logic of penetrations for openings remained an issue. In this intermediate version of the scheme, from October 1931 and approved by the client, Le Corbusier utilises projecting translucent volumes as compositional elements in their own right. Arranged in a

 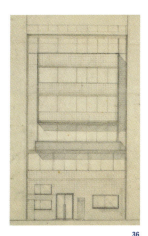 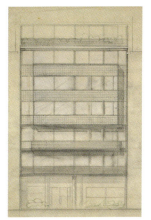

29 Immeuble Molitor glass walling; sliding doors and 6th floor balcony (FLC, L2-10-13).
30-37 Sequence of development for two facade variants, 5 or 6 floors plus ground floor level. The envelopes increase in thickness, enriched with bow-windows (in numerical order: FLC, 13538, 13474, 13473, 13709, 13539, 13556, 13703, 13548).
38-40 Variants with bow-windows in Nevada brick set out in a quincunx (FLC, 13541, 13656, 13545).

35 36 37

23   1931-1934: CONSTRUCTION

30 Préfecture du Département de la Seine, Direction du Plan de Paris, Report by inspecting architect on construction permit request n° 3817 1931, 30 October 1931 (Ville de Paris archives V012, n° 409).
31 Letter from Marc Kouznetzoff and Guy Noble, Société Immobilière de Paris-Parc des Princes, to the Mayor of Boulogne-sur-Seine, 16 October 1931, requesting construction permit (Boulogne-Billancourt municipal archives, dossier 208-W-251).
32 Marie-Jeanne Dumont, *op. cit.*
33 'Immeuble de rapport à Boulogne-sur-Seine', in *L'Architecture d'aujourd'hui*, n° 5, 1934, pp. 38-39: 39.
34 Vladimir Jovanovic architect, 1990-1991.

quincunx in alignment with the balconies, they produce, through juxtaposition with the sleek, reflective surfaces of the other windows, a highly subtle play of volumetric effects. The graphic, and indeed the plastic effect of the envelopes, also shown in the plans submitted for the construction permit but not realised, is highly successful. To illustrate the point Le Corbusier later published a wonderful axonometric drawing in *L'Œuvre complète*, in an act of rebellion against overly rigid municipal regulations that had obliged him to renounce a solution he felt to be formally more interesting.

The proposal submitted simultaneously to the Municipal authorities of Boulogne and Paris (October 1931), was in fact amended on account of the bow-windows, or more precisely "closed constructions corbelled from the wall with a cumulative area greater than one third of the facade"[30]. This did not satisfy an ordnance of 13 August 1902 still in force across the Paris district. As for the Boulogne side, the derogation seeking approval to "occupy the window space at a height of 4 metres from pavement level rather than the regulation 4.40 metres, and on Rue de la Tourelle, 4 metres in place of the regulation 4.80 metres"[31] was also refused. In the architects' archives there are versions of the facade modified to respect the legal prescriptions—notably by removal of the lower level of bow-windows. But the option was abandoned in favour of a simplified envelope design.

Following initial joint rejection by Boulogne and Paris—we will come back to this question of the non-respect of roof-profile and setback limits—Le Corbusier turned to a more fitting, "quasi haussmannian"[32] solution (as Marie-Jeanne Dumont puts it). Perfect symmetry was thus re-established as detailed design progressed. The radical nature of the early proposals was toned down; the dynamism afforded by the chequerboard of translucent and transparent surfaces worked into the depth of the envelope gave way. In its place appeared a more restrained facade, inserted without rupturing the Nungesser-Tourelle block as a "veritable 'sampler' of architects' work"[33] (in the phrase used to describe the block by *L'Architecture d'aujourd'hui* in relation to Number 28 of the same street, by Jean Fidler and Alexandre Poliakoff).

In contrast to what was specified in the construction contract, the two facades are identical except in the ground floor and superstructures. On both Nungesser-et-Coli and Tourelle, they are made up effectively of a continuous glazed wall through the full height of the building, up to the sixth floor, which is set back. The background plane is made up either of glass brick spandrels beneath sliding transparent windows, or a fully glazed surface along the first floor level (cathedral glass spandrels and clear glass sliding units, the option of perforated metal in the lower section, as shown in published plans, having been hastily discarded). The facade surface is enlivened by projecting elements. Note that the floor of the first balcony was at one time also in glass brick, but probably disappeared when the facade was renovated in 1991[34]. Whether in the second floor balcony with its painted (in a deep shade of grey), perforated sheet metal parapets, or the large bow-window extending from the third to the fifth floor, echoing the rhythm of the side portions by means of

41

alternating translucent and transparent openings, the scansion is perfectly balanced. The openings to the cheeks on either side at first floor level were removed just after the Second World War, during one of the Immeuble Molitor's several facelifts.

This "flat transparent facade, designed to be a realisation of the "essential joys" of modern life", was well received, with a good deal of focus on the architectural language of the "facade de verre", which was compared to emblematic works by Van Tijen, Barbiano di Belgiojoso or Neutra. The sixth floor, its setback forming a balcony strongly defined by its tubular steel railing, is handled almost literally as the "crowning glory" of the building in the plans appended to the construction permit in February 1932, and also in the perspective views for publication.

As for the detail of these two uppermost storeys, which would contain the apartment-studio of Le Corbusier himself, more patience would be needed... In February 1932, before the eventual granting of construction permits in November 1932 (Paris) and January 1933 (Boulogne)—work on site commenced using plans drawn up in summer 1931 and approved by the Société Immobilière on 16 October of the same year, although they finished at floor seven. The superstructure was completed in November 1932. But Le Corbusier's office at that time was still working on the details for these two upper levels...

41-43 Facade development on Rue Nungesser-et-Coli: bow-windows in chequerboard layout were abandoned after being rejected by the authorities. Thereafter a more suitable arrangement was adopted. Nevada brick remained a key material component (FLC, 13351, 13383, 13384A).
44 Advert, Société immobilière de Paris-Parc des Princes; the "situation unique" was the key selling point for leasehold units (FLC, H2-2-488).

42

43

44

45

46

45 Shot of the west facade on Rue de la Tourelle by Alfred Roth during construction of Immeuble Molitor.
46 The same facade photographed by Lucien Hervé in the 1950s (FLC, L2-10-8).
47-48 Open plan and glass walls: interior perspective views by Atelier Le Corbusier (attributed to Charlotte Perriand) showing layout of the apartments (FLC, 13849).
49-51 Apartments on the 1st (above) and 6th (below) floors captured by Albin Salaün for the publication of Immeuble Molitor in Vol. 2 of *Œuvre complète*, 1929-1934.

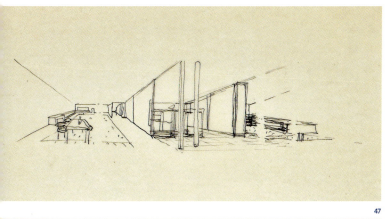

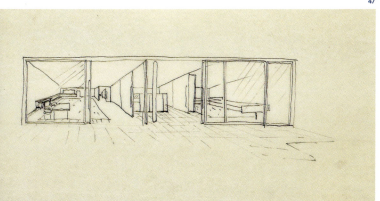

27   1931-1934: CONSTRUCTION

35 Letter from Le Corbusier to his mother, 10 March 1931, in *Le Corbusier. Correspondance*, vol. II, op. cit., p. 320.
36 Handwritten note, Le Corbusier, Vézelay, 14 April 1941 (FLC, H2-7-210).
37 Letter from Le Corbusier to Marc Kouznetzoff and Guy Noble, Société Immobilière de Paris-Parc des Princes, 7 August 1931 (FLC, H2-2-519T).
38 Letter from Le Corbusier to the Société Immobilière de Paris-Parc des Princes, 22 August 1931 (FLC, H2-6-19).
39 Ibidem.
40 Lease contract "Madame Jeanneret, dite LC", registered 18 July 1932 (FLC, H2-1-427). See also: État locatif, 7 January 1935 (FLC, H2-1- 426).
41 Antoine Le Bas, 'Maison, immeuble et compagnie: le singulier pluriel du logement de banlieue. 1840-1940', in *InSitu*, n° 6, 2005, pp. 2-31: 16.
42 Jean P. Sabatou, 'Immeuble à Paris. MM. Le Corbusier et Pierre Jeanneret architectes', op. cit., pp. 41-46: 44.
43 Jean P. Sabatou, 'Un appartement dans le gabarit', in *L'Architecture d'aujourd'hui*, September 1934, pp. 47-49: 49.
44 Letter from Le Corbusier to the Mayor of Boulogne-sur-Seine, September 1932 (FLC, H2-2-446).
45 Letter from Le Corbusier to la Société Immobilière de Paris-Parc des Princes, 22 August 1931 (FLC, H2-6-19).

"Townhouse" on the rooftop: the apartment-studio of Le Corbusier

"They are asking us for a mansion block to lease in Boulogne. If it happens I'll have a roof over my head"[35], Le Corbusier wrote to his mother in March 1931. During the awarding of the commission to the architects in Spring 1931 it was agreed informally that Le Corbusier would build the top two floors of the Immeuble Molitor, where his own home was to be, at his own expense. "The verbal agreement" with Paris-Parc des Princes, then headed by Marc Koutznetzoff, President of the Board—"a White Russian"[36]—and his associate Guy Noble, the Chief Executive, was only made official in August 1931: the architect purchased, in the name of his wife Yvonne Gallis "the floor area permitted to be enclosed under roofline and setback limits; to this floor area was added the cost of communal services, such as elevator, stairs and ground floor entrance lobby"[37]. Le Corbusier thus became the buyer of a seventh-floor unit at the price of 110,000 francs, part of it payable during construction and the rest in the form of rent, plus a Société Immobilière de Paris-Parc des Princes share subscription[38]. He made his intentions plain: "It is understood that in pursuing a desire for certain experiments that I wish to have control over while living in this apartment myself, I undertake this part of the construction (the built part of my apartment only) fully at my own expense"[39].

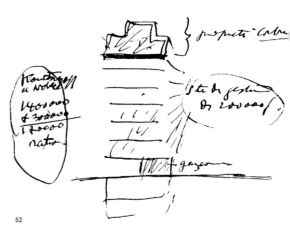

Perched on the top of the Immeuble Molitor, the apartment-studio, therefore, was always a relatively independent entity. Le Corbusier nominally set about occupying himself with "how to make the construction he was financing a continuation, in terms of materials, character and style of the building constructed at the agency's expense"[40]. But the apartment-studio displays a certain autonomy in terms of expression of the envelopes and internal spatial as well as material identity. This strategy, which Le Corbusier had already tried out in the apartment he designed for Charles Beistegui, a new structure grafted onto the roof of an existing building in the Champs-Élysées (1929), was certainly not new. Indeed, the practice of "upending the vertical hierarchy of apartment blocks"[41] in which the established division of functions was inverted, dated from the early twentieth century and was relatively widespread: bedrooms for domestic staff below street level, cars in the basement, and "townhouse" or master residence on the roof level (abetted by the introduction of elevators of course). Conditioned by profoundly limiting codes governing the roof profile—a "line that can't be crossed"[42] but which Le Corbusier nonetheless tried to "step over or push through, to get the highest yield on the area"[43]—the architect made the most of this option at the Immeuble Molitor. Through the design of his own "appartement-atelier", he wanted to explore very subjective ideas about 'habitation' in such an environment, while furthering the "research he had long pursued into the improvement of dwellings"[44].

The relative independence of the "penthouse" in relation to the general scheme of the Immeuble Molitor is also in evidence in the phasing of the two stages of work. The architect stipulated at the outset that the apartment "would be the result of further studies"[45]. The constraint of height limits imposed by the commune of Boulogne provided further justification. Le Corbusier felt the restrictions made it "extremely

52 Le Corbusier sketch with note "propriété Corbu" for the top apartment on the 7th and 8th floors of Immeuble Molitor (FLC, H2-7-218).
53-54 Roofline, variant for building of ten floors! (FLC, 13494, 13608).

46 *Ibidem*.
47 *Ibid*.
48 From the site timetable established by the Entreprise Cornet for February 1932 to October 1932, six stages of primary construction were anticipated (FLC, 13900).
49 As a "propriété alignée", right-of-way codes applied to the facade plane on Rue Nungesser-et-Coli only; the sixth floor was set back from the facade plane, the height limit for the roofline principally corresponding to the upper horizontal of the fifth floor, at 18.29 m, calculated "from a straight line parallel and at 7.5 m from the axis of the road" at 15 m. Préfecture de la Seine, Ville de Paris, Bureau des alignements, request lodged 20 October 1931 (FLC, H2-2-434); permission de grande voirie n° 2416 conditionally issued, 28 November 1931 (Boulogne-Billancourt municipal archives, dossier 208-W-251).
50 Projet Le Corbusier, Demande de tolérance, handwritten note, undated (FLC, H2-2-428).

difficult to lay out a normal apartment higher than the sixth floor", which is why he "hoped to obtain certain exemptions in order to make the studio and its dependencies useful (for him)"[46].

The apartment-studio—which Le Corbusier had earlier said he "wanted to build light"[47]—was therefore deferred slightly, as shown by the construction permits for which additional documentation to this effect was submitted[48]. The first set of plans lodged simultaneously at Boulogne and Paris in October 1931 sketched the profile of the two upper levels in elevation and section in quite cursory fashion. Measured floor plans were not included in the dossier at all (note that the dossier lodged at the Mairie de Paris concerned a 6-storey block)[49]. The addendum material submitted in August 1932—a plan of the eighth floor and a schematic section through the two upper floors—seems to have been drafted with the aim of obtaining the necessary exemptions in relation to the height limit in Boulogne. It is a far cry from what would eventuate when the roof levels were carved up, their garden areas and accessible parts considerably reduced. Negotiations with Boulogne went on into 1934, the "tolerances" demanded by Le Corbusier having been partly accepted by the Commune, but the latter would not budge either on the natural ventilation of the WC in the studio, or on the useable floor areas in the laundry (which, contrary to the architect's formal agreement, would end up being the maid's room).

Between the early sketches probably dating from autumn 1931 and the first full set of plans of July-August 1932, explorations to determine the outline of the building predominated. Volumetrically, a great number of variants for "treatment of the 7th and 8th stories as a townhouse"[50] were explored. The axonometric, section and elevation show the addition of four more levels above the roof of the Immeuble Molitor (10 floors in all!) by means of a stepped form, a solution Henri Sauvage had successfully achieved at Rue Vavin (1912-13). They depict in graphical form the effort to explore the upper limits permissible under the 1902 regulations drawn up by the City of Paris Principal Architect, Louis Bonnier. Besides these, retained in the architect's archives (a provocation?), we have a series of studies made to systematically re-configure the building profile to meet the height and setback restrictions. This series is immensely important and fundamental to grasping the genesis and logic of the project. The vault, in its multifarious forms, would become its essential theme.

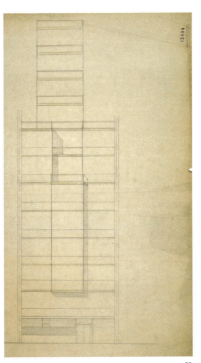
53

54

29 1931-1934: CONSTRUCTION

51 Charlotte Perriand, *Une vie de création*, Éditions Odile Jacob, Paris, 1998, pp. 55-56.
52 André Wogenscky, *op. cit.*, p. 31.
53 Maurice Diricq, photos Willy Rizzo, 'Génial et amer, admiré et injurié, architecte du bonheur, visionnaire de la cité future: Le Corbusier', in *Paris-Match*, n° 253, 30 January 1954, pp. 26-33 et 54: 33.
54 Le Corbusier, radio interview with Robert Mallet, 1951, in *Le Corbusier, entretiens avec Georges Charensol (1962) et Robert Mallet (1951)*, La Librairie sonore, Frémeaux & associés, 1987.

Up against it: roof line and envelopes

Aside from a few adjustments, notably an office as an extension to the studio, and finalising the bedroom (apparently a long and difficult process), the design of the general layout of the apartment seems to have happened quickly, resulting, as Charlotte Perriand noted, from a very clear idea about its use: "Corbu had a couple theory: Monsieur and Madame in different spaces, separate but communicating, with a meeting point in the centre. That's what gives the plan of the dwelling. On the right, as you enter, on the east side is the "atelier du Maître"—strictly off limits. There he would write or paint, master of his own domain. On the left, or west side [...] Madame's area, including the kitchen, dining area and Monsieur and Madame's bedroom (a flaw in the couple theory). Where the two spaces intersected you have the reception area for friends, stair access to go up to the other bedroom, and the roof terrace where little birds would come and tend the wild lawn dotted with violets, daisies, dandelions blown in on the wind"[51]. As a designer at the Rue de Sèvres studio, Perriand had worked on the interior design and built-in furniture, especially in summer of 1932. Her description is key to understanding the apartment. The portrait has an element of caricature (her account of Monsieur and Madame's relations however is confirmed by André Wogenscky—"you have no right to come in here!"[52], Le Corbusier apparently cried before "bluntly despatching" Yvonne from the atelier...), but Perriand clearly renders the sharp separation established within the dwelling, the spaces reserved for Le Corbusier who divided his working day into artistic work at the studio in Nungesser-et-Coli in the morning, and architectural practice in the afternoon at the Rue de Sèvres design office.

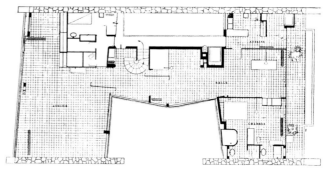

55

The establishment of the floor plan of "Le Corbusier's attic"[53]—as *Paris Match* wryly named it—was therefore fairly immediate. On the Boulogne side there are the kitchen, dining room and bedroom. On the Stade Jean Bouin side of the building is the painting studio, separated from the western part, at main courtyard level, by the living room and entry hall with fine spiral stair leading to the guest bedroom and roof terrace. Though a well lit space, the architect-painter was well aware that the double orientation east-west of the studio was not optimal for the painter-architect. As he confided to Robert Mallet in a radio interview in 1951: "That is the paradox. It's a painting studio and when I got the seventh floor, where I am, to put a roof on it and create my painting studio there, where I work in the mornings, I noticed that I had no north, because of the layout of the place. I was going to have

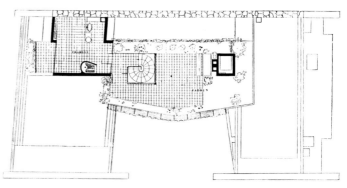

56

55-56 Le Corbusier's apartment-studio: plans of 7th and 8th floors, intended for publication.
57 Portrait of Le Corbusier in his studio by artist-photographer Michel Sima in the 1950s (FLC, L4-9-40).

a studio with no light from above because the city regulations wouldn't allow me to have any. But I do have light from the floor up to 2.2 metres, the full length and width of the studio, twelve metres by seven. I thought that was going to be an awful light for painting, changing all the time, going east to west... But I think in the end that is excellent for painting because in painting you are up against a thousand different effects of light and that's a good thing, as opposed to the north key of Mr Caravaggio"[54]. Notwithstanding his enthusiasm, it was a major problem and Le Corbusier was forever trying to get around it as long as he lived there with alteration after alteration to the glazed wall infill. At the same time, though, we can certainly see this real limitation as one point of departure for the project.

55 Immeuble de Rapport à Paris, in *Le Corbusier et Pierre Jeanneret, Encyclopédie de l'architecture. Constructions modernes*, 7th series, Éditions Albert Morancé, Paris, 1937, n.p.
56 *Le Corbusier et Pierre Jeanneret. Œuvre complète. 1934-1938*, published by Max Bill, vol. 3, Birkhäuser, Basel-Boston-Berlin, 19th edition, 2015, [Les éditions d'architecture, Zurich, 1946], p. 131.
57 With a plan and main section, this drawing would have been penned on board the steamer Massilia, en route to Buenos-Aires, in *Le Corbusier et Pierre Jeanneret, Encyclopédie de l'architecture. Constructions modernes*, op. cit.
58 See: Jacques Sbriglio, *Immeuble 24 N.C. et appartement Le Corbusier*, op. cit. et Rémi Papillault, *L'éblouissement et le contre-jour dans l'atelier du 24 N.C.*, in *Le Corbusier et l'œuvre plastique*, XII Rencontres de la Fondation Le Corbusier, Fondation Le Corbusier-Editions de la Villette, Paris, 2005, pp. 203-215.

Solidity vs translucency: the vaulted roof

Published on the last page of the *Encyclopédie Morancé* entry featuring the Immeuble de Boulogne in 1937[55], and later in volume III of the *Œuvre complète*[56] is a series of sketches dated 26 September 1929, with a handwritten note with the words "Ma maison"[57]. This is recognised by historians as a benchmark for the apartment-studio[58]: a relatively closed volume, lit from above asymmetrically by shafts of light obtained by the arrangement of conical vaults inspired by an architecture that weaves together mediterranean architectural references with elements of a more industrial character. The first sketches for the apartment-studio follow this principle on what seems to be, on the Paris side, a very jagged plan. The arrangement would have posed some issues of integration with the language of the smooth, continuous glass wall of the floors below, and was hastily simplified using a series of variants in which the number of truncated cone or barrel vaults was gradually reduced. The single barrel vault was the solution eventually adopted, either, at first, springing from the low floor of the seventh storey, or "supported" on a vertical wall plumb with the facades of the Immeuble Molitor.

From these ideas we see Le Corbusier is not yet pursuing the Catalan vault. Since his Barcelona visit in 1929 Le Corbusier seems to have been fascinated by this concept, and he would go on to use it on several projects: the weekend house at La-Celle-Saint-Cloud in 1935; the Maisons Jaoul of 1951-55; a series of unbuilt schemes including the Roq et Rob at Cap Martin (1949-55) and La Sainte-Beaume at Trouinade (1948). This low-set, thin vault was really an improved version of the famous flat roof which, since he first theorised it in the *Cinq points d'une architecture nouvelle*, had suffered from ongoing waterproofing issues. At the apartment-studio, the vault evolved. Juxtaposed with parallelepipeds against the party walls, the vaulted space shows a degree of structural independence (notably in the version supported directly on the floor). Moreover it demonstrates genuine formal experimentation, curved surfaces exploiting the contrast between their solid nature and the transparency of the walls at each end.

One working version provided for a saw-tooth roof configuration, facing north, much as Le Corbusier had done for the Atelier Ozenfant in Paris (1922). Another had glazing built into the thickness of the vault and following the path of curvature to create a continuous slit lengthwise through the space. In both cases the characteristic feature of the studio, at this juncture at least, is a neat separation between east (or street) and west (courtyard) facades, to maximise light from above, well suited to the morning labour of the sculptor. Although in one of the variants the curved wall is partly translucent, most often the facade facing towards Stade Jean Bouin has a solid wall, meant to protect the painter from strong, direct light from the east.

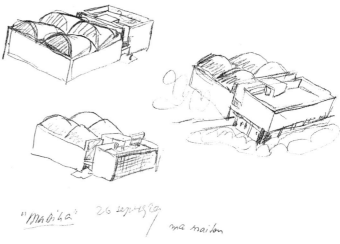

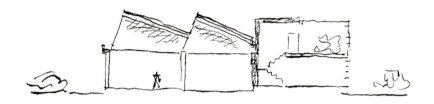

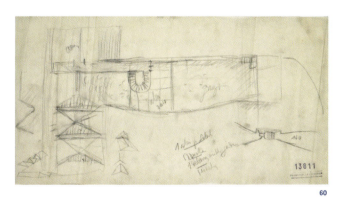

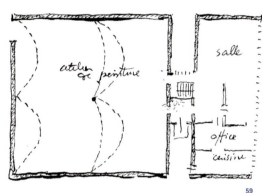

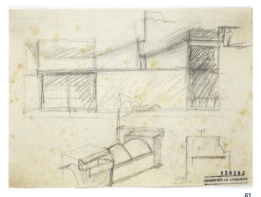

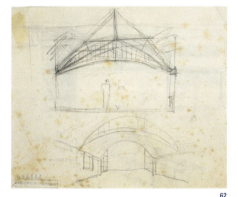

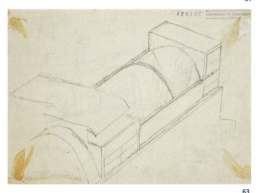

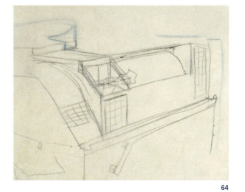

58 Le Corbusier, sketch "Ma maison" dated 29 September 1929, "done on board the "Massilia" en route to Buenos-Aires" and published in *Encyclopédie Morancé* in 1937.
59 Plan and section illustrating the section *Ma maison* in Vol. 3 of *Œuvre complète*, 1934-1938.
60-64 Volumetric variants for the top-floor apartment-studio, which bring in daylight from above, the east facades being somewhat opaque (in numerical order: FLC, 13811, 13836E, 13836E-R, 13836C-R, 13726).

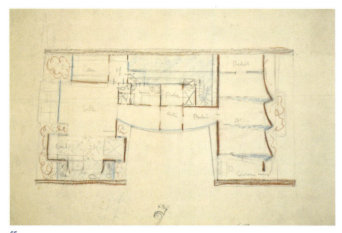

65

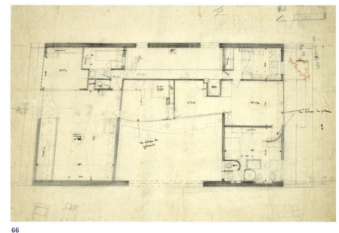

66

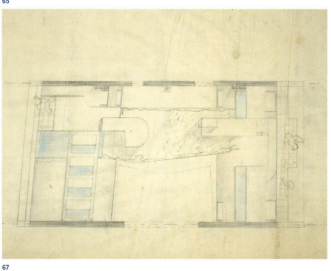

67

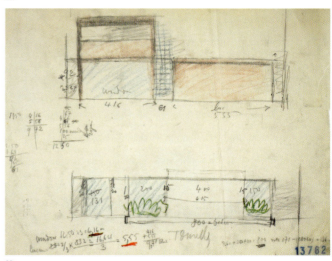

68

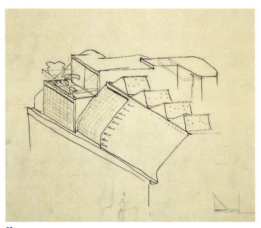

69

70

65 One of the first variants for the apartment-studio characterised by a very lively studio facade. Note the orientation of the layout is reversed (FLC, 13690).
66-67 Concept: top-lit studio space and mainly opaque facades (FLC, 13784, 13540).
68 and **72** East facade, concepts with an opaque wall in the centre (FLC, 13762, 13412).
69-70 Concept: top-lit studio; translucent glass wall following the roofline on the east facade (FLC, 13602, 13549).
71 Studio glazing in 2014.

THE MANY LIVES OF STUDIO-APARTMENT LE CORBUSIER   34

59 The dossier of plans dated 7 July 1932 would be the basis for lodgement of the construction permit application, and is marked "completed 7 August 1932". Several plans are stamped "Ch. P." i.e. Charlotte Perriand who probably used them as a basis to work off for the interior design.

The profile of the zone where the office and guest room upstairs were to be follows the outline of the statutory roofline regulations quite faithfully—tracing its curvature almost to the millimetre—and as such seems to have gelled quite rapidly. In contrast, the main vaulted space would be reworked over and over again, developing in terms of proportions, relationships between the volumes, and materials, the latter being precisely described in the sheaf of plans dated 7 July 1932.

This variant would be radically revised again in the plans submitted for an amendment to the construction permit, bearing the date 7 August 1932[59]. At this point there was a complete U-turn: the space now opens to the exterior and uses the glass wall concept that would be used for the two facades. The barrel vault, slightly lowered, now springs from two transverse beams supported on one or two intermediate uprights, decoupling the large facade openings completely. Le Corbusier gave no explanation for this apparently sudden change of direction. It probably came about due to the difficulty of incorporating overhead light within the shape of the permissible roof profile and it would have major repercussions on his conception of the transparent envelopes and the structural frame. Largely neglected by the huge body of literature on the apartment-studio, it is indispensable for understanding the both interior spatial layout and some of the architectural details which, as a consequence, take on a whole new meaning.

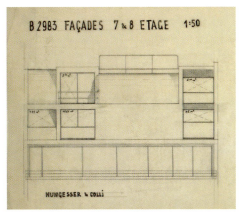

71

72

35   1931-1934: CONSTRUCTION

60 Jean P. Sabatou, 'Un appartement dans le gabarit', *op. cit.*, p. 52.
61 *Ibidem*.
62 Kenneth Frampton, 'The League of Nations, the Centrosoyus and the Palace of the Soviets, 1926-31', in *Architectural Design*, vol. 55, n⁰ˢ 7-8, 1985, pp. 41-54: 41.

"To avoid the eyesore of glass walls with breaks in them we did it as barrel vaults". Load bearing structure

Le Corbusier always stressed that his apartment "cut through the anomalies in the regulations"⁶⁰ and he protested at the anachronism of laws governing alignments. In 1934 he offered to Jean Sabatou, in *L'Architecture d'aujourd'hui*, a reading of the building that married legal prescriptions with structural imperatives and architectural challenges. The ideas are revealing: "Roofline and setback regulations should come from the truss. If the roof of a construction can be flat, the principle is idiotic; applying the regulation leads to considerable expense and misuse of the most favourable plot of land. This is happening right across the city. Its consequences are grave. In reinforced concrete constructions the regulations prevent one from having posts going from the foot of the facade right to the top. One is bound by economic necessity to occupy the space inside the setback of the roof, the four upper floors being stepped in successively. In the apartment in question, there were no longer any facade posts or interior posts, these being proscribed by having to use the meagre spaces left free under the regulations. One then has to have force arms and big beams formed between one party wall and another. The height of the facade tolerated by the regulation was just 2.05 metres. To avoid the eyesore of glass walls with breaks in them we did it as barrel vaults"⁶¹.

The vault thus became an essential part of the project. It was an effective way of staying inside the permissible alignment while tangentially occupying the roof setback of the Immeuble Molitor. The device also lent itself to the open spatiality the architect wanted. For both the studio and the "enfilade" of kitchen-dining room-bedroom on the western side, the absence of a central line of uprights helps to define the architectural form of the apartment-studio. As for the building of it, as we have mentioned, it coincided with a structural gambit that, though no technical achievement per se, brings into play a number of subtleties. Inseparable from the spatial conception but also from the definition of the envelopes, it deserves to be analysed in detail.

Statics of the vaults

Le Corbusier, seconded by Pierre Jeanneret on whom, as Kenneth Frampton remarks, he was "technically dependent"⁶² for the constructional and material definition of his projects, was interested above all to minimise load points. As such, it was not a question of free columns being made apparent as they were in the

73-74 7th floor: study for roofline and ceiling heights (FLC, 13746, 13749).
75 Cross section of Immeuble Molitor through the main courtyard (FLC, 13366).
76 1:50 scale section of the apartment-studio, following the calculation of the maximum permitted roofline (FLC, 13398).

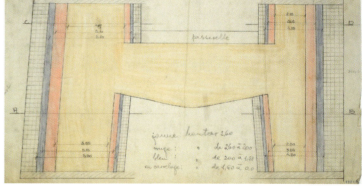
73

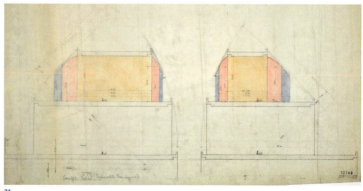
74

63 Note from the Société Immobilière de Paris-Parc des Princes, undated typescript, (FLC, H2-2-556).
64 Jacques Sbriglio, *Immeuble 24 N.C. et Appartement Le Corbusier*, op. cit., p. 52.
65 Correspondence, in the form of expert assessments and counter-assessments, with Société Immobilière, the owner of 26, Rue Nungesser-et-Coli in 1937 is quite illuminating on this matter (FLC, H2-2-550 and later).
66 Note from the Société Immobilière de Paris-Parc des Princes, undated typescript, (FLC, H2-2-556).
67 Counter-assessment, Parc des Princes' Affair, Response to the adversary's technical note, undated typescript, (FLC, H2-2-568). Martinaud, the bank engineer who endorsed the loan to Société Immobilière, also demanded some detail of the statics of "the 12 m beam on the Rue de la Tourelle side". Letter from Pierre Jeanneret to Arsène Cornet, 22 October 1932 (FLC, H2-3-47).

upper floors of the Immeuble Molitor, but rather of eliminating any intrusion of load bearing structure into the spaces. Thus, in the studio, the principle of lateral beams bonded into party walls is maintained, indeed 'declared' by electing to make these walls visible—brick on the south, rubble-stone on the north. Chased into the party walls on a "continuous joist cast into the slab"[63], the two beams also rest on intermediate supports so as to reduce their span: two points on the courtyard side (one superimposed on the structure of the Immeuble Molitor, where the staircase is, the other placed around one third of the way along the facade to the main courtyard) and one point one the street side. The latter, an asymmetrical "curious V-shaped post"[64] detectable from the street, behind the translucent glass bay, stands on the post of the floor below. Cleft into a type of crutch, which improves it structurally, it also helps support the span of the beam. The static schema of the vault is completed by a tie bonded into the tympanum on the office side and an inverted impost on the side with the rubble-faced wall, separating the principal vaulted space from the slightly higher, flat-ceilinged area abutting the party wall.

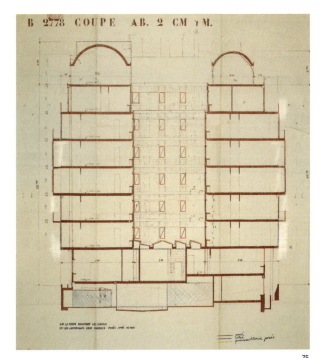

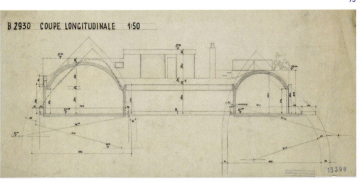

The living and bedroom spaces on the west are structurally even more radical: from the two sides (courtyard/facade) the continuous beam is anchored only into the party walls, with a huge 12 metres span and no intermediate support. A series of metal ties (one built into the tympanum adjoining the bedroom, another exposed in the kitchen and another in the bedroom, serving as a curtain rail!), ensure good transverse behaviour of the barrel vault. This structural solution, which the neighbours deemed "foolhardy and dangerous"[65], a device "(liable to) compromise the stability of the walls"[66], "grossly overloading the party wall and causing the materials in some places to work at dangerous rates"[67], is literally exposed by Le Corbusier. Clearly visible in the west facade, at the ends of the balcony, the longitudinal beam effectively floats free, independent of the envelopes that follow the curvature of the vault, either as a glass brick wall as in the kitchen, as the niche reserved for the 'frigidaire', or as glazing over the bathtub, providing ventilation to the bathroom. On the courtyard or east side, the beam traverses and continues outside, in front of the curved glass-brick wall behind the washbasin. Not only does the exposed load-bearing structure play a part in shaping the design of the envelopes, but the absence of intermediate posts is also expressed internally: an alcove is formed off-centre where the

68 Sketch, undated
(FLC, H2-4-16).

transition from living room to dining room occurs; this recess, 'in place of' the corner post of the main courtyard, underlines the absence (the support here is stepped back from the beam, and simply stabilises the central core). Whether it's a gimmick to showcase the 'technical challenge' of the long-span reinforced concrete beam, or a sign of the designer's sharp sense of irony in 'replacing' structure with void, this detail, heightened by a bright colour treatment, is especially significant. In the same vein one might also mention the projecting half column in the entrance lobby, significantly out of line with the cross beam and brought forward of the white wall behind by means of a light grey finish.

Composition of the vaults

As for the composition of the vaults, they have very clearly moved away from the Freyssinet-type thin shells that the early sketches suggested. A sketch preserved among the architect's correspondence indicates a structure of metal beams[68], with vaulted canopies made of reinforced concrete arches and hollow block infill, like the floors of the Immeuble Molitor. The only contractor's construction plan of the high floor of the seventh storey gives no exact directions on the vault's exact nature or thickness. A handwritten note in the margin where the floors are described—ribbed in concrete with the voids filled with hollow brick and Héraclite-type cement-bonded fibre insulation—supports the hypothesis that it was generally consistent with the concrete structural/hollow brick infill system used for the rest of the building.

The apartment-studio in 2014:
77 West vault, dining room: an alcove in the place of the intermediate support emphasising continuity of the longitudinal beams.
78 West side of Rue de la Tourelle, dining room; west vault supported on a continuous beam between two party walls.
79 Main courtyard, east facade of the bedroom: the horizontal beam clearly expressed in front of the curved glass brickwork.
81 Facade on Rue de la Tourelle, west balcony: longitudinal beam extending to the outside, over the Nevada brick alcove of the kitchen.
80 and **82** Entrance, central core: the connecting beams discernible as 'ghosting' on the mixed concrete and hollow-block ceiling structure.

77

78

Central core

The two relatively independent vault structures are joined at the central core of the building, between the two courtyards, by a transverse beam at the facade facing the main courtyard, as well as a series of joists in the thickness of the floor that play a role in 'stabilising' the ensemble. One beam, at an offset angle, connects the post at the left of the staircase (bearing the cross beam of the workshop) and the square-section pier of

the facade, which sits on the structure of the Immeuble Molitor. These spaces, corresponding to the living room and lobby, therefore have much lower ceilings, lit only by a strip of daylight in the upper part of the facade facing the main courtyard as well as by the light coming in from the stairwell, i.e. the glazed opening giving access to the roof terrace. The rooms at the centre of the building were relatively dark and were originally treated with fairly bright finishes. They contrast with the very bright feel of the living spaces on the Boulogne side and the studio on the Paris side, both of which had the advantage of large glazed window bays.

69 Willy Boesiger, Hans Girsberger, *Le Corbusier 1910-1965*, Les éditions d'architecture, Zurich, 1986, pp. 64-66: 64.
70 Letter from Le Corbusier to his mother, 17 January 1935, in *Le Corbusier. Correspondance*, vol. II, *op. cit.*, p. 493.
71 Maurice Diricq, photos Willy Rizzo, "At his home the lift machinery is in the living room", in 'Génial et amer, admiré et injurié, architecte du bonheur, visionnaire de la cité future: Le Corbusier', *op. cit.*, p. 33.
72 'Fermetures', in *L'Architecture d'aujourd'hui*, n° 11, 1937, p. 58.
73 'Le Pavillon Suisse à la Cité Universitaire', in *Chantiers-Organe technique de L'Architecture d'aujourd'hui*, January-February 1933, pp. 3-14: 9.

"A new life has begun, thanks to the glass wall". Envelopes

As we have said, Le Corbusier turned to the option of overhead lighting at an early stage. This was not just for the studio but also the living areas. The fine series of sketches for the interior design, signed by Charlotte Perriand, give us an impression of the "ship's hold" atmosphere created by a continuous opening in the crown of the vault. In a similar way to the light-tube type openings elsewhere (notably for the guest room, which one might say has more of a submarine flavour), it was a solution that did not really work, not only—once again—in terms of the roof regulations, but also in terms of the idea of spatiality that the architect was trying to put into material form.

The idea of wide-spanning barrel vaults as the guiding principle was a critical step in the project's genesis and would also influence the conception of the envelopes, which henceforth became free of any structural constraint. This strategy would produce an extraordinary interior ambience shaped by direct, very strong natural light entering "from the whole of the glass walls, floor to ceiling"[69], diffused by the white-painted curved face of the vault. "A new life has begun, thanks to the glass wall", Le Corbusier would later say of the Immeuble Molitor apartments. It was an idea he would pursue even more freely for his own dwelling, where "visitors will be excited by the bright apartment!"[70], as he wrote to his mother in 1935.

West facade

This is especially obvious in the west facade, a spectacular glazed wall section, extending left, from the dining room, into the kitchen and right, to the bedroom, juxtaposed with a wall of Nevada glass bricks in a metal frame. This "wall of glass giving onto the balcony with its high (1.13 m) parapet, which Le Corbusier calls an 'anti-vertigo balcony'"[71], incorporates room-height modules of clear plain glass. Sliding on a system of rollers integrated into the ultra slim frames made up of painted pressed steel angles, the two opening windows—of equal dimensions—are fixed one on top of the other to ensure proper continuity with the exterior. As shown in the backlit photos published in *L'Œuvre complète*, the relatively deep balcony with its wide bench seat, soon embellished with planter boxes, aims to be an extension of the dining room, fully open onto the Boulogne-Suresnes countryside. Mahogany "persian blinds", sliding "accordion fashion and guided top and bottom by rings threaded on rails"[72], produced by Établissements Périer at Bonneuil-sur-Marne (a leader in the field) allow for filtered light or near complete darkness to predominate in the living room and bedroom. These "wooden shutter blades are hung vertically against the window and fold back to left and right against the side walls" so as not to be an obstruction. The Périer shutters are a signature feature of the apartment (Le Corbusier had used the same "heaven-sent" detail[73] for the Pavillon Suisse). They would survive countless alterations to the envelopes in the years ahead.

83 Dining room sketch, western glazing and balcony (FLC, U1-9-51).
84 Portrait of Le Corbusier on the west balcony, towards Boulogne. Sliding window in pressed steel in the foreground (FLC, L4-9-26).
85 Enfilade, bedroom-to-dining room: continuous glazing the full width of the building, between party walls (FLC, L2-10-126).
86 The west facade originally included a translucent glass-brick section at the northern end, near the bathroom (FLC, L2-10-119).

83

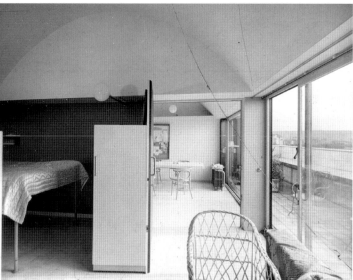

41   1931-1934: CONSTRUCTION

74 As with the general contracting firm run by Arsène Cornet, and Maison Quillery of Paris who succeeded them, Dubois & Lepeu took on the work from Établissements Bézier for "metal joinery and other mirror works" during construction owing to "disagreement between contractors and clients on amounts claimed". This controversy was already apparent in 1932, and in May 1933 the site was shut down completely for some months. Whereupon, "to try to avoid new issues, the Architects handed the remainder of the works to regular contractors in whom they had total confidence, namely: Maison Quillery for the masonry; Maison Dubois & Lepeu for metalwork; Self, electrical appliances; Crépin, gardening; metal ornamentation, numbers and lettering; Célio et Perron, glass. [...] The work was finished thus and the tenants were able to take possession of the apartments". Société immobilière de Paris-Parc des Princes, Note on Immeuble 24, Rue Nungesser-et-Coli, 5 January 1935 (FLC, H2-1-416).

Envelopes of the studio

On both the east (street) and west (courtyard) elevations, the glazed walls of the studio are huge. The extremely slender hardware, as for the whole of the 7th and 8th stories, was built by Établissements Dubois & Lepeu, with whom Le Corbusier had worked for the Cité de Refuge. The Paris based firm, who won the metalwork contract for the building phase of the Immeuble Molitor[74], took on the entirety of the envelopes of Le Corbusier's apartment at the same time (west facade balcony, studio, living room and rooftop pavilion).

For the window-wall on the street frontage, the one facing the main courtyard, and the even taller vertical panel adjoining the rubble party wall, the construction principle is the same as that of the west bay window, namely an assemblage of grey-painted pressed steel flat bar and angle. The detail of the middle transom—a U-profile with the exterior channel visible on the facade—is noteworthy. Visible on the courtyard-side facade, this negative joint is integral to the highly refined glazed wall set-out of the top floor, perfectly complementing the curtain wall of the Immeuble Molitor.

87 Studio in the 1930s: transparent envelopes, east facade on Rue Nungesser-et-Coli (FLC, L2-10-47).
88 View of the studio published in Vol. 2 of *Œuvre complète*, 1929-1934.
89-90 Établissements Dubois & Lepeu, facade on Rue Nungesser-et-Coli, details of pressed steel window units; courtyard facade (left, FLC, 13333) and street frontage (FLC, 13332).

75 Rémi Baudoui, *Edmond Wanner (1898-1965)*, in Jacques Lucan (ed.), *Le Corbusier. Une encyclopédie*, Centre Georges Pompidou, Paris, 1987, pp. 477-478.
76 For the openings for the studio, directions are given in a handwritten note on the Dubois & Lepeu construction plans, drawn between November and December 1932 (FLC, 13692 et 13901).
77 The Dubois & Lepeu construction drawings show clearly how the opening system works, with sliding frames hanging from rollers. The "guichets Wanner" are shown on only one drawing, neither dated nor signed by the contractor (FLC, 13457), and very probably referring to the envelopes for the Immeuble Molitor (as it includes a shutter box, which was never a consideration for the apartment). As shown in correspondence between Établissements Bézier and Pierre Jeanneret, in spring 1932, "the two large panes of the large street-facing facades of Immeuble Molitor will be top-hung from rollers" in the as-built version. See: Letter from Établissements Bézier to Pierre Jeanneret, 14 March 1932 (FLC, H2-3-442).

The opening windows consist of two sliding units, one at the far southern (Paris) end, the other at the courtyard, joined to the intermediate post. Instructed by Le Corbusier, the manufacturers took inspiration from the sliding sashes developed by Edmond Wanner for the Immeuble Clarté in Geneva and which he also provided for the Pavillon Suisse[75]. The reference is clearly cited in the construction drawings done between December 1932 and January 1933 ("sliding Wanner frame, plain glass"[76]), although we don't know whether the Swiss maker was contacted directly or whether it was merely a reference to the "high-spec" model sold by Wanner. The technique—opening sashes supported at the bottom on a steel bar and sliding in a rail—was probably an adaptation of the more modest engineering pioneered by Dubois & Lepeu, which was more like a standard frame-surround model with roller bearings, as shown in numerous details[77].

88

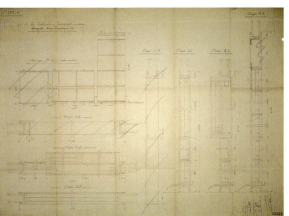

89

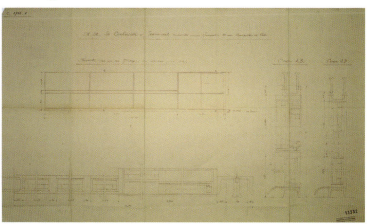

90

43   1931-1934: CONSTRUCTION

78 Letter from Le Corbusier to M. Deloye, M. de Saint-Gobain, 29 December 1932 (FLC, H2-6-22T).
79 'Les briques Nevada', in *Glaces et verres*, 3rd année, n° 14, February 1930, pp. 16-21: 16.
80 'Les matériaux de verre', in *Techniques et architecture*, n°s 3-4, 1944, pp. 56-66: 60.
81 J. Le Braz, 'Les verres prismatiques', in *Glaces et verres*, 6th année, n° 32, February-March 1933, pp. 2-10: 3.
82 The wooden blinds shown on the construction plans were never built, and the architect provided hanging curtains in coarse cotton on all the facades to protect against light.

Glazed infill

"Dear Monsieur, [...] I thank you most kindly for the generous gesture you wish to make. Saint-Gobain glass will triumph in my apartment as it already triumphs in other 'glass wall' constructions we are currently building (Clarté Geneva, rental home in Boulogne, Cité de Refuge, Cité Universitaire), and is becoming vital to projects in development at Algiers, Zurich and our design for the Centrosoyuz building in Moscow. One day, I think, when you create the 'Order of Saint-Gobain', I should be entitled to its finest ribbon!"[78] In December 1932, requesting a supply of Saint-Gobain products free of charge (and receiving them!), Le Corbusier made no bones about the importance of glazed panels. As he stressed, the apartment-studio was effectively a three-dimensional catalogue of Saint-Gobain components, opportunely selected for their particular characteristics for application in different places.

Thus, plain glass sheet (preferred over standard window glass owing to the large dimensions of the panels) was intended to "extend" the dining room towards the exterior, whereas "reinforced cathedral glass" for the inward-opening casements of the window strip above the living room and entry hall was to protect against possible glare while coming down the stairs (as we shall see, Le Corbusier will add a sunshade here in the early 1950s for these very reasons).

The architect similarly made extensive use of Nevada glass bricks. These are moulded units "20 centimetres square and 40 millimetres thick, with a fairly deep throat to secure it in the slab"[79]. The bricks had a "textured face (on one side) and a concavity shaped like a spherical cap which reduced the weight of the brick while maintaining adequate resistance"[80]. They are found in the bedroom wall, in the extension section of glazing in front of the bathroom, as well as in the vaulted recesses behind the washbasin, in the kitchen, and in the office, and the luminous translucency of the surface preserves a certain intimacy. Contrasted with the grid-like pattern of fine concrete joints encasing the armatures embedded inside the throats of the blocks, the sculptural effect is highly successful.

In the studio (excluding the window next to the office, which is plain glass), the need to control natural light impelled Le Corbusier to use a huge range of translucent components, including cathedral type glass printed on one face and reinforced with an ultra fine mesh, placed in spandrel sections. For the area where the painter's easel stood the translucent infill was critical, and here he opted for prismatic 'verre parasol'. Grooved on the internal face, this glass produced a softer, muted glow—"the rays break up as they pass through a surface of separation"[81]—avoiding glare completely. Overhead light having been rejected, all the painter could do was find ways of using infill in the glazed wall to tame the easterly morning light[82], a ceaseless quest that would continue into the 1960s...

91

91 Le Corbusier's mother at the studio window, stills from the movie shot by the architect in July 1937 (FLC, sequences 114816 and 114817).
92 Le Corbusier in his studio, by Lucien Hervé; glazed infill was partially replaced after the war (FLC, L4-9-14).
93 Studio in morning light captured by Lucien Hervé in the 1950s (FLC, L4-9-121).
94 Portrait of Le Corbusier by Robert Doisneau in front of the studio glazing in 1945. Cathedral-type prismatic or reinforced glass, textured on one side, the glazing being carefully chosen by the architect according to its function in the bay.

Rooftop pavilion and guest room

For the composition of the rooftop pavilion that serves as a transition from the grand curving staircase to the roof garden, a wholly different logic held sway. Glazed (except for the metal door to the terrace) it was in fact made up of a series of welded, painted pressed steel flat and angle profiles with fully transparent infill. From the annotations on the construction drawings it seems that particular care was taken in the definition of the details, notably the efforts to align the finished face of the envelopes with the exterior profile of the reinforced concrete corner posts. The posts carry a relatively thick awning, projecting outwards from the volume of the pavilion—note the asymmetrical placing of the exterior metal post which helps to maintain the overhang on the hood; artificial lighting is incorporated into it.

Metalwork for the pavilion—which, unlike the construction drawings, always had a horizontal transom—extends out from the guest bedroom. Here, where two steps mark a change in level, metal joinery of the same type is placed. In other words two transparent panels frame the steel entry door to the bedroom. From the little documentation available—notably sequences from the portrait of his mother, filmed by Le Corbusier in July 1937—we can make out, near the access to the guest room balcony, a largely glazed opening panel.

95 Roof terrace pavilion; polychromy of the concrete canopy and lighting incorporated into the awning support (FLC, L2-10-129).
96 Établissements Dubois & Lepeu, partitions for the 8th-floor terrace, details of pressed steel units (FLC, 13335).
97 Roof terrace in the 1930s, looking towards the main courtyard (FLC, L2-10-130).
98-99 Views of the glass box on the 8th floor from the terrace (left, FLC, L2-10-138) and from the stairway looking up (FLC, L2-10-40).

95

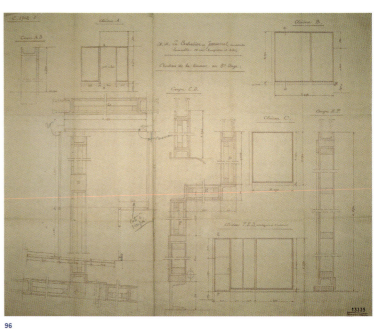

96

97

98

99

47 1931-1934: CONSTRUCTION

83 'Le stand Héraclite', in *L'Architecture d'aujourd'hui*, n° 4, 1934, no page numbers.
84 There is a brochure in the archives for a French distributor of Athermex multicellular concrete, Établissements Chollet-Lefèvre, of Lunéville (FLC, H2-2-45).
85 Estimate for various works, specification, subset 'béton armé maçonnerie', undated (FLC, H2-2-225).
86 See plan FLC, 13390. A note of May 1933 from Arsène Cornet does also mention Solomite—highly compressed straw panels—which he would have been responsible for. Solomite was found to be present in the guest bedroom on the 8th floor.
87 Estimate for works, specification, subset 'peinture, vitrerie, miroiterie', undated (FLC, H2-2-153).
88 *Ibidem*.
89 *Ibid*.
90 *Ibid*. A handwritten note clarifies that this was for the exterior, the interior being finished with "oil paint with special primers".
91 See: Anna Rosellini, *Le Corbusier e la superficie. Dal rivestimento d'intonaco al "béton brut"*, Aracne, Ariccia, 2013.
92 Société immobilière de Paris-Parc des Princes, Le Corbusier and Pierre Jeanneret architects, Estimate for various works, 1 December 1931 (FLC, H2-2-230).
93 *Ibidem*. For the small courtyard they proposed that lintels be treated using "exterior cement-lime mortar, float-finish. This render is to be lime-based again on the existing party wall and composition again on the stairwell and landings".

Opaque envelopes

Both the Immeuble Molitor and the apartment-studio reveal the attention the architects channeled into the composition of the non transparent walls. They wanted increased thermal performance, regarded as an "indispensable corollary of modern, durable architecture"[83], and highlighted this in the application for a construction permit. The option of mineral insulation, especially the new multicellular concrete product Athermex, from Belgium[84], was probably rejected due to its excessive weight to volume ratio. So they turned to a more radical solution, a multi-layer wall, insulated on the inside with panels of bonded (or "petrified", in the vocabulary of the time) vegetable fibre. So, after having used Solomite in all its forms at the Clarté in Geneva, "the cheeks of the bow-windows comprise [...] a hollow brick wall of 0.11, an air cushion, (and) héraclite on a roughened backing"[85]. The opaque facades of the courtyard had a similar treatment, including on the seventh floor: a multi-layer system with (from outside to inside) mortared hollow brick, an air cavity and insulation laid on Héraclite-type fibre board panels[86]—the same "élite material" that would become very widespread between the wars and that Le Corbusier had in fact already used for the opaque walls of Pavillon Suisse.

For the treatment of opaque exterior surfaces, the option of *simili-pierre* or unpainted stone-like mortars was mentioned in the (undated) first description, which limited itself to "indicative" materials schedules "defining rather the limitations and general approaches adopted"[87]. In fact, although the architects had early on suggested "coloured cement mortar", and only for "reinforced concrete wall members for the main courtyard with glass bricks bedded into them"[88], they hastened to add the requirement to supply "separate prices to paint in Cimentol"[89], a product with "applications for several small parts of the ground floor and small courtyard"[90]. The option of render as a backing for paint rather than a finish in its own right seems to have been imposed quite quickly

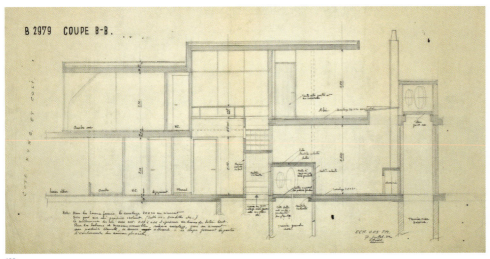

100 Transverse section through pavilion and roof-light, 7 July 1932; note the sound insulation on ducts housing the mechanism for the lift and service hoist (FLC, 13414).
101 North facade facing main courtyard, living room and entry, in 2014.
102 Recent view of the balcony on the west facade, Rue de la Tourelle.

94 Société immobilière de Paris-Parc des Princes, Le Corbusier and Pierre Jeanneret architects, Inventory, May 1933 (FLC, H2-3-87). On the same occasion the architects regretted that "set back from the seventh floor, the concrete was left form-finished". Although the quote from the painting contractor B. Bossenko & V. Mikhaylik is only for a six-storey building, this note suggests that wall treatment for the apartment-studio should have been the same as the courtyard facades of Immeuble Molitor.
95 Estimate for painting work to be undertakern by Consortium Financier et Foncier, November 1931 (FLC, H2-4-401); See also: Estimate for works, specification, subset 'peinture, vitrerie, miroiterie', undated (FLC, H2-2-153).
96 B. Bossenko & V. Mikhaylik, Peinture, Estimate, 8 March 1932 (FLC, H2-4-419). The contractor's record has no details on the product eventually used. A later estimate dated February 1934, mentions Cimentol only for interiors. The undersides of balconies were finished in Monblan (H2-4-429).
97 'La croisade pour la couleur', in *L'Architecture d'aujourd'hui*, n° 10, 1933, pp. 117-118: 117. Silexore—from the family of silicate paints—was invented in Germany in the 1860s and distributed by Établissements Van Malderen in France. It was proposed due to its superior adhesion to cement surfaces, and its waterproofing and protective properties. In the 1930s it was seen as a tried and tested product (also available in a vast range of colours), but was supplanted in the 1960s by plastic paints. 'Les peintures pour le bâtiment des Établissements L. Van Malderen', in *L'Architecture d'aujourd'hui*, n° 2, 1935, p. 102; 'Silexore', in *L'Architecture d'aujourd'hui*, n° 12, 1935, p. 82.
98 Interview with Bernard Bauchet, architect, Paris, 21 March 2014, conducted by Giulia Marino. Ariel Bertrand, *Rapport de sondages: appartement de Le Corbusier, 24, rue Nungesser-et-Coli*, mars 2006 (FLC, recent archives).

101 102

knowing that for solid walls to the courtyard which were not particularly visible, the added value of "*ciment-pierre*" was not justified—Le Corbusier was probably burned by recent issues of cost overruns for pre-coloured Jurassite at Villa Savoye![91]

For the composition of the backing, the specification of 1 December 1931 already called for "reinforced concrete to be cement rendered externally"[92] for the main courtyard. If the idea of "*enduit-ciment*" render was never in question for reinforced concrete on the courtyard side[93], the surface treatment did seem to pose some problems for the architects. When an inventory was made in May 1933, they stated that "the cement renders are float-finished and not smooth"[94] as prescribed. The finish coat, according to the quote of the successful tenderer B. Bossenko & V. Mikhaylik of Paris (dated November 1931), conformed to the specification, while they envisaged "fascias, mullions and transoms of Nevada brick (panels), supports for frames, party wall, to be brushed and painted with Silexore two coats"[95] (a silicate paint product). The firm's next quote, dated March 1932, seems to confirm this, stating explicitly "Silexore", and in a handwritten annotation "or similar product approved based on sample"[96]. This "product possessing particular petrifying qualities akin to those of typical silicate formulations"[97] was put forward for its excellent benefits as a waterproofing material but no instructions were given on the colour selection, there being a wide palette of options available from Établissements Van Malderen, who produced Silexore in France. When the rooftop pavilion was repaired in 2004-2006, an ochre colour was exposed on the cheek of the guest room. This may have been, at least for the roof terrace, the original 1934 colour[98] (although, as we will see, the facades underwent several phases of renovation).

99 'Cordonnier est-il toujours mal chaussé?', in *Le Décor d'aujourd'hui*, n° 30, 1938, pp. 1-27.
100 G.D., 'Où ils vivent, ce qu'ils construisent', in *Beaux-Arts*, 9 April 1937, p. 1.

101 Letter from Le Corbusier to his mother, 29 April 1934, in *Le Corbusier. Correspondance*, vol. II, *op. cit.*, p. 470.
102 Le Corbusier, radio interview with Robert Mallet, 1951, *op. cit.*

"A machine for living in for the machine age, designed by Le Corbusier". Interiors: partitions, materials, polychromy, furniture

The magazine *Le Décor d'aujourd'hui* produced a special issue on architects' homes in 1938. The article "Cordonnier est-il toujours mal chaussé?"[99] is a revealing insight: compared to the Art Déco interiors of Francis Jourdain's house, the marble and mouldings of the 1820s-style residence of Maurice Dufresne, the ruthless modernity of René Drouin's apartment, or even Pierre Chareau's take on the industrial interior, Number 24, Rue Nungesser-et-Coli looked discordant. This "*machine à habiter de l'époque machiniste conçue par Le Corbusier*"[100], as the magazine *Beaux-Arts* described it in 1937, was a departure from contemporary style not only for its spatial originality, but also because of the avowedly inventive nature the interiors, the result of a design process that allied the rigour of the architect's theories to a highly personal idea of domesticity. Although—at least in 1934, the beginning of its history—the apartment at Rue Nungesser-et-Coli can be seen to possess some of the traits of the "purism" on display at the Pavillon de l'Esprit Nouveau of 1925, this was by no means a direct translation of the precepts of the 1920s; the appropriation of the space by its own designer, his experimentation with somewhat extreme solutions—"architectural strategems"[101], as he wrote to his mother—make this one of a kind in the Corbusian catalogue.

"It is the open plan, which, once the mason has finished, offers you these exposed wall faces, inconsistent in a way, grey or white as the case may be, and you are surrounded by this monotony which may be bothersome for some people, but it doesn't bother me at all, I find the white admirable, but nevertheless by the use of colour you manage to impose order on it. You classify the events, you create hierarchy, you give intent to it. You enhance obscure architectural phenomena, like ordinary looking walls, with a bold dash of vermilion against a bit of white for example, or a very dark grey alongside, you begin to create an extraordinary architectural energy. This is polychromy. This is the complete novelty we have in modern times from reinforced concrete and free-plan construction"[102]. These insights from Le Corbusier in 1951 clearly show that the thinking in regard to the apartment interiors was much more than the mere adding of colour. The way the interior material substance is defined was a driving factor in the design of the apartment-studio, over and above the success of specific architectural devices (like the bedroom) or the pleasing integration of built-in furniture (some of it designed with Charlotte Perriand). From the large vaulted spaces like the studio or the dining room, to more elaborate spatial complexes like the living room, the attention given to the material substance, colours, textures, is fundamental. Likewise, the various niches, recesses, shelves, become the support for a diverse assortment of objects and artworks and these in turn become inseparable from one's interpretation of the architecture itself.

103 Portrait of Le Corbusier in the living room, by photographer/designer Willy Rizzo in 1959.
104 Living room in 2014; view towards dining room.
105 Entry to the apartment-studio at the time of Le Corbusier's death in 1965; view towards the wall adjoining the main courtyard to the north (FLC, slide collection).
106 Recent view of the entry looking towards the living room and dining room to the west.

103

104

105

106

51   1931-1934: CONSTRUCTION

103 Marie-Jeanne Dumont, *op. cit.*
104 Rémi Baudoui, *Edmond Wanner (1898-1965), op. cit.*, pp. 477-478.

Pivoting doors and vitrified ceramic tiling

In the preceding paragraphs we have looked at the overall floor plan, with the clean separation that Le Corbusier sought between living spaces and painting studio. This distinction seems to have been one of the main starting points for the project. But the architect wanted to retain a degree of connectivity from one end of the seventh floor to the other, with the central block, low ceilinged and relatively dark, opening onto the very bright vaulted rooms. The photograph taken from the living room, published in *L'Œuvre complète*, illustrates this: lit from behind, it shows the change of scale—and ambience—between the outer rooms and the central core, an aspect the architect will try to accentuate using a stronger colour scheme for the living room. Transverse views from the studio also stretch all the way to the glazed wall of the dining room, presenting a continuous space, a loose parcours even, accented by a number of major events. The shots by Peter Willi and Lucien Hervé taken in the early 1950s illustrate how this reading "through" the dual-aspect apartment is strongly conditioned by devices for separation of the vaulted rooms: large swinging doors placed off-centre to either side of the entry, creating separation respectively for studio and living-dining areas. These elements, which Le Corbusier would have picked up from a trip to Majorca, where he spent his holidays in summer 1932[103], are an extremely successful spatial artifice. In the open position, on the axis of the swing—a sophisticated technical component supplied by Edmond Wanner[104]—the thickness of the veneered timber doors disappears; in the closed position, these large elements, as wide as the central core of the building, maintained the requisite intimacy by total enclosure of the different spaces. Chromatically,

107-108 Views through the length of the studio; the continuous white vitrified ceramic tile flooring reinforces spatial continuity through the space, with pivot doors in the open position (FLC, L2-10-34, L2-10-33).
109 Portrait of Le Corbusier climbing the stairs to the rooftop, by Willy Rizzo in 1959.

105 These are the "white vitrified ceramic 14 × 14 cm" tiles "laid square with no border. Around the base of the walls, white vitrified tile plinths 15 × 15 cm with chamfer"; Memo from the firm Lucien Peretti, Asnières, undated (FLC, H2-5-532). Tiles were laid on a 2-3 cm asbestos screed, for best acoustic insulation.

106 Le Corbusier, radio interview with Robert Mallet, 1951, *op. cit.*

109

we can see how the two faces continue the colour scheme of the room in the closed position, almost melting back into the wall (separation from the living room for example involved a rather dark shade—a natural dark umber—next to the wall to the staircase, and a paler shade—light sienna—on the living room side).

Each room appears to be orchestrated according to a design blueprint of its own, yet together they read as a consistent whole. Much like the sheets of oak-veneered plywood added in several places in the later 1930s, the choice of a single floor finish—the white vitrified ceramic that Le Corbusier would use again and again in later works[105]—lends even greater emphasis to this. As he confided to Recteur Mallet of the Académie de Paris who asked him why he did not opt for the (far more noble) wood parquet: "It's a white cement tile, 20 by 20, there's nothing cheaper. But I didn't do it to save money: I like the poverty of it. I find it lends dignity to everything else. I dont like rich materials. I like rich ideas, manifested by simple means, intense, tight, and condensed; I don't want a parquet grabbing my attention. This white tile makes a pleasant reticulation across the whole apartment from end to end. The unity is very interesting. Instead of going from one room to another, you are always within the one thing, and I feel that is very important. A snail shell, for example, seeing as we are like snails in our shell-like apartments, is of a single substance from the tip of the spiral to the outside"[106]. In the kitchen, the same tile type is one third of the standard module size, but everywhere else the unbroken expanse, the bright, matte surface formed by the regular layout of tiles with a ceramic wear resistant finish (not, as Le Corbusier indicates, white cement), laid on a mat of asbestos fibre, preserves the unity and coherence the architect wanted.

53   1931-1934: CONSTRUCTION

107 E. Ringuet et Cie à Paris, Estimate addressed to Le Corbusier, 24 August 1933 (FLC, H2-5-578).

Kitchen

The kitchen lies between the small courtyard—from here it has separate access from the walkway—and the balcony on the west facade. It is inserted at the point of juxtaposition where the profile of the main vault meets the end vault. Set against the party wall and with an oculus at the crown the latter has a more emphatic curve, beginning at the seventh storey floor level and supported by the main internal beam. The recess framed by the profile of the tympanum as well as the exposed tie—meaningfully underscored by its dark colour against the light background—accentuate the complex shape of the ceiling, which, due to the cramped nature of the room, is not seen in full.

Partnering this lively volumetric structure in section is a very rational layout in plan, ordered by the built-in furniture designed with Charlotte Perriand. It creates a sort of 'room within a room', the area for meal preparation (courtyard side) being separated from the area for eating by means of a clever device: the niche projecting out onto the balcony and intended to house the frigidaire. This device allows for the floor area to be optimised while maintaining the regularity of the floor plan.

Fixed furniture comprises two separate elements. One of these is the "*cloison épaisse*", a thick partition, partly built of masonry, perpendicular to the development of the room, essentially forming a storage element with openings on both sides: a broom cupboard and some very deep drawers below on the balcony side, and sliding doors in the upper part close to the kitchen area. The other element is an L-shaped block, with a tin double sink-drainer (manufactured by the famous Entreprise Ringuet, specialists in cafe furnishing and billiard tables![107]) under the tilting window that opens onto the small courtyard, opposite a Nevada glass brick wall. The sink carries through to the worktop of the second storage unit, the materials, dimensions and details of which match those of the *cloison épaisse*. These two units are effectively made of two parts, a lower part up to a height of 82 centimetres, and an upper shelving section supported by four metal tubes at the corners. This "break" allows one to appreciate a space which is, after all, relatively restrained, without disrupting the organisation of the kitchen, intended to be very functional. A gas stove in the alcove formed by the services duct and broom cupboard, ensures linkage between the two blocks of built-in furniture.

Materials here are particularly well thought out, chosen with the aim of creating a unified ambience. Hence the wall finish abutting the party wall, white faience tiles (22 × 7 cm), continues on the thick partition, and through and behind the worktop with its rounded edges. The one exception to the rule of continuous floor finish throughout the apartment is the ceramic tiling

110 Variants for kitchen fit-out with overhead lighting (FLC, 13553).
111 Kitchen as-built, in a plan stamped by Charlotte Perriand, 7 July 1932 (FLC, 13658).
112 View of built-in furniture, at the time of Le Corbusier's death (FLC, slide collection).
113-114 Details of built-in furniture before the 1990s remodelling.
115 Plans, sections, elevation of built-in furniture designed in association with Charlotte Perriand (FLC, 13870).
116 Yvonne in the kitchen in a photo published in *Œuvre complète*, 1929-1934.

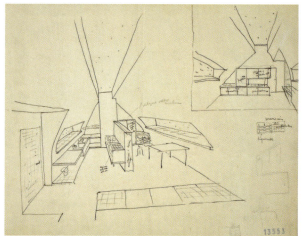

110

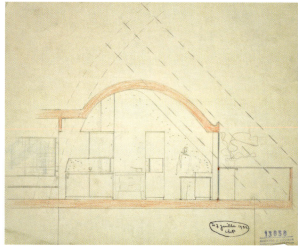

111

THE MANY LIVES OF STUDIO-APARTMENT LE CORBUSIER

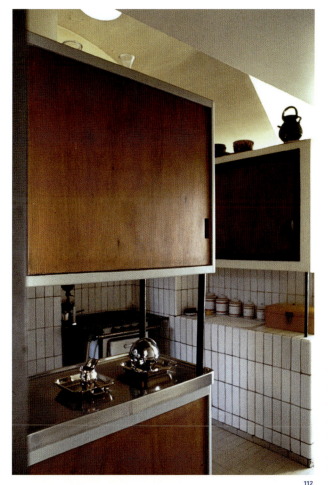

of approximately one-third the size of the module, to match the "hygienic cladding" on the walls. Built-in furniture in painted Okoumé wood has sliding doors in natural oak—aligned in clear sight opposite the door to the dining room—and painted metal tube supports ensure consistency of the furnishing. The ambience is very sober with polychromy in natural shades. Drawers on the balcony side in natural oak framed in dark-brown painted timber follow the same rules of coloration.

Note that the technical services—radiator, pipework, downpipes, etc.—are exposed, in accordance with a precept we find elsewhere throughout the apartment. Lighting—a metal rod with a bulb in the form of a droplet attached to the end, like those in the bedroom and dining room—is a later addition, added by Le Corbusier when the kitchen furniture, which in the 1960s seems to have become unstable, was "restored".

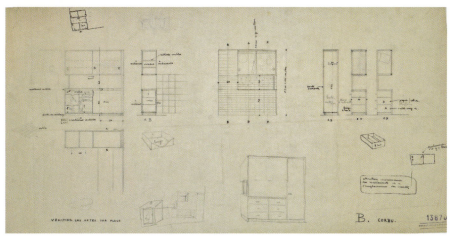

55   1931-1934: CONSTRUCTION

108 Arthur Rüegg, *Le Corbusier: meubles et intérieurs 1905-1965*, Scheidegger & Spiess, Zurich, 2012, p. 308.
109 Jean P. Sabatou, 'Un appartement dans le gabarit. Le Corbusier et Pierre Jeanneret architectes', *op. cit.*
110 'Cordonnier est-il toujours mal chaussé?', *op. cit.*

Bedroom

The bedroom is certainly one of the more "reworked" spaces not just of the apartment-studio but in Le Corbusier's œuvre as a whole. Alongside research on the roof profile, the rather laboured process of designing the bedroom involved numerous sketches aimed at mastering proportions as well as formal aspects. Like the kitchen, the bedroom is located at the juxtaposition of main vault and second vault adjoining the party wall and required intricate planning so as to control the volumetrics, which, by necessity, are extremely complex. Le Corbusier used a variable section owing to the fairly deep alcove in the bathroom which is aligned to the change in ceiling level; the alcove area gradually decreases as studies progress. Likewise the projecting volume of the shower, on the side of the main courtyard, hides the step-in created by the set-out of the curves.

Built-in furniture in the kitchen is aligned with the extrados of the beam and doesn't touch the ceiling, but in the bedroom Le Corbusier opts for a totally different strategy: the interpenetration of the shower and bathroom volumes with awkward floor areas. The shower is particularly successful, its somewhat organic forms melding, in the vertical direction, with the double curve of the ceiling. Spatially this produces an extraordinary richness of form, accentuated by the rounded openings of the wet areas. The set-out of volumes internally corresponds to a very balanced facade on the main courtyard, solid planes coinciding with the slight projection of the bed head and the shower (which is lit on both sides by a thin band one glass-brick in width and a small opening sash for ventilation). Opaque planes contrast with the translucent plane abutting the party wall and pushed forward by the free transverse beam.

As we have seen, the kitchen layout was conceived as a room within a room. The built-in bedroom furniture—ascribed by Arthur Rüegg to the trio Le Corbusier-Perriand-Jeanneret[108]—has a very different logic, inseparable from the functional organisation to the extent that it completely determines the way the architecture is defined. As the press noted, "one of the room's wardrobes is attached to the door and swings with it"[109], the opening on an off-centred axis being a solid timber shelf unit accessible from two sides (laminated sliding doors at the front, and a roller door on the short side). Similarly the unit housed perpendicular to the wall of the bathroom serves as a storage element (studies for the internal layout defined to the millimetre) and as a separation between bedroom and lavatory, i.e. the WC and handbasin in front of the elegant Nevada brick wall on the courtyard side.

The wood and sheet metal dressing table, with glass top, fixed to the bathroom partition, and the bed complete the furniture. The bed, "which has only two feet and is attached to the wall at the head"[110], is one of the objects the architect's biographers have been most intrigued by... for his bedroom, as told by Charlotte Perriand, "Corbu wanted an abnormally high double bed, at hand height. Was this to better see the sky through the

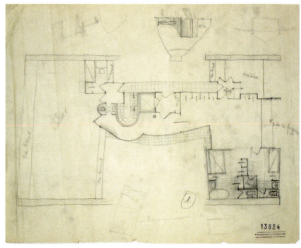

117

118

119

120

117 Study for fit-out of the western part of the apartment-studio; sketch of the bedroom interior layout (FLC, 13824).
118 View of the bedroom in the 1930s (FLC, L2-10-118).
119-120 The bedroom shown in *Œuvre complète*, 1929-1934.

111 Charlotte Perriand, *op. cit.* See also: Jacques Barsac, *Charlotte Perriand. Un art d'habiter, 1903-1959*, Norma éditions, Paris, 2005, p. 119.
112 Arthur Rüegg was consultant to the bed restoration program in 2007, at the time of Bernard Bauchet's work to the bedroom. The bed height had been reduced in the mid-1950s at Yvonne's request, and was returned to its original height during the works, re-using the rear legs which had been part of the original but cut down to suit. The colour *"gris argent"* that Rüegg used was arrived at from samples taken during restoration. See: Arthur Rüegg, *Le Corbusier: Meubles et intérieurs 1905-1965, op. cit.*, p. 308. Interviews with Bernard Bauchet architect, Paris, 21 March 2014 and Arthur Rüegg, architect, Lausanne, 7 April 2014, conducted by Giulia Marino.
113 Jean P. Sabatou, 'Un appartement dans le gabarit. Le Corbusier et Pierre Jeanneret architectes', *op. cit.*, p. 49.
114 Arthur Rüegg, *Le Corbusier: Meubles et intérieurs 1905-1965, op. cit.*, p. 131.
115 Le Corbusier, *Clavier Salubra*, Éditions Salubra, Basel, 1931.

large glass bays [over the top of the "antivertigo" parapet], or to have something more suited to the "*jeux de la nuit*"? Corbu used to joke about it"[111]. Fixed against the wall of the main courtyard and slightly offset so as to restore the alignment of the room, the bed does indeed consist of just two supports for the base, 140 centimetre-high metal tube legs painted "silver-grey"[112]. The structure is quite closely related to the bed he would attempt to produce in series after 1935, whereas the headboard—solid timber screwed to a black painted steel strip—prefigures the one he would design for his "Cabanon" in Cap Martin, 1951-52.

As we have mentioned, the many studies that went into the bedroom were concerned especially with the bathroom, where the depth of the alcove gradually came closer into line with the tie for the main vault. Dimensioned around the size of the bathtub and tiled with light blue-grey *pâte de verre* mosaic and faience (the same as in the kitchen), the bathroom has no protection at all; on the contrary, positioned opposite the swinging door through a very wide asymmetrical opening with rounded corners, it is literally in full view—*L'Architecture d'aujourd'hui* likened the bedroom to "a village square" en 1934![113]

Much ink has been spilled by historians on the exposition of the sanitary fittings as "*objets techniques*", featured alongside lightbulbs, electrical wires, pipes and radiators in the apartment. For his own home the architect explored this theme without trepidation, as illustrated by the bidet contrapuntally situated opposite the dressing table, in front of the bathroom, and subtly dignified by the painting *Nature morte au compas* by Fernand Léger (1928)—a wedding gift from Jeanne Léger[114].

A final fundamental aspect should be mentioned as far as the bedroom architectural concept is concerned. Along with the living room, it is one of the rooms where colour design has been developed the furthest. Sadly, information gleaned from the archives and black and white photographic records is patchy; the same applies to the Salubra wallpapers, no doubt steamed off during the room's numerous refurbishments—"remove the Salubra, blue and red", as an undated note in Le Corbusier's hand tells us. There are precious few surviving material remnants of original polychromy to enable us to reconstitute the exact tones, which it seems were probably distorted in recent surveys. Instructions in Le Corbusier's sketch illustrating the series "application of 'plain colours'" in the first volume of the Salubra colour charts[115] also do not seem to be in accordance with the shots published in *L'Œuvre complète* (notably the volume for the shower which appears to be light in colour, and the mirror, of which the outer face was painted yellow only in the 1950s).

121 Sketch of bed fitted into the partition behind, and solid wood bed-head (FLC, H2-6-603).
122 Bedroom as seen in *Œuvre complète, 1929-1934*. Painting *Nature Morte au compas*, by Fernand Léger (1928).
123 Sketch and note written by Le Corbusier "copy given to Célio", 12 March 1934; bedroom colour swatch (FLC, H2-7-203).
124-125 First Salubra colour chart, series *Les Unis, Mur I*. A sketch of his bedroom illustrates Le Corbusier's "*application des Unis*"; in reality, the design mixes colours that never co-existed.

121

122

116 Sketch, handwritten note 'double remis à Célio', 12 March 1934 (FLC, H2-7-203).
117 'Cordonnier est-il toujours mal chaussé?', op. cit.
118 Arthur Rüegg, *Le Corbusier: Meubles et intérieurs 1905-1965, op. cit.*, p. 309.
119 Le Corbusier's definition. Letter from Le Corbusier to Fernand Gardien, 22 April 1961 (FLC, U1-8-169).

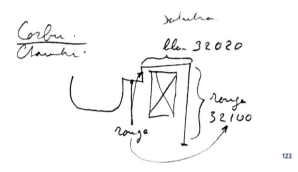

The reference to shades "*bleu 32020 tête du lit*" and "*rouge 32100 angle miroir et paroi lit*" in the margin of the sketch (a copy of which would have been given to the painting contractor Célio in March 1934[116]) is precious indeed. The palette submitted to the painter seems to confirm the impressions received by a journalist in *Décor d'aujourd'hui* who appreciated "the contrasts of plain coloured wallpaper creating the atmosphere of this room, to the left and overhead, white; above the bed, dark ultramarine; to the right, red"[117]. As for built-in furniture, the treatment in light ochre, cream white and pale grey—as for the north cupboards and wall—emphasises the colour of the walls around the bed.

In the bedroom, as in the dining room, a metal rod fixed horizontally at right angles to the bed with a droplet-shaped bulb at the end—a "fixture of commercial opalescent glass"[118]—constitutes the main artificial lighting. "Table lamps '*à serpent*'"[119] with adjustable stems, placed strategically around the room (on each side of the bed, beside the mirrors, etc.) complete the light fixtures for the integrated bedroom-bathroom.

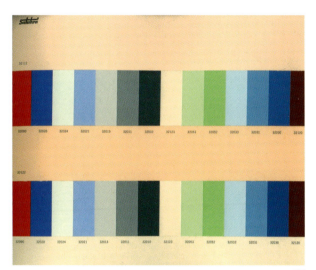

59 1931-1934: CONSTRUCTION

120 In the July 1937 film shot by the architect in the dining room, we can also see a darker wall, the northern one, probably in natural burnt umber. FLC sequence 14820, in Tim Benton, *Le Corbusier, Secret Photographer*, Lars Müller, Zurich, 2013.

121 *Ibidem*.
122 Order from Le Corbusier to Établissements Thonet, 23 November 1934 (FLC, H2-6-65); the 22 January 1935 invoice says the colour was "gris 111".
123 Jacques Barsac, *Charlotte Perriand. Un art d'habiter, 1903-1959, op. cit*.

124 On the table, see FLC, H2-5-106 and FLC, H2-6-26. Mr Pierrefeu, a sixth-floor tenant, asked Le Corbusier to design an identical one for him, except for the top which was Cipollino marble. Produced by the same makers, it faithfully replicated the

same dimensions and bracket fixings for the top as Le Corbusier's ("quatre champs d'équerre sur la face"); Letter from Pierre Jeanneret to Compagnie des Grands Marbres, 27 March 1934 (FLC, H2-5-1934).

Dining Room

Under the vault on the west side is the dining room—the principal space. It is contiguous to the living room (the void for the chimney flue and service hoist separates the two), and opens onto the balcony. The curve of the ceiling and the vast sliding glass door panels shape the rooms characteristic identity. Despite the spatially monumental nature of the room, the furnishing originally was rather bare, with just a few select pieces. All the walls and vault seem to have been finished (if one can trust the descriptions in the press) with off-white Salubra wallpaper (except for the darker wall against the bedroom)[120]. The natural burnt umber door and grey radiator, placed in front of the glazed wall, may well have been the only traces of colour in a relatively "neutral" ambiance (furniture also having a neutral presence). Relief is provided only by the paintings, which, opportunely displayed, are an integrated part of the furnishing. Originally, this collection included *Composition avec profil* by Fernand Léger (1926) and *Nature morte aux nombreux objets* by Le Corbusier (1923). After 1945 it would include *Nature morte Vézelay* of 1939, and one of the *Totem* series, as well as several other paintings...

The 1934 photographs capture an erudite setting: a large void occupied only by a table and chairs, the stem-lamp poised discreetly overhead. The film made by the architect in July 1937[121] also offers a crucial account of the dining room in its first iteration. Aside from a cane armchair that the couple had brought from Rue Jacob, the dining room furniture essentially comprises the table and a collection of four Thonet Model B9 bentwood chairs, "cane-seated, similar to the last three just delivered to the Pavillon Suisse at Cité Universitaire, grey lacquered, the same colour as at the pavilion"[122]. The table has lacquered cast iron legs and a white marble top made by the French and Italian "Compagnie des Grands Marbres" in Nanterre (72 × 213,5 × 80 cm)—Yvonne, according to Charlotte Perriand, had spread the rumour that Le Corbusier's source of inspiration was "a morgue table in a dissecting room"[123] on account of the shallow rim of the table edge! Delivered in March 1934, the table revisits the general tenor of Le Corbusier's designs for the Cité Universitaire some years previously, the legs being simply fixed to the underside. The legs for 24, Rue Nungesser-et-Coli were made by Dubois & Lepeu when they manufactured the hardware for the apartment, and were probably inspired by a commercial model (Le Corbusier, with Perriand and Jeanneret, had used them before for the standard locker units; Perriand would later propose them for the *Maison d'un jeune homme* at the Exposition Universelle in Brussels in 1935)[124].

The red carpet, the Aalto vase, the sculpture by his friend Jacques Lipchitz, the small table, the countless objets arranged under the ceiling at the tympanum, and of course the monumental electric heater that serves as a support for a sculpture by Joseph Savina: this relative "minimalism" in the dining room would not survive for long once the Le Corbusiers took possession...

126-127 Dining room in *L'Œuvre complète, 1929-1934*. Furnishing is fairly minimal; a purist Le Corbusier painting and a work by Fernand Léger, strategically positioned in the room, create the ambience (FLC, L2-10-105).
128 Dining room seen from the living room in a Robert Doisneau photo taken soon after the war.

61   1931-1934: CONSTRUCTION

Living Room

On the other levels of the Immeuble Molitor, the spaces that face onto the main courtyard become the entrance gallery (while living spaces get to enjoy the main glass-wall facade). But for his own home Le Corbusier inverts it, setting the living room in the central core of the apartment. Sandwiched between the vertical void for the chimney flue and service hoist and the volume used for the lift shaft ("his lift is in the living room !", chuckled Maurice Diricq, the *Paris Match* journalist)—the "reception area" however was by no means a residual space. On the contrary, the refined solutions for the interior, notwithstanding its rather intimate character, render it a space of considerable spatial richness.

The constraints were numerous. The chimney void, coupled with the service hoist juts into the space separating it cleanly from the dining room. On the other hand, Le Corbusier, in order to acquire more area for his "*jardin suspendu*" on the roof, stopped the house lift at the 6th floor, but this meant he had to deal with the lift gear emerging into his living room. Between the chimney nook—featuring an extremely simple orifice sealed by a metal screen—and the volume of the lift a small space cuts in at the middle door of the landing opening onto the walkway. The architect turned this constraint into an opportunity with some clever integration of building services. The lift machinery is concealed in a deliberately soundproofed bulkhead incorporated into the furniture, namely a shelf unit against the vestibule wall; the tubular metal post supporting the pavilion awning on the roof and carried on the "cube" of the lift doubles as an electrical duct and support for the light fixture "in the shape of a pear" fixed to the end of a metal bar. The volume of the chimney, meanwhile, is pierced with fairly deep, "very practical" (in the designer's words) rectangular niches.

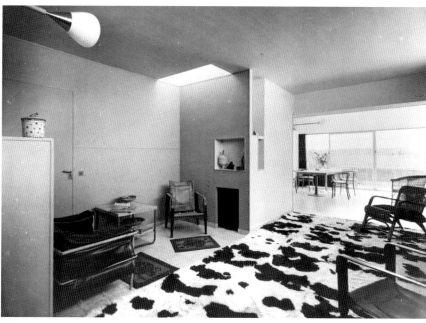

129 Living room in *L'Œuvre complète, 1929-1934*.
130 View of the glazing on the west, seen from the living room; fireplace and alcove let into the shaft.
131 Living room looking towards the lift machinery, made into a piece of fixed furniture by the architect, photographed by Albin Salaün around 1934 (FLC, L2-10-91).
132 Living room from the dining room; photograph by André Steiner, taken in 1936.

129

125 Jean P. Sabatou, 'Un appartement dans le gabarit. Le Corbusier et Pierre Jeanneret architectes', *op. cit.*
126 'Cordonnier est-il toujours mal chaussé?', *op. cit.*, p. 22.
127 Jean P. Sabatou, 'Un appartement dans le gabarit.

Le Corbusier et Pierre Jeanneret architectes', *op. cit.*, pp. 47 and 50.
128 Sketch by Le Corbusier with directions for Salubra colours, and note "double remis à Célio", 12 March 1934 (FLC, H2-7-203).

129 Arthur Rüegg, *Le Corbusier: Meubles et intérieurs 1905-1965, op. cit.*, p. 281.

"The smallness of the rooms is not perceptible, the polychromy of the walls helps to extend the space"[125], Le Corbusier suggested to Jean Sabatou in 1934. The use of colour in the living room obeys the same principle, aided, moreover, by the perfect control of natural light. Thus, "the walls are covered with grey and white wallpapers; the opposite walls are spring green and pure burnt sienna"[126]. On the walkway side, the surfaces are lighter, with raised joint strips (wall to walkway and alcoves), enhanced by a "roof light above the fireplace bringing sun into the apartment at around noon in winter"[127], subtly positioned over the furnished area of the living room proper. Opposite, the slightly bowed envelopes facing the main courtyard are essentially opaque, with the thin strip of window in the upper part interrupted only by the middle upright. These envelopes are painted in darker, stronger colours such as 'Vert 32053'[128] from the first Salubra colour palette, as confirmed in a note from the architect to Célio.

There are some "vestiges" of tubular steel furniture from the late 1920s, notably the *Grand Confort-grand modèle* armchair of 1928: Le Corbusier had bought the prototype of the third version, exhibited at the *Salon d'Automne* of 1929 ("blue tube, grey frame for the base, brown leather cushions"[129]). There is also his first living room table (grey-painted metal with natural timber veneer top and shelf beneath). Though rather spartan when the Le Corbusiers moved in, the living room became richer towards the end of the 1930s with one or two larger pieces specially designed for the space.

As we will see, the living room would become one of the spaces most subjected to modifications over the years, Le Corbusier himself making alterations to polychromy and material fabric as well as furniture.

130

131

132

63   1931-1934: CONSTRUCTION

133

134

Entrance

The apartment's entrance lobby has none of the logic of a bourgeois apartment. The contrast with the smart glazed halls of the other floors of the Immeuble Molitor could hardly be more striking. The entry door from the walkway leads in fact to a very tiny space. On the right, the pier—a half-column—is attached to the studio wall. On the left, the staircase begins its ascent, curving around to the upper floor; the steps, painted a darker blue-grey, accentuate the very fluid movement, and the absence of a handrail (replaced by a central tube) appears strategic. Opposite, the solid wall to the main courtyard was originally painted Salubra "Vert 32053" in continuation of the adjacent living room. At the sides, the space is contained (or not) by the two large rotating doors we have already mentioned. The entry lobby is a pivotal design element in the apartment-studio, and is much more than an interstice between the living spaces and the "master's cavern". The perception of a double-height or very elongated volume and its extreme brightness owing to the roof light and glazed rooftop pavilion, make this a very evocative space.

135

133-134 Double-height lobby, with curved stair, 1930s (left, FLC, 2-10-35; Vol. 2 of *Œuvre complète, 1929-1934*).
135 Le Corbusier at the entry to the apartment-studio, by photographer Robert Doisneau, 1945.
136 Transverse section, study of volumetric and internal fitout (FLC, 13525).
137 Transverse section, eastern side, studio and guest room, 7 July 1932, completed 7 August 1932 (FLC, 13415).
138 View of the guest room towards the roof terrace; the volume in the foreground with the curved surface encloses the shower.

[130] Arthur Rüegg, 'Le charme discret des objets indiscrets', in *Archithèse*, n° 1, 1985, pp. 41-45.

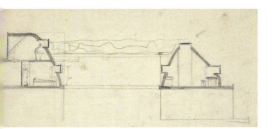

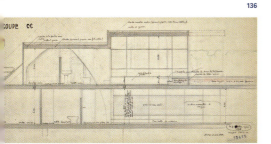

Guest room

Decidedly more "organic" in feel, the 8th floor guest room has its own spatial identity. This is due not only to the shape of the vault against the party wall—a shape, as we have seen, determined by the roofline regulations—but also to the curved volume of the shower, bulging out in relief against the wall/tympanum of the studio—several studies were made of its rounded form, notably the detail of its juxtaposition with the wall, with a curved metal sheet.

The "discreet charm of indiscreet objects", to borrow Arthur Rüegg's assessment of the open bathroom[130], is even more pronounced in the guest room where the ambiance is strongly conditioned not just by the exposition of the washbasin and attached plumbing but also the expansion tank for the Immeuble Molitor central heating system. This "technical object" is literally on show, the centrepiece of the room, on a thick half-height partition that turns into a storage unit, separating the sleeping area from the bathing area or the "*salle d'eau*".

The only 1934 photograph we have, published in *L'Œuvre complète*, is taken from the balcony on the street side: the volume of the shower is in the foreground, the walls appear to be stripped of all finishes. The contrast with its appearance today, plywood in natural oak now dominating the space, is striking indeed. This was a later addition dating from the late 1930s.

Originally Salubra wallpapers covered the curved surfaces of the guest room; the few traces surviving behind the cladding—the coloured sheets were

probably just covered over and not steamed off as they were in the rest of the apartment—reveal a light blue-grey shade at least for the solid wall to the street elevation, left of the bed and the wall that extends from the glass panel of the rooftop pavilion. The pavilion is the counterpart to the glazed access to the balcony on the opposite side, creating a very strong light through the apartment that is conducive to the spatial idea of the bedroom. The bedroom is essentially open to the staircase and, by extension, through the transparent envelopes, onto the raised garden backing onto the small courtyard. The only protection is the double curtain (perhaps the "green tarpaulin", ordered on 23 April 1934?). Note that colour was originally used to render the step between the guest room and the pavilion more emphatic.

131 Letter from Le Corbusier to his mother, 23 June 1935, in *Le Corbusier. Correspondance,* vol. II, *op. cit.,* pp. 505-506.
132 Letter from Le Corbusier to his mother, 29 April 1934, *ibidem,* p. 470.

The garden

"My dear little *maman*. At last warmth and long days. I write from up on the rooftop, in the garden, at eleven in the evening, the pink and white rose bushes and palissades of ivy, the tall grass of the lawn. It's extraordinary, a rooftop garden. Yesterday we dined on Albert's roof, bathed in sunlight, trees all around us, dominated by a thuya grown to immense size. Once again an astonishing sight"[131]. These words of Le Corbusier to his mother in 1935 are very revealing: the roof terrace, largely laid out as a garden—an aspect even more evident in the preliminary design—needs to be regarded as an interior in its own right.

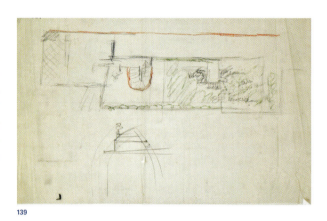

Located between the extrados of the vaults, the terrace is situated between the two courtyards, in the central section of the plan. The glazed pavilion with its very pronounced awning opens onto a space treated with hard landscaping (cement tiles) bounded, on the Boulogne side, by the projecting volume of the service hoist and chimney, deliberately clad in smooth cement tiles. A bench extends from the "*lanterne*" or roof light illuminating the living room. This and the concrete bases are the terrace's only integrated furniture. Le Corbusier equipped the terrace with green-painted garden furniture, the same kind of run-of-the-mill "standard" products that one comes across here and there in the living spaces.

"The garden, a poem. Lawn, lilac, roses and more, and what a horizon!"[132], Le Corbusier said in 1934. The central part, a "hard" area extending from the landing of the pavilion, is encircled by greenery planted in raised beds running along the haunches of the vaults and around the metal grills overhanging the courtyards on each side. The benefits ascribed to rooftop planting in terms of insulation of the roof is a subject we will come to in the chapter on the all-important issue of waterproofing of the terrace. For the present we should signal the primordial importance of vegetation, the delimiting feature of the accessible rooftop, in creating a veritable open-air room. Indeed, this was an aspect the architect consistently emphasised. Le Corbusier we find, at his own residence, not merely experimenting with what is without doubt a central tenet of his *Cinq points*

133 René Burri, quoted in Patrick Moser, *René Burri. Le Corbusier intime*, exhibition catalogue (Corseaux, Villa Le Lac-Le Corbusier, May-October 2011), éd. Castagniééé, Lausanne, 2011, p. 50.

134 L. Crépin & H. Rogier, Gardening contractors, estimate addressed to Pierre Jeanneret architect, 10 April 1934 (FLC, H2-5-581).

d'une architecture nouvelle—as the bird's eye axonometric drawings which he repeatedly uses to illustrate his residential designs of the 1920s and 1930s show—but deriving personal enjoyment from it, and displaying a genuine attachment to his plants.

On the subject of plants, he approached L. Crépin & H. Rogier, a gardening business, with whom he had collaborated several times before, with particularly successful results on the exterior works for the Maisons La Roche-Jeanneret. "I planted nothing myself, it all blew in on the breeze. That was so wonderful! Agreed, it wasn't the good Lord, but it all came from the skies, everything growing there. Such a lovely story"[133], or so René Burri was told in 1958. But the idea that the garden was totally spontaneous, as Le Corbusier would have us believe, is just that—a story. The vegetation was selected with great care. Following the advice of Lucien Crépin, the architect laid out the scheme with harmony in mind. There were "four spindle trees and two thuyas, one pyramid shaped and the other oval"[134] (which soon started to look like substantial trees!), plus many shrubs and numerous aromatic species. A rosebush which seems to have been Yvonne's pride and joy completed the scheme. As for the two ivy bushes climbing up the "kennel fences"—the garden's metal grilles—these were regarded by Le Corbusier as partitions in true form, and indeed they contribute to shaping the interior character of the garden. When Le Corbusier undertook his radical re-shaping of the plantings after 1945 they remained crucial.

139 Garden layout, undated sketch (FLC, 13789).
140-143 Roof terrace and garden layouts, 1930s (FLC, L2-10-150).
144 Portrait of Le Corbusier by Felix H. Man. After the war the 8th-floor garden was especially verdant, and perfectly maintained.

1931-1934: CONSTRUCTION

Service Rooms

The service rooms: WC, store cupboard and servants' room on the walkway side, as well as the store room on the studio side, are concentrated in a "cut-out" under the main vault of the studio. The store cupboard and WC are treated as utility spaces. But the maid's room has a certain interest.

The first noteworthy feature is the courtyard facade, identical to that of the kitchen opposite: a relatively high spandrel in Nevada brick surmounted by a pivoting sash on a horizontal axis casement window (made by Dubois & Lepeu). Despite its tiny dimensions—to obtain the construction permit Le Corbusier promised that it was "just a laundry, impossible to fit a bed in there..."—the room is "dilated" by natural light and benefits from fixed furniture controlled to an optimum degree in dimensional terms. With a washbasin and cupboard built into the wall with sliding doors (it impinges partially on the store cupboard), the furniture is designed for optimising space.

145

146

147

145 The facade of the maid's room, small courtyard in the 1970s: the Nevada brick spandrels with a casement window above.
146 Maid's room in 2014, with the original spandrels replaced.
147 Recent view of the maid's room: with in-built fixtures and handbasin.

148 Walkway above the small courtyard; reinforced cathedral type glass inserted to half-height in the pressed steel balustrade (FLC, L2-10-14).
149 The walkway in 2014; glazed infill has been replaced several times—currently provided with commercial reinforced glass.
150-151 Recent view of the 7th floor walkway, with entrance to the apartment-studio (left), and one of the standard floors. Nevada brick partition gives access to the landings serving the apartments.

135 Le Corbusier, radio interview with Robert Mallet, 1951, *op. cit.*
136 André Wogenscky, *op. cit.*, p. 62.

Studio

The painting studio occupies the whole of the vaulted section on the side looking towards Paris and the Stade Jean Bouin, apart from the service rooms which back onto the little courtyard. It is essentially composed of two parts: a main space adjacent to the north party wall, and an area on the south for his own personal office, between the facade and the services block. The distinction within this narrow band is striking. Once again it is strongly shaped by the "small vault" at the end in glass bricks, and the clear volume of the artist's workspace.

For the studio space, compositionally speaking, the extremely bright ambiance created by the double window in the facade is undoubtedly fundamental. Whether from the glazed panels, the vertical strip up against the party wall on the courtyard side, or the opening high up in the opposite wall, the very intense light across the room helps too define a very generous spatial configuration (in 1934, solar protection was planned only for the opening to the street—a curtain

152

hanging on a Ridorail curtain rod). By the same token, the effects of diffused light, from the step-out of the cross beams and over the curved surface of the vault, are remarkable. It should be noted that at this stage in the project the vault soffit was simply rendered and not lined with painted ply.

The party wall that Le Corbusier wanted to retain in its "rough" form is an element of primary importance in the definition of the painter's studio. The architect stressed this on several occasions: "Don't you see how beautiful that wall is? That is my neighbour's wall. It's a common Paris rubble wall, there are even two red brick flues running through, toothed in among the rubble-work. When I saw it, I said: this wall is just marvellous. Such beautiful construction. I had it pointed very flat to avoid dust so I have the grey of the cement, the beige of the stone and the red of the brick giving a wonderful colour, and for painting it's an enemy of the first order, it's a tough judge because these are the most solid of colours, the most magnificent, the densest that a painter can have before him and if he paints on a wall like that, I assure you, he really has a struggle on his hands"[135]. "This living vertical surface"[136], a surface "worked" by the architect in order to equalise it without harming the appearance of a strongly wrought material identity, is enhanced by the raking morning light from the high window on the street wall. This "constant friend", as he symbolically defined it, would be the support for his canvases, placed on deep projecting plinths of ceramic tile, and of course would enter into Corbusian "mythology". The painter's easel literally "displayed" in photographs taken for publication, is the indispensable finishing touch.

152 Painting studio furnished for the exhibition *Les Arts dits primitifs dans la maison d'aujourd'hui*, organised by Louis Carré and Le Corbusier in his own apartment in July 1935. On the rear wall a tapestry by Fernand Léger, in the foreground, a statue by Laurens.
153-154 Studio as seen in Peter Willi's photographs from the 1960s. View towards the main courtyard (top) and office (FLC, L2-10-53, L2-10-46).

153

154

71 1931-1934: CONSTRUCTION

For interiors and finishes, the studio appears in the early photographs to be relatively empty. Aside from the inevitable easel the only items are an oval table, some assorted armchairs, and two watchmakers' drawer cabinets brought from La Chaux-de-Fonds. The latter, which would remain in the studio until the architect's death, are freely placed in the main space and used—or so it seems in the setup for publications—to support canvases.

Lastly there is the tray for washing paintbrushes—placed on the floor so that the family dog, Pinceau (paintbrush), can also avail of it! In substance it continues the ceramic tile theme, in the half-module version, and extends up the wall at the tap.

At this time the area intended for the office also seems relatively bare—Le Corbusier seems to have worked at the oval desk where a small bronze by Chauvin has pride of place. The shelving unit with its large plywood sliding doors, stretching along the wall of the service rooms, had already been completed in collaboration with Charlotte Perriand.

The small table literally embedded into the translucent vault and the filing cabinet separating the office from the great void of the studio, behind the radiator, appeared in 1939. The fixtures within the office area in fact appeared neither in the first photographs of the apartment, nor in the film of 1937 during his mother's stay in Paris. Like the selection of furniture and some of the lighting, they were among the furniture introduced during the couple's early years in Paris. As we will see in the next chapter, between moving in in 1934 and their departure from Paris during the Second World War, the architect and his wife gradually settled into the spaces by carrying out transformations which, far from being anodyne, would shape way the apartment was seen and represented in scholarly literature on twentieth century architectural history.

155

156

155 Studio captured by photographer Étienne Bertrand Weill; tray for washing brushes at lower left.
156 Portrait of Le Corbusier in the studio, by Lucien Hervé; raking light on the party wall (FLC, L4-9-86).
Following pages Le Corbusier on the roof terrace, by Robert Doisneau, 1945.

Immeuble Molitor was one of the 'grands projets' initiated at the end of the 1920s. Along with Cité de Refuge de l'Armée du Salut (1933) and the Pavillon Suisse at La Cité Universitaire (1930), the glass wall is a characteristic feature. As with the Nungesser-et-Coli building, the envelopes of these iconic interwar objects have undergone numerous modifications.

1934-1965: THE LE CORBUSIER PERIOD

"IT WAS RISKY FOR ME TO GO AND LIVE IN MY OWN ARCHITECTURE. BUT IT'S ACTUALLY WONDERFUL"

In 1931, Le Corbusier was actively looking for funds to support the Société Immobilière de Paris-Parc des Princes and get results in the promotion of the Immeuble Molitor, mobilising his extensive network—Josephine Baker, Fernand Léger, Blaise Cendrars, Raoul Dautry, Elie Faure, James Joyce, the Princesse de Polignac, and his "friend, the famous aviator and writer Mr Saint-Exupéry"—to this end. In 1933, he again had to "manoeuvre, act, discuss, persuade and win out"[1] in the controversy with the businesses who had downed tools in 1933. The magnitude of the task tested him: "I wish this confounded house were finished! That we might leave our dingy cave in Rue Jacob and start living in more civilised conditions!"[2], he ranted at the time.

In 1934, with work complete, the architect was once again at the centre of a legal wrangle that impacted the apartment-studio, after the Société Immobilière went bust and there was a risk of seizure by the Société La Nation who had put up the funding with a line of credit in the early 1930s. Stressing its significance as "a model building profiled in detail in the biggest journals in France, America, England, Italy, etc."[3], Le Corbusier defended his project—his property in the literal sense. Judging from the correspondence, the legal-financial imbroglio was taking its toll on Le Corbusier. It would not be settled until 1949 when, "by means, seemingly, of the sale of a Picasso and a Braque, his co-ownership rights were at last confirmed"[4]. In the meantime, he took possession of the Rue Nungesser-et-Coli apartment[5].

1 "We had to hasten Piquey's return to fix up the Boulogne building which had gone to pieces through lack of money and, relentlessly, for weeks, we had to manœuvre, act, discuss, persuade and win out. Now it's done. Or at least we think so", Letter from Le Corbusier and Yvonne to his mother, 6 October 1933, in Rémi Baudoui, Arnaud Dercelles (eds.), *Le Corbusier. Correspondance*, tome II, Lettres à la famille 1926-1946, Infolio, Gollion, 2013, p. 452.
2 Letter from Le Corbusier and Yvonne to his mother, 23 December 1933, *ibidem*, p. 460.
3 Letter from Le Corbusier to Monsieur Germain, Trustee in bankruptcy for the Société de Paris-Parc des Princes, 12 September 1935 (Archives Fondation Le Corbusier, Paris, FLC, H2-1-579).
4 Dominique Lyon, Olivier Boissière, *Immeuble Nungesser-et-Coli*, in *Le Corbusier vivant*, Telleri, Paris, 1999, pp. 88-95: 88. The deed of acquisition by Yvonne is dated 10 November 1949 (FLC, recent archives).
5 The occupation certificate was officially approved by the Bureau Municipal d'Hygiène on 18 October 1934 (FLC, H2-1-357).
6 Letter from Le Corbusier to his mother, 29 April 1934, in *Le Corbusier. Correspondance*, vol. II, *op. cit.*, p. 470.
7 *Ibidem*.
8 *Ibid*.
9 Société Immobilière de Paris-Parc des Princes, marketing brochure, around 1932 (FLC).
10 Letter from Le Corbusier to his mother, 1 July 1934, in *Le Corbusier. Correspondance*, vol. II, *op. cit.*, p. 474.
11 Letter from Le Corbusier and Yvonne to his mother, 28 May 1934, *ibidem*, p. 472.
12 *Ibidem*.
13 Musée du Quai Branly, Resource Centre, Département Patrimoine et Collections, Paris, fonds Louis Carré.

1934-1939: The Corbusiers move in

"My dear little *maman*. A rough week. We've moved all the paintings and papers. Seventeen years' of paper! A trip down memory lane. My arms are dropping off! Note. One thing to recognise: in my own way I had it all in remarkable order. Nothing amiss. [...] I won a moral victory with Yvonne. The apartment was presented to her finished, curtains, most of the furniture (new) after a good lunch at Schniewindts [tenants on the first floor]. She was thrilled, happy, but pretended to say nothing. It was the first time in Boulogne for her. The apartment is good. It was risky for me to go and live in my own architecture. But it's actually wonderful"[6]. In April 1934, Le Corbusier left his apartment in the Saint-Germain quarter for the superstructure of a building he himself had built in one of "the most lively localities in Paris"[7]. "It's a fresh start, he would say. The end of a cycle. After eighteen years at Rue Jacob, old town"[8], at last he could enjoy the comfort of a modern apartment block: "soundproofing in the floors and partitions, oil-fired central heating with an automatic boiler, radiators in each room, hot water all year round for the baths, bidets, basins, kitchens, maid's rooms, lift, laundry and drying room, large garage"[9]. He was enthused: "our gorgeous home, wonderful. Hive of activity!"[10]. His wife, however, was more subdued—"I'm finding it hard but it will get better. I do miss Rue Jacob and our friends in the area"[11]. And yet, as Le Corbusier said, "Yvonne, after having kicked up a fuss on principle, has done what cats do: she's walked round and round her new box and now she's purring away. Meaning with broom in hand and incessant polishing she's keeping house with the joy of a conqueror. She'll never say so, she's stubborn as a little donkey. [...] What I can say is that her taste and mine go well together, they agree even though they are different. Also we're practising the "freedom of the seas", meaning we're leaving each other alone. The apartment responds admirably to this wisdom"[12].

1

So what happened to the interiors? As we saw, in spring 1934, the apartment looked quite bare. This is evident in the photos for the exhibition *Les arts dits primitifs dans la maison d'aujourd'hui*, organised by Louis Carré, renowned *galeriste* and 4th floor tenant at the Immeuble Molitor, in July 1935, with Le Corbusier in the apartment-studio itself[13]: aside from the few select items of furniture mentioned in the previous chapter, the spaces, still relatively empty, lent themselves well to hosting the exhibition, where «archaic Greek art sits comfortably alongside a Fernand Léger tapestry or a Laurens sculpture, and a Baoulé statue from Côte d'Ivoire fraternises with a freshly painted canvas by Le Corbusier"[14].

But "the Purist echo" of the apartment would not last long. The time between moving in, in April 1934, and leaving for Ozon, and later Vichy, in 1940, was spent settling in: "Yvonne 'cracks the whip'. Their apartment gleams, it's turned into a wonderful place"[15], she "keeps it spick and span at all times. An impeccably well kept house"[16]; nor did the architect let up in completing the interiors with furniture as well as one or two more major adaptations.

2

14 A. B. (André Bloc?), 'Les arts primitifs dans la maison d'aujourd'hui', in *L'Architecture d'aujourd'hui*, n° 7, 1935, pp. 83-85: 83.
15 Letter from Le Corbusier to his mother, 23 June 1935, in *Le Corbusier. Correspondance*, vol. II, op. cit., pp. 505-506.
16 Letter from Le Corbusier to his mother, 1 July 1934, ibidem, p. 474.
17 For a description of the couch, see archival documents FLC, H2-6-45, FLC, H2-6-54 and FLC, H2-6-71. See also: Arthur Rüegg, *Le Corbusier: meubles et intérieurs 1905-1965*, Scheidegger & Spiess, Zurich, 2012, pp. 133 and 306.
18 "Structure by Établissements Berl, October 1934, joined with a 40 × 40 angle frame from which steel laths are suspended, 2.50 m × 0.78 m wide" (FLC, H2-6-54).
19 Letter from Le Corbusier and Yvonne to his mother, 21 or 26 November 1934, in *Le Corbusier. Correspondance*, vol. II, op. cit., p. 487.
20 Letter from Le Corbusier to his mother, 10 January 1937, ibidem, p. 554.
21 Letter from Le Corbusier to L. Rapaport architect (Bucharest), 11 March 1939 (FLC, recent archives).
22 *Plaisir des Arts*, television programme, 18 January 1959.
23 Letter from Le Corbusier to M. Bheuillot, 10 January 1939 (FLC, recent archives).

"How homely everything looks": furniture and carpets

First, in October 1934, came the couch, a seat with a steel frame of 30 mm tube and 40 × 40 mm angle, grey lacquered,[17] made by Dubois & Lepeu and Les Établissements Berl to a Le Corbusier design[18]. The cushions, in a light coloured coarse cloth ("white cotton"), would soon be embellished with Yvonne's embroidery, which would only accentuate the excitement at the arrival of this first piece designed specifically for the apartment: "Major event this morning: they brought up, though not without some fuss, the big settee in the fire nook. And how homely everything looks, how we've "gone up in the world"! Yvonne is thrilled. Now we too can serve coffee on the couch. What a palaver earning your right to join bourgeois society!!!"[19] By the same token the seat, which would be placed between the volume containing the lift gear and the chimney—where it still is—demanded a low table, something that Le Corbusier, after having "searched desperately"[20], decided to design himself in 1937. This occasional table, fashioned from a slice of tree trunk attached to a structure of painted flat-section steel, is without doubt one of the most characteristic items of furniture in the apartment. It is also "celebrated" historically in numerous studies comparing it, deservedly, with the designs of Pierre Jeanneret and Charlotte Perriand.

3

Next came the carpets. These play a crucial role in the apartment's ambience, and even shape its spatial identity in some instances: the "cowhide carpet from the Argentine pampa" brought into the living room in 1935 by Pelleteries J. Vanek, the "Rumanian peasant carpet" he ordered from Bucharest in 1939—"No point looking for a rare collector's carpet. Any cheerful carpet in a good state will give me pleasure"[21]—and of course the traditional Chandigarh carpet, which, as Le Corbusier tells us, was "a gift from Pierre Jeanneret's cook in India"[22].

In addition to these artisan pieces laden with diverse meanings, Le Corbusier designed and had made a carpet for the dining room. As he wrote to the Tlemcen factory in 1939: "I am making a few adjustments in my apartment to try and make it more "feminine" (so my wife says!). Among other things, I want to have a carpet under my dining table, of pure wool, mid-red in colour, 2 × 3 metres, one colour only mind you, no border, 14,000 points per square metre; pure wool manufacture"[23]. In 1939 the red carpet was duly laid under the marble dining table—which is impossible to move, so two longitudinal slits had to be provided to slide it between the heavy legs. This carpet, a seemingly anodyne piece that is in fact essential to the way the space is read, was the first stage in a progressive change of mood in the great vaulted space, which, through a few details of great sculptural power, gradually began to lose its rather restrained character.

Previous page Portrait of Le Corbusier in his living room, by photographer/designer Willy Rizzo, 1959.

1 Furnishings in the living room 1950s (FLC, L2-10-92).
2 Living room pieces: tubular steel-framed couch, low 'tree trunk' table, Chandigarh carpet, cowhide (FLC, L2-10-93).
3 Indirect lighting in the dining room, towards the end of the 1950s. The console for the telephone, in the corner near the kitchen, was designed by Le Corbusier (FLC, slide collection).

24 See bill from the firm of P. Deux et Cie., Paris, for supply and installation of oak-plywood panels on battens (FLC, H2-6-223).

Natural and coloured wood. Colour and lighting

After the furniture—including the metal bookcases for the studio, in *"gris 33 artillerie"* finish, made by Les Forges de Strasbourg—Le Corbusier turned his mind to two fundamental aspects both of which would have huge repercussions for the apartment-studio: the plywood linings and the artificial lighting scheme that he would radically revise.

Because of degradation due to industrial pollution affecting walls and ceilings and because of the early water leaks that appeared in several places around the apartment[24], the architect effectively opted to line the interiors. The great vault of the studio was covered with white or cream-painted plywood on timber battens following the profile of the beams, and the horizontal ceilings were clad in sheets of timber, fixed with cover strips in high relief. Furthermore the architect made use of this new grid-work on the ceiling to complete his office; newly fitted out it became a highly intimate space strongly defined by the presence of natural timber. By the same token, the guest room was lined too; curved natural oak sheeting, nailed onto a substructure of boards and incorporating Solomite insulation, follows the curvature of the vault and carries on up through the section of the volume. The pavilion ceiling is also sheeted with timber. In the living room, Le Corbusier did away with the polychromy on the wall to the main courtyard, re-covering the face of the "wall under the bays" (painted "vert Salubra 32053"in 1934) with natural plywood too. The wood curves up to the ceiling and along the side of the lift gear volume opposite the chimney. These changes, needless to say, are highly visible.

4

These major transformations—the plywood option was one he had explored not long before at the holiday house in La-Celle-Saint-Cloud (1935) and would make use of many times again (the "Cabanon" is its apotheosis!)—are accompanied by an equally radical intervention to the artificial lighting. Coinciding more broadly with a new direction we can detect in his postwar architecture, Le Corbusier was explicit in this respect. In an April 1939 letter to his mother, he recapped on the "refurbishment": "My dear little *maman*. Here we are, *'hors d'ouvriers'*. The painters have gone. We've renovated and its good! It's great, my apartment looks finished at last. The problem was the blackening caused by the Boulogne soot: ceiling coated with black, pale green walls likewise. I've had the ceiling lined with natural oak panelling. Green wall likewise. Staircase likewise. The wall where the little chimney is, grey before, is now a slightly overwhelming shade of vermillion. The dining room has been repainted white (walls and vault). The big part of it was modifying the electric lights, too harsh, no atmosphere or ambience. And I found out that I didn't know a thing about lighting. But by racking my brains, I understood. Lighting its all about lighting what you want to light. So you just have to know where you want strong light, where you just want ambient light, where you want to light up a statue, an object or a bouquet. I've had some lights made up in glass sheet, so cheaply, but effective, precise. So now we've got light the way we want it, doing what it's meant to do.

4 The living room today retains some of the features of the 1950s.
5-6 Guest room: plywood linings in a photo taken at the time of the architect's death (left, FLC, L2-10-128) and in 2014.
7-8 Living room: plywood linings to the wall onto the main courtyard in the 1950s (left, FLC, L2-10-90) and in 2014.
9-11 Studio: "study area" with its built-in furniture (left, FLC, L4-9-74).

5

6

7

8

9

10

11

81   1934-1965: THE LE CORBUSIER PERIOD

25 Letter from Le Corbusier to his mother, 8 April 1939, in *Le Corbusier—Correspondance*, vol. II, *op. cit.*, pp. 614-615.
26 Assuming that not many changes occurred during the war—remember that the couple came back to the property in 1942—the Robert Doisneau images dating from 1945-1946 and the colour photos by Felix H. Man, taken in the same period, might show, barring a few details, the "1939 works".
27 Memo from the firm of Guilux, Paris, 1 February 1939 (FLC, H2-2-6 et FLC, H2-227).
28 Pierre Lagard, architect, interview 2 March 2014, Paris, conducted by Giulia Marino.
29 Le Corbusier, radio interview with Robert Mallet, 1951, in *Le Corbusier, entretiens avec Georges Charensol (1962) et Robert Mallet (1951)*, La Librairie sonore, Frémeaux & associés, 1987.

It has such a profound effect in some cases. It's alive but also intimate. Exactly what we needed. It's really not bad now. 'We can have visitors'. It gives me such joy this 'discovery' of electricity. It was time to figure out something, which proves that you have to go back to square one on every question"[25].

This "discovery of electricity" was something he would have occasion to experiment with at home. The natural wood cladding effectively obliged the architect to rethink his interior polychromy—the wall of the chimney, originally grey, would change a little in shade over the years but remained red until his death in 1965. The lighting also had to be made suitable for this new, much darker ambiance. There is little information in the archives on the exact transformations Le Corbusier made at this time[26]. But one example would be the "Marseille" lamp as it was known, designed and purchased by Le Corbusier for his own apartment at this time, as we can see from an invoice from the Société des Applications Guilux (1 February 1939)[27]. This double-orientation light fixture, which would be used extensively in his postwar works (Villa Sarahbai in Ahmedabad, the "Cabanon" in Roquebrune, Cité Radieuse in Marseille), produced an indirect, raking light, and embodied ideas about lighting that Le Corbusier pursued throughout his career. The industrial lamp hanging from the V-shaped pillar in the studio—a standard model used by the railway agency, according to André Wogenscky[28]—was probably bought at this time too. "Street" fittings of this kind would endure in the architect's lighting vocabulary into the postwar era (for instance at the Claude & Duval Factory, Saint-Dié-des-Vosges).

A few years later, in 1951, Le Corbusier would come back to this foundational moment, these initial steps in his subsequent research. His thoughts are revealing and worth repeating at length: "It's a problem I became aware of at a certain moment. Again it was my wife who drew my attention to it. One day she said to me it's like a barracks in here. "Why is that?" I said. Then, well, I thought for a moment—it was a Sunday evening and we were there together—and I said: "it's the lighting that's doing that! There's too much lighting everywhere, the light is too intense, too harsh". I went for a walk around each of the rooms: "now I understand", I said. Who was it who said that? Archimedes I believe. I discovered the law of lighting, you see: lighting is to illuminate walls and objects. That's it! It's not about manufacturing and selling chandeliers, or fittings. It's a primary, fundamental truth, unknown to most people. That's what led me even just recently into agreements with a huge firm that has patent rights for fluorescent lights, because I refused to use fluorescents then, as I'd just come back from the Americas; I'd seen these two civilizations, these Americas North and South, poisoned by this invasion of wan, depressing, ghostly fluorescents. I said: "I don't want this", and I was made to see that it was just a question choosing what powders to put in the tubes. And my task was to find the human powder, the thing that would humanise lighting, something which was actually sowing depression in the North American soul"[29].

12 Le Corbusier, sketch showing principle for indirect lighting, annotated "24 NC, pour salle à manger, pour atelier", September 1950 (FLC, H2-7-154)
13 Portrait of Le Corbusier in the living room, by Nina Leen for *Life Magazine*, shortly after the war; fireplace wall changed from grey to red in 1939.
14 Portrait of Le Corbusier by Willy Rizzo in 1959; the wall adjoining the walkway is now painted black in contrast with the bold red of the chimney.

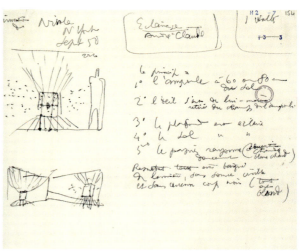

12

30 Le Corbusier, sketch, New York, September 1950 (FLC, H2-7-155). The citation by André Claude seems relevant but the note in the margin "invention of Nivola", is rather more mysterious.
31 Letter from Le Corbusier to Monsieur Rozen (S.I.P.), 4 September 1959 (FLC, K2-17-401); Letter from Le Corbusier to Monsieur Rozen, 28 September 1959 (FLC, K2-17-402).

13

14

By the same token we see Le Corbusier developing this principle in a series of annotated sketches showing the main rooms of the apartment that he must have penned in September 1950 in New York. The famous lighting designer André Claude is mentioned at the top of the page, so we assume there must have been contact between the two men, Le Corbusier noting afterwards: "The principle = 1° lightbulb 60 or 80 cm from the floor; 2° the eye of the viewer outside the field of the bulb; 3° the ceiling is lit; 4° the floor is lit; 5° [illegible] radiating softly (warm sensation, warm white); [...] everything bathed in light, no visible sources and no black bodies (all white)"[30]. We see these ideas in the apartment lighting at the end of the 1950s: Le Corbusier moves away from direct lighting by "stem lamp", adding fluorescent tubes in the recessed space created by the tympanums of his vaults in the dining room on a metal rail along the length of the living room following the window, as well as behind the upside-down impost in the studio, all the while making sure the shadows produced are not excessively «cadaverous, purplish" and won't "distort the colours"[31].

32 Caroline Maniaque, 'Artisanat et petites entreprises dans l'activité parisienne de Le Corbusier après 1945', in *Le Corbusier et Paris, Rencontres de la Fondation Le Corbusier*, FLC, Paris 2001, pp. 81-94: 83.

33 Letter from Le Corbusier to Monsieur Contesso, 29 July 1948 (FLC, K2-17-333).

1945-1951: the apartment goes "brutalist"

"Le Corbusier would choose collaborators especially accredited in the practice of construction and relationships with the contractors, people in whom 'he had total confidence'. In other words, as one of them confirmed, 'adaptable' collaborators, 'with little personal ambition' who 'would respect his ideas'. He needed 'loyal' partners capable of understanding him almost without words. 'A spirit of mutual trust' for example bound Le Corbusier to Fernand Gardien, who described himself as 'merely a designer' without any architectural credentials, a staunch 'Corbu fan' to whom Le Corbusier had entrusted his major postwar construction projects"[32]. That remark by Caroline Maniaque applied perfectly to the "permanent construction site" that the Rue Nungesser-et-Coli apartment-studio became after the Second World War. The history of this emblematic place, where a sequence of fairly heavy interventions would take place from 1948, would also be a story of the relationships between Le Corbusier and his close collaborators. André Wogenscky—his right-hand man, in the role of project supervisor; the "youngsters" Teodoro Gonzalez de Léon, Pierre Faucheux and Alain Tavès, Robert Rebutato, and of course Fernand Gardien himself, undoubtedly the key protagonist in this ongoing tale. The "*collaborateur*" was regularly tasked with managing works of repair and maintenance—including after Le Corbusier's death—but would often enjoy, with the architect's blessing, a certain autonomy. By the same token, Le Corbusier—who often demonstrated an undoubted "self-referential" streak in the architectural solutions he used—would call on trusted contractors and artisans: Jules Alazard, Salvatore Bertocchi, and not forgetting Ancienne Menuiserie Sylva, the joinery business run by his friend Jean-Jacques Duval. Pierre Jeanneret too, seemingly the brains behind his technical solutions for the Immeuble Molitor in 1934, would be called upon in some of the more problematic situations owing to his excellent knowledge of the premises and his mastery of all things constructional.

15

1948: west side timber facades

In 1948 Le Corbusier wrote acerbically to the manager of the Owners' Corporation: "Monsieur, please find enclosed a sample; worthless, but as a document it will be of interest to you. It is from the Immeuble 24, Rue Nungesser-et-Coli. It is a piece of the rust that has catastrophically attacked the window of the building this year—the fifteenth year of no maintenance. Perhaps you are unaware of the significance of rust in a metal window. Well, here is the evidence of what happens. This piece of rust from a window frame is in contact all around with the glass. It's invincible—nothing can withstand it. The very Bible itself talks of the all-killing rust; this little piece is the proof"[33]. The following year he reiterated his complaint, in the same ironic tones, about lack of maintenance at the Immeuble Molitor since its completion in 1934: "By letter of 6 May, the *New-York Times Photos* asked my permission to circulate the photos of Immeuble 24, Rue Nungesser-et-Coli, for the press. [...] Yesterday the *New-York Times* sent two photographs of 24, Rue Nungesser for me to sign. I refused to authorise the photographs of a building

16

34 Letter from Le Corbusier to Monsieur Contesso, 16 May 1949 (FLC, K2-17-347).
35 Drawing collection (FLC, 13460 and following).
36 Drawing collection (FLC, 13518 and FLC, 13519). On dismantling of existing frames in November 1943, see: FLC, H2-6-245.
37 Letter from Le Corbusier to Jean-Jacques Duval, 27 July 1948 (FLC, dossier Usine Claude et Duval, E1-20-458).
38 'Le montage du double-vitrage Atherson', in *Glaces et verres*, n° 98, October 1948, pp. 13-14.
39 Before taking over his father's business, Jules Alazard, master glazier in the XIX° arrondissement, worked with the Le Corbusier's office in the 1930s. Pierre Lagard architect, interview 2 March 2014, Paris, conducted by Giulia Marino. See also: Caroline Maniaque, 'Artisanat et petites entreprises dans l'activité parisienne de Le Corbusier après 1945', *op. cit.*, and Jules Alazard, Jean-Pierre Hebert, *De la fenêtre au pan de verre dans l'œuvre de Le Corbusier*, coll. Actualité du verre, Dunod-Glaces de Boussois, 1961.

in such a state of disrepair, disrepair that was plainly apparent in the photographs and gives a quite miserable impression, to be distributed. Every day we have foreign visitors to see this house. Before the war the American Express touring coach would unload a batch of visitors daily to look at the facade of this building, a building known all over the world. I would like that this small anecdote of a reminder will signal the beginning of repair work to this building. It is deteriorating most awfully"[34].

Le Corbusier's report, scathing as it is, appears fully justified. The apartment had been left unmaintained and without heating, in fact practically disused for a long period, and was in a pitiful state. The warm outfits Le Corbusier and Yvonne are wearing in Robert Doisneau's 1946 photos—standing by the electric stove they had installed despite having oil heating in the building—testify to the restrictions which seem to have continued after wartime. The famous portrait by Nina Leen in this same period has Le Corbusier immortalised in front of the chimney, where extra heating in the form of a wood-burning stove has been installed, confirming the sense that a chill had invaded in the apartment. This prolonged and chronic lack of heating is certainly one of the causes of severe degradation in the 1934 steel window bay, the metalwork of which, as Le Corbusier recounts, had become extremely corroded. The sliding mechanisms no longer worked; the glass had cracked on the diagonal, and shattered under pressure due to the frames increasing in volume. The weather tightness of the facade had become seriously compromised by the glass bay's general condition and led to water ingress in the floor below. Faced with a frankly quite disastrous condition report Le Corbusier decides on a radical solution: the western and guest-room facades will have to be replaced.

The option of a new steel facade was dismissed outright, not only because of shortages of metal in the construction market after 1945, but also because Le Corbusier seems to have learned the hard way that the technique, as he wrote to Pierre Jeanneret, seemed to offer no guarantee of durability. So the plans drawn by Gonzalez de Léon—stamped by Le Corbusier on 27 July 1948[35]—show solid timber profiles simply fixed to "existing metal pieces" which were in some cases reused (for example the angle piece for fixing the original glass bay to the floor, still in place as shown in Gardien's report of 1961[36]). The construction drawings had been prepared at the Rue de Sèvres studio, and for the building work Le Corbusier, with the help of André Wogenscky, called upon his friend Jean-Jacques Duval, owner of the joinery firm Sylva in Saint-Dié-des-Vosges,[37] for whom the architect had realised during the same period (also aided by Gardien), the Claude & Duval factory at Saint-Dié (1945-47). In addition to the construction system, which, because of the incorporation of certain existing elements is slightly different, the envelopes for the apartment-studio have numerous similarities with the ones for the Duval hosiery factory. There is the same solid timber fabrication, the Atherson infill units (the first double glazing produced by Saint-Gobain[38]), an invention strongly endorsed by Jules Alazard[39], but also the proportions, a Modulor scheme adapted to the dimensions of the apartment's primary structure. Le Corbusier described it thus: "This year 1948 we started with a

15-16 Portraits of Le Corbusier and Yvonne by Robert Doisneau.
Taken in 1945, the images show the uncomfortable interior conditions at the end of the war. An electric stove has also been installed in the dining room, near the kitchen.
17 Le Corbusier posing in front of one of his wooden sculptures in the studio, shot by Willy Maywald in 1948.

40 Le Corbusier, *Le Modulor*, collection Ascoral, III section, Normalisation et construction, vol. 4, Éditions de L'Architecture d'aujourd'hui, éd. 1950, pp. 165-166.

1930 construction commissioned at a time when building regulations had the effect of limiting the height of this bay to 204 cent. under a reinforced concrete head beam, a haphazard limit that dictated the whole proportioning of the apartment behind this bay. We didn't apply the 'Modulor' in 'feet-inches' 183-53-226-s.b., but on *this occasion* we built a special 'Modulor' (a kind of *trompe-l'œil*) based on 165-204. This is very interesting and explains our attitude to formulae, sniff out, feel evaluate and decide. Here we decided, sure enough, the 'Modulor' 183-226 might cancel out what, in the current situation, would have been the emotional cause of the architecture: the glass wall. We were agreed on the master organ here, the architectural sensation: it's the glass wall. Realising it consecrated our undertaking: no-one expects subterfuge. Harmony reigns throughout the room"[40].

18

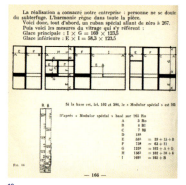

19

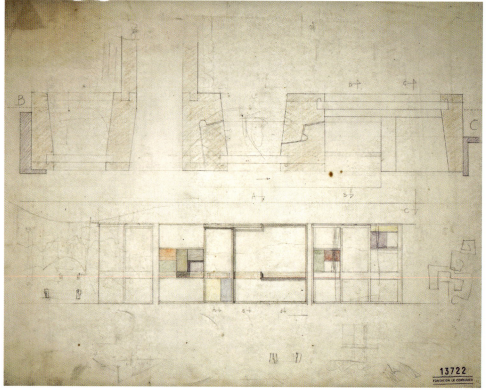

20

21

18-19 Timber framed glazing of the dining room illustrated in *Le Modulor* in 1950.
20 Internal view of the glazing on the west side; in this intermediate version the timber joinery frame incorporates a number of coloured glass (FLC, 13722).
21 Dining room facade. The photo was taken before the coloured glass was installed in accordance with the proportions of the Modulor; built by the glazier Bony (FLC, L2-10-113). On the left of the photo, Périer blinds in the open position.

    Subtlety or bricolage, the painted timber bay of the west facade is carefully proportioned in its three parts, kitchen, dining room and bedroom. The last of these is relatively simple—three panes of decreasing sizes (the smallest being a door opening inwards)—while the dining room facade appears to be especially well thought out in its design. This applies not only to the dimensions in the elevation (following the 'false' Modulor), but also to the remarkable work in the thickness of the envelope: the 20-centimetre deep transom, placed approximately one-third of the way down the facade, is worked into the thickness either by means of a bracket fixed on the inside of the large pane, or—more spectacularly—by forming an outward-projecting "niche" approximately 30-centimetre thick, next to the door. This feature, framed by metal profiles adapted to guarantee perfect watertightness, was completed, not long afterwards, by coloured glass inserts, carefully designed to the (true) Modulor. The effect of light filtered through the coloured panel and diffused in the vaulted space which at this stage was still relatively "neutral" in its colour scheme (except for the famous red carpet of Tlemcen) is very suggestive. In both cases (console or niche), of course, the parts built into the facade thickness are used for the display of all manner of small objects...

41 Plan FLC, 13855C.
42 Maurice Silvy, Paris, Repairs to 7th floor terrace access stairway, 26 September 1983 (FLC, recent archives).

22

23

For the guest room, the architect's initial scheme picked up the theme of the "*baie équipée*" with built-in storage (the coloured niche in the upper part with a system of units serving as a base for the non-opening part). But this was much simplified for construction, with a simple opaque timber panel on which is placed a protruding timber "box".

The roof pavilion, in contrast to the sketches by Le Corbusier in which the same principle is suggested (much more evolved graphically[41]), was modified in the early 1950s, with very different construction methods. Le Corbusier chose an easy and quick "low cost" solution for the pavilion, with its very thin, very corroded pressed steel profiles. This consisted of solid oak joinery fixed simply to the main 1934 structural frame. These form a relatively thick, fairly intricate grid, a structure capable of accommodating double-glazed units (Atherson again, supplied by Alazard), fixed to "exterior beads simply nailed"[42]. Glazed sections alternate with opaque panels of Plymax, an industrial product comprising a sheet of plywood on the inside and aluminium on the

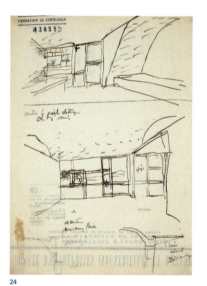
24

25

THE MANY LIVES OF STUDIO-APARTMENT LE CORBUSIER

26

27

22 West facade timber glazing; before the addition of coloured glass, the projecting box had transparent glass (FLC, L2-10-11).
23 Dining room, late 1950s (FLC, 13722).
24 Le Corbusier, sketch of the new guest room arrangement on the 8th floor (top), and dining room (FLC, 13855D).
25 Guest room: plywood linings and new timber structure of the east facade (FLC, L2-10-11).
26-27 Portraits of Le Corbusier by Lucien Hervé (left; FLC, L4-9-15), and Willy Rizzo, at the end of the 1950s; in the background, the new timber and steel pavilion.
28 Le Corbusier on the roof terrace in 1959 in a photo by Willy Rizzo. Oak timber joinery now painted.

28

89   1934-1965: THE LE CORBUSIER PERIOD

[43] *Ibidem*.
[44] Lettre from Georges Blanchon to Établissements Pingère in Paris, 20 June 1950 (FLC, U1-11-147).
[45] Letter from Le Corbusier to Pierre Jeanneret, 14 June 1950 (FLC, H2-6-268).
[46] Advertising by Peintures Berger, Matroil, in *L'Architecture d'aujourd'hui*, n° 2, 1933, p. 101.
[47] Barbara Klinkhammer, 'After Purism: Le Corbusier and Color', in *Preservation, Education and Research*, vol. 4, 2011, pp. 19-38.
[48] Letter from Peintures Berger to Fernand Gardien, 23 November 1950 (FLC, U1-11-154).
[49] The bill from Miroiterie-Vitrerie Alazard in Paris, addressed to Messrs Jeanneret and Blanchon, 24 July 1950, concerns supply and installation of all the infill pieces: reinforced, prismatic and textured glass, as well as plain window glass (FLC, U1-11-124).

outside, also used in the studio (the original vent in the south face was kept). According to Maurice Silvy, the architect engaged in 1983 to handle the pavilion's second makeover, "joinery had been varnished, then painted on the outside faces. The aluminium panels seem to have been coloured although no traces survived"[43].

1950: back to the steel frame of the studio

At the time of the replacement of the glass bay on the west—this being particularly exposed and hence badly decayed—Le Corbusier was thinking about what should be done with the studio envelopes. These too showed obvious signs of age but did not justify complete replacement.

It was in fact a strategy of "repair". It was a difficult business and Pierre Jeanneret was brought in to help. The requirements issued by Georges Blanchon—who was working with Jeanneret at the time—to the painter from Établissements Pingère in Paris were clear: "partial works to make the apartment of Monsieur Le Corbusier waterproof. Strip and repaint the studio glazing. Glazier and ironworker to de-glaze the window, after which you will strip it, apply a coat of anti-rust, then the glazier will reglaze it and you will follow up with the paintwork. For the stripping stage, the process and product Le Corbusier requires you to use is 'Framalite'"[44].

For the rust treatment—which had already become an obsession—the architect was unswayed. He wanted at any cost a complete process, and in particular the Framanol-Framalite brand of paint strippers and passivation products for metalwork, an acid chemical treatment for stabilising steel that he seemed especially keen on—"My orders are Framanol-Framalite at whatever the cost"[45], he told Pierre Jeanneret.

For the finish coat, Le Corbusier seemed happy to specify Berger products, especially Matroil, a British patent available in France since 1926 for a zinc-based, "guaranteed lead-free" paint[46]. More stable than oil paints, the product allowed him to achieve the matt surfaces he favoured in the postwar years[47]. Once again the information we have on the colour selection is incomplete—we know only that samples of black Matroil and green Matroil "which will enable Monsieur Le Corbusier to define the exact shades for his apartment"[48], were sent through via Gardien.

During works to repair the steel envelopes of the studio Le Corbusier replaced all the windows[49], but he also took the opportunity to make some substantial alterations to the facades. He added opening sashes to the glass walls on both sides of the studio, undoubtedly to increase natural cross-ventilation, which he felt would reduce the overheating

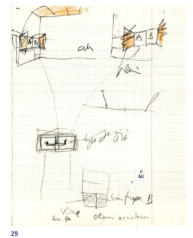
29

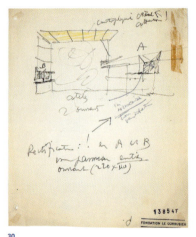
30

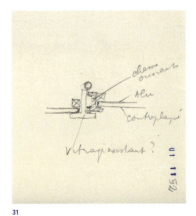
31

32

50 Letter from Georges Blanchon to Établissements Barre, Mathieu et Passedat, 22 June 1950 (FLC, U1-11-51). Plymax panels were supplied by Romard & Dumuids of Monfermeil in June 1950 (FLC, U1-11-187).
51 Letter from Le Corbusier to his mother, 18 February 1951, in Rémi Baudoui, Arnaud Dercelles (eds.), *Le Corbusier. Correspondance*, vol. III, Lettres à la famille 1947-1965, Infolio, Gollion, 2016, p. 163.
52 Memo from Entreprise Pingère, 20 December 1950 (FLC, H2-6-302). Some years later, Le Corbusier complained to Monsieur Brue of Peintures Pingère over how the Matroil paint had been applied, "by brush rather than by spray"; letter from Le Corbusier to M. Brue, Peintures Pingère, 26 April 1951 (FLC, K2-17-193).
53 Letter from Le Corbusier to his mother, 8 April 1939, in *Le Corbusier. Correspondance*, vol. II, op. cit., pp. 614-615.
54 "Mr LC told Gardien that during LC's next trip to the Indies he would need to: 1° change the curtain (see LC's sample) silk velours (red) [illegible]; 2° S.M. Salubra, door red, wall black; 3° bedroom, black wall near bed, blue at foot of bed; 4° aluminium window to vault, see Orsay"; unsigned note 29 September 1961 (FLC, U1-8-170).

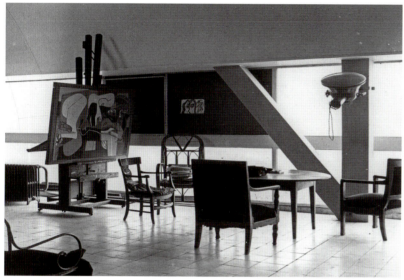

33

34

problem that had been a thorn in the side of Le Corbusier the painter since 1934. There are sketches (sent to Gardien or Pierre Jeanneret? we are not sure) showing one double operable casement in the upper part of the second module from the party wall, on the stadium side, and the other in the second volume from the floor of the part adjoining the party wall. In both cases, as Blanchon instructed the contractor Barre, Mathieu et Passedat, this meant "altering the frame in question by adding an opening light to each. In the four empty spaces, instead of glass we will have plywood sheets covered in aluminium on the exterior, '*Système fabrication Plymax*' "[50] (the courtyard bay in reality would have one opaque and one translucent opening light; the handle on the courtyard side was re-used).

The roof light over the living room was also replaced on this occasion, as were the plywood panels that had been added to the ceiling adjoining the party wall. The "ventilator" through the wall to the right of the bed-head, protected by a metal cover pivoting on a vertical axis, also dates from this time.

At this time also a complete repaint of the internal walls was undertaken—"the house is repainted, clean, heated"[51], he wrote to his mother. This included the dining room, as we can tell from the only trace of polychromy in this majestic space, probably corresponding to the "8 kgb of Matrone rouge" shown on the bill from Pingère in December 1950[52], a shade that would have served as a counterpoint to the "rather overwhelming vermilion"[53] of the chimney, altered in 1939.

The choice of Salubra wallpaper for the bedroom—black on the south wall (next to the bed), and blue on the east (at the head of the bed)—dates from the same time and would be the subject of a major revision ten years later[54]. Between 1959 and 1960, René Burri's famous photos, with the painting by André Bauchant *La glorification de la vierge* and the very small niche to the right, provide major evidence of this new colour scheme and its impact on the spatial quality of the bedroom and the apartment-studio as a whole.

29-31 1950: notes by Le Corbusier on alterations to the studio envelopes in 1950; new opening frames fitted into conserved original frames (FLC, H2-7-159, 13854F and U1-11-52).
32 Le Corbusier in front of a new window in the studio, east side, photo by André Villers.
33 Studio in the 1950s in an image by Lucien Hervé (FLC, L2-10-60).
34 Le Corbusier at work in the studio, by Willy Rizzo; in the background, the new window and Plymax infill.

91 1934-1965: THE LE CORBUSIER PERIOD

55 "MATONE, white, black, natural ochre, yellow ochre; MATROIL white for interior, Matroil yellow ochre, Matroil bright red; BERGEMAIL light pearl grey and Napier green; bill from Peintures Berger to Mme Le Corbusier, 27 June 1952 (FLC, K2-17-190).
56 Plan FLC, 13855B.
57 Letter from Le Corbusier to Auguste Mione of Bordeaux, 30 May 1950 (FLC, H2-6-265).

1950-1951: brise-soleil

At the beginning of the 1950s, a multitude of small interventions occurred throughout the apartment. Though very localised, these transformations were nonetheless important ones, especially in terms of polychromy, reinforced in the same tones with Peintures Berger products[55]. In particular, a few years after designing the Claude & Duval Factory in Saint-Dié-des-Vosges, Le Corbusier replicated the brise-soleil device in a diverse range of shapes and functions.

The first of these was a series of brise-soleil in oak plywood, placed at 45 degrees in the reveal of the ribbon window of the living room. Internally, these elements (taken down in the early 1960s), were judged to protect the living room from direct light, diffused through reinforced glass. The installation of a "shade in the Mont-Saint-Michel fashion"[56], as Le Corbusier noted on a sketch, was probably also a response to problems of glare.

Le Corbusier also looked at another brise-soleil for the west facade. In a March 1950 letter to Auguste Mione—"boss" of Construction Moderne Française, a public works contractor with whom the architect had collaborated on several occasions—Le Corbusier described these elements in considerable detail: "My apartment needs some small modifications: a type of brise-soleil on the window of the dining room (see profile actual size, also location plan, enclosed). Would you calculate the steel needed; it will need to be very weak steel of course. PS this awning is on the west facade on the seventh floor. Prevailing winds are quite strong, westerly and southwesterly. The beam to attach it to is 12 metres long, very thick concrete section. It's carried on the two party walls; it's braced by the dining room vault. The awning profile, in my view, will need to have a sufficiently good fixing. I think it may even be an idea to use newspaper when the concrete is poured to separate them from the concrete beam. The formwork for the shade is 'Eternit' wide gauge corrugated; it will stick to the concrete"[57]. This variant designed by Le Corbusier's firm (Iannis Xenakis was the design lead) was preferred over the parabolic-hyperbolic vault in aluminium—more elegant but much harder to construct. There are no images in the Le Corbusier archives of this brise-soleil. The horizontal line in the render still visible on the west beam today might be a remnant.

In the same series of solar control additions one other device should be mentioned: a brise-soleil—or rather hood ("*casquette*")—in aluminium fixed to the upper part of the east facade on the guest room balcony. Fairly discreet, this sheet metal element is still in place.

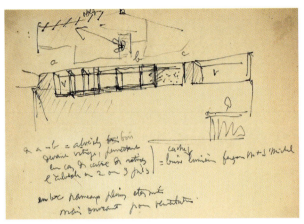

35

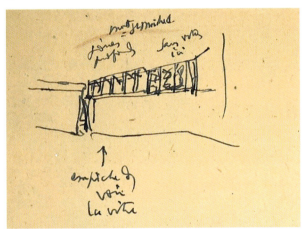

36

35-36 1950: brise-soleil added to the living room (FLC, 13855B and 13856E).
37 Undated plan of the apartment-studio, including the brise-soleil (FLC, 13524).
38 Living room in the 1950s, photo by Lucien Hervé (FLC, L2-10-60).
39 Study for metal brise-soleil, west facade, September 1950 (FLC, 13534).
40 Aluminium "hood" to the guest-room balcony (FLC, L-11-8).
41 Study for Eternit brise-soleil, June 1950 (FLC, 13745)
42-43 Technique for the brise-soleil in Eternit in the form of the remarkable "paravent à poussettes" proposed at this time by Le Corbusier for the Immeuble Molitor lobby (photo: Willy Rizzo, 1959, FLC, H2-7-159).

THE MANY LIVES OF STUDIO-APARTMENT LE CORBUSIER   92

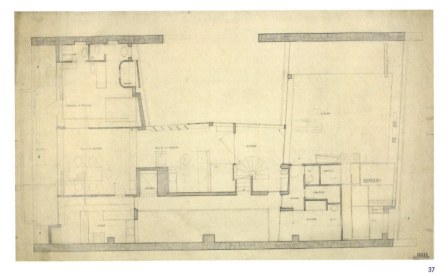

37

38

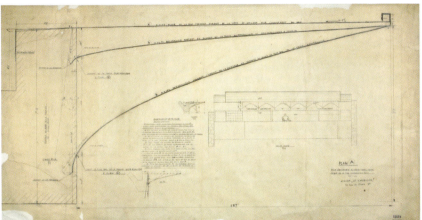

39

40

42

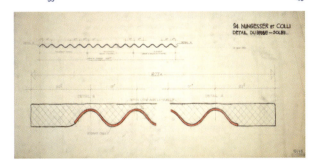

41

43

93   1934-1965: THE LE CORBUSIER PERIOD

58 Letter from Le Corbusier to Pierre Jeanneret, 3 November 1950 (FLC, K2-17-45).
59 Note from Le Corbusier for the attention of Jean Martin, Salvatore Bertocchi, Jules Alazard, Dujourdy, Subject: facade renovations to main courtyard 22/24, Rue Nungesser-et-Coli, 5 November 1956 (FLC, U1-8-122).
60 Letter from Fernand Gardien to Monsieur Henri, Rennaise de Préfabrication, 16 September 1959 (FLC, K2-17-67).
61 Letter from Fernand Gardien to Charles Barberis, 16 September 1959 (FLC, K2-17-281).

1957-1965: experiments

As we mentioned, from the beginning of the 1950s Le Corbusier was preoccupied with the state of the envelopes of the Immeuble Molitor, demanding a prompt and radical intervention. In the absence of funds from the Owners' Corporation the negotiations in the spring of 1950 led nowhere. After this, owing to some major defects notably with the Nevada balconies which seem to have been structurally compromised, Le Corbusier, alarmed, approached Pierre Jeanneret in an urgent tone: "I've been to Mr Andrieu's apartment (5th floor Tourelle). We're not taking this seriously enough: what if Mr Andrieu, who is an important aviator, were to offer cocktails on his balcony in the last fine days of autumn, and 10 people are on the balcony. That would be 10 deaths. I think we have to get on top of the question of these Nevada balconies whatever it takes (brackets to reinforce them or whatever it needs). It's not the round bar of the Nevadas that has given out, it's the supporting flange which has pulled away from the tenons of the support bars eaten out by rust"[58]. In reality the structural measures Le Corbusier ordained, executed by Dindeleux of Paris—the firm that installed the Nevada bricks in 1934—would be only a temporary reprieve. A more comprehensive intervention tackling the lightweight envelopes as a whole would not occur until the 1960s. Meanwhile, in 1957, Le Corbusier awarded the tender for the transformation of the curved envelopes to the main courtyard. The 1930s glass brick facade was transformed into a waveform glass ("*pan de verre ondulatoire*") wall in the manner of the Couvent de la Tourette, which was under construction at the time...

1957-1959: from "undulating glass" at the Immeuble Molitor...

Thus, in November 1956, Le Corbusier alerted his team of trusted firms: Jean Martin, the painter-finisher from Luynes who had created the doors for the Chapelle de Ronchamp (1950-55), Dujourdy, a metalsmith from Maisons Jaoul (1951-55), and the ever-present Salvatore Bertocchi and Jules Alazard. As the architect put it: "the problem can only be seen by a team comprising mason, metalworker, painter, glazier, working as one, on good terms, coordinating everything with a team of tradesmen working together to put it into practice. [...] The characteristics of the work are that the facades have not been maintained since 1933. They are victims of rust. You need to use modern methods for stripping back with heavy water products; that's what the painter, with quality workmen and materials, can achieve"[59]. The preferred solution was a radical one; the interwar glass wall transformed into something altogether more contemporary—the "*pan ondulatoire*".

In September 1959, Fernand Gardien sent the construction drawings for the 60 stanchions (2.80 × 0.24 × 0.7 m) forming the new facade to La Rennaise de Préfabrication, who undertook to make them from "reinforced concrete, in rubbed cement finish"[60]. The "12 ventilators (Maison du Brésil-type)" were ordered from Charles Barberis at the same time[61]. The "small

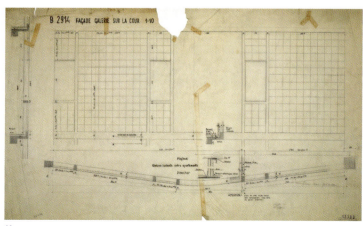

62 Note from Le Corbusier to Fernand Gardien, 28 October 1959 (FLC, K2-17-72).
63 Note from Le Corbusier to Salvatore Bertocchi, 27 November 1959 (FLC, K2-17-199).
64 Letter from the Owners' Corporation to Entreprise Jean Martin, 8 March 1960 (FLC, K2-17-202).

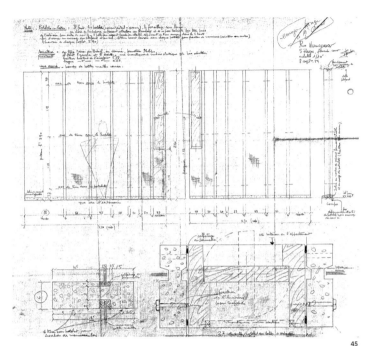

44 Immeuble Molitor, concept, proposal for corridor facade in Nevada brick, undated (FLC, 13389).
45 Immeuble Molitor, replacement of envelopes to main courtyard; glazing with posts in concrete and reinforced glass including Maison du Brésil-pattern vents, September 1959 (FLC, U1-9-28).
46 Facade to main courtyard (north) in 2014.

horizontal bars for the '*ondulatoires*' for 24 N-C", Le Corbusier suggested, could be "copper or aluminium"—adding a note in the margin: (WATCH OUT for rust!)"[62].

Before leaving for Chandigarh Le Corbusier gave instructions to Salvatore Bertocchi for the opaque surfaces—including envelopes on the main courtyard front: "Can you make note that I think this would work well: courtyard facade walls painted white, concrete wave-forms in natural concrete colour, wooden aerators painted grey (exteriors) after having installed copper-sheet fly-screens"[63]. The paint coats themselves—Jean Martin's responsibility—were clearly spelled out in the letter of engagement from the Owners' Corporation: "We confirm our order for painting works to be carried out on the courtyard facades of 24, Rue Nungesser-et-Coli, following recent repairs. These works shall be executed on the higher areas of the building (Mr Le Corbusier's apartment and terrace) and the vertical parts of the facades to the top of the first floor level and do not include painting work to be carried out for the first floor and floor of the courtyard. We also do not envisage any painting of the stanchions of the glass wall which will remain in natural concrete. For painting on masonry: brush down, first coat SILIFILM, second coat SILEXORE, third coat SILEXORE or SILICONE V.M. (formulation recommended by Établissements Silexore); for the metal elements: exterior and interior face of frames, bars, brackets, 7th floor rungs, handrail and grilles at the roof terrace, brush down, scrape back any rust, degrease and apply one coat zinc chromate or red lead and graphite. Paint coats in glycerophtalic oil paint; for wooden frames: brush and two coats superfine varnish for the exterior"[64].

65 Deed of Succession of Mrs Gallis Jeanne Victorine, Le Corbusier, n. 2705, 11 July 1958 (FLC, recent archives).
66 Note for the attention of Fernand Gardien, 2 September 1960 (FLC, H2-6-353).
67 Note from Jeanne (Le Corbusier's secretary) to Fernand Gardien, 10 December 1960 (FLC, U1-8-149).
68 FLC, U1-12-s.n.
69 Note from Le Corbusier for the attention of Pierre Faucheux and Alain Tavès, 19 October 1959 (FLC, K2-17-384).
70 Note from Le Corbusier for the attention of Fernand Gardien, 14 December 1961 (FLC, K2-17-141).
71 Note from Le Corbusier for the attention of Fernand Gardien, 8 March 1962 (FLC, U1-11-348).

1962: … to "prefab concrete glazing" at the apartment

At the same time, Le Corbusier, who in the meantime had gained ownership of the apartment following Yvonne's death on 5 October 1957[65], was wondering about the facades. The diagnostic assessment was not encouraging. On the Boulogne side, the timber glazed wall was suffering from lack of maintenance: ten years after its completion, it was severely deteriorated and leaking. On the Paris side, the piecemeal repairs to the metal joinery were showing signs of weakness—"We will have to keep an eye on the threat of rust at 24 Rue Nungesser-et-Coli", he wrote to Gardien in September 1960[66].

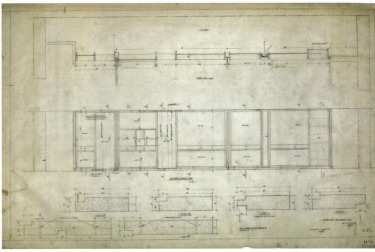

47

All possible avenues were explored, from "de-rusting windows without removing the frames"[67] to replacement with "sliding aluminium French doors by STEP-Arcadia", for which there is a brochure in the archives[68]. More radical solutions to replace the glazed wall in the dining room were also envisaged. For this the architect dipped into his arsenal of recent projects: "URGENT. Draw my glazing at Rue Nungesser-et-Coli: dining room, which will perform the same role as the ones at [the Unité d'habitation de] Meaux. Have the metal parts made up by Budin as a trial as soon as possible. Remind me to telephone Budin myself to arrange a meeting"[69], he commented in a note to Faucheux and Tavès dated October 1959. In the antipodes, two years later, he explored an even more radical solution which involved reproducing the details of the Maison du Brésil at the Cité Internationale Universitaire, in Paris (1953-59) as we can see from the detail sheets drawn by Robert Rebutato in January 1962: a glazed bay with a rhythm to match the timber glazing but built using prefabricated concrete elements and infill panels of plain glass, sealed with mastic on the outer face. Studies for this "in-situ prefabricated concrete glazed wall"[70] were developed between December 1961 and April 1962 and seemed well on the way to completion when the solution was rejected. The Owners' Corporation was by now in a position to fund the work, and the opportunity for a larger campaign of renovation for all the Immeuble Molitor's envelopes was on the cards again. Le Corbusier tried to get his apartment project included in this effort.

47 Apartment-studio, west facade, proposal for new glass wall: glazing between concrete posts, January-April 1962 (FLC, 13714).
48 Immeuble Molitor, east facade. Alterations to the studio envelopes are visible in this 1950s photo by Lucien Hervé. Condition of envelopes to the rest of the building, however, is very close to the original (FLC, L2-10-5).
49 The east facade in 2014: metal joinery of the Immeuble Molitor replaced in the 1960s, and now much thicker in section than the 1934 frames.

72 Letter by registered mail from Le Corbusier to Docteur Delatour, President, Trustee for the Owners' Corporation for 24, Rue Nungesser-et-Coli, 5 February 1962 (FLC, U1-8-173). **73** Letter from Le Corbusier to André Malraux, 14 June 1962 (FLC, recent archives); Malraux would welcome the request:

"As you know, I decided to have the building protected, but I have to submit the dossier to the Superior Commission on Historical Monuments, which has to be consulted. I will be making sure this progresses without delay, and I will be sure to inform you when it has concluded"; Letter from André Malraux to Le Corbusier, 1 September 1964 (FLC, recent archives). Ironically in May 1969, "The Superior Commission on Historical Monuments determines against the inscription to the Supplementary Inventory" of the Immeuble Molitor " it having been effectively the subject of major restorations";

Letter from Antoine Bernard, for the Minister delegate for Cultural Affairs, to L. Miquel, Secretary of the Fondation Le Corbusier, 23 May 1969 (FLC, recent archives). **74** This applied also to the sliding windows "an innovation in 1931, which has become standard practice today";

letter from Le Corbusier to Delatour, Trustee for the Owners' Corporation, 5 February 1962 (FLC, K-16-s.n.). **75** Minutes of the Owners' Corporation Meeting, Immeuble 24, Rue Nungesser-et-Coli, 17 December 1962 (FLC, U1-12-6).

1962-1964: Immeuble Molitor and apartment renovations

The question was probably already the order of the day in March 1962. By this time Le Corbusier was suggesting to Gardien that he should style himself as "Clerk of Works" to the Owners' Corporation[71], and looking into the funds on offer from the *Commission Nationale d'Amélioration de l'Habitat*. In fact the architect had always been concerned with the appearance and integrity of the facade of which he himself had been the "author". The Corporation wanted to replace the original sliding doors with pivot-opening windows, and Le Corbusier pushed back: "I am very formally opposed to the Owners' Corporation taking their own initiative in connection with this house. May I point out, Mr President, that the facade of this house is the work of Le Corbusier and Pierre Jeanneret; these facades accordingly are protected by law. It is prohibited to touch them in any way without the architect's consent. I remind you of a recent vote of the owner's committee recognising this house as part of the modern architectural heritage of Paris. The then-President, Mr Guénassia, had obtained the consent of all the owners in order that this heritage may be conserved"[72]. Some weeks later, as he did in the case of the Villa Savoye at Poissy, Le Corbusier addressed his complaint to André Malraux, the Minister of Culture, demanding urgent protection for the Immeuble Molitor: "This house was built thirty years ago, with no money, with paltry funding. Some fine folks have lived there. Death or the avatars of life have dispersed this initial cohort of the sympathetically-minded. The apartments have since been bought at high prices: 25 million or more each. The new tenants talk about it as a 'luxury residence' and are furnishing it correspondingly. Some talk about altering the windows as they fancy; others altering the balconies. Not long ago I happened upon a workman who said to me: 'I'm going to carry this overhang up to the ceiling' (he's talking about the principal beam of the entire house). 'But all the steel is inside' said I; 'don't fret; we'll cut 'em with the blowtorch' he replied"[73].

48

49

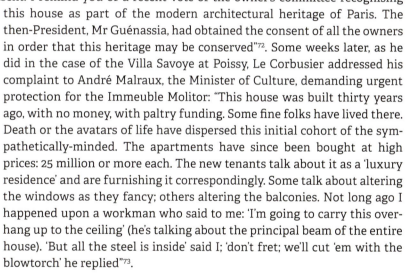

Restoration versus replacement

Despite his tough talk, however, Le Corbusier actually wanted to bring in a very radical solution for the facade, far more radical than the mere replacement of existing elements that the Corporation had earlier envisaged. His proposal was a new facade: stainless steel, Nevada bricks replaced with "enamelled glass", "opaque triplex glazing" or "Vitrex, translucent plastic" (several different enterprises were consulted in summer 1962). Le Corbusier saw the wholesale replacement of the curtain wall as an opportunity to "correct" some of its design faults[74]—he was preaching the same solution at Villa Savoye. The discussions between the Owners' Corporation, which would have happily gone with a simple repair job or at most a "restoration"[75] for economical reasons, and Le Corbusier, advocating a

76 *Ibidem*.
77 Letter from Bernard Lembo of Murinox at Montereau, to Le Corbusier, 30 June 1962 (FLC, U1-12-199).
78 Immeuble et Copropriété, 24, Rue Nungesser-et-Coli, Estimate for works of restoration to the facades (unsigned), 9 January 1963 (FLC, K2-17-22).
79 Letter from Le Corbusier to Monsieur J. Canetti, 18 July 1962 (FLC, U1-10-79).
80 Letter from Fernand Gardien to Roger Michoud, 8 September 1962 (FLC, U1-12-188 and FLC, K2-17-73).

"definitive" fix, were rather lively. "A three-person committee presided over by Monsieur Le Corbusier" was set up, tasked with "ruling on the policy for undertaking the works and its technical application"[76].

During preliminary studies, consulting firm Murinox provided a condition report. It was unsparing: "These facades have been autogenous welded in situ, presenting difficulties for dismantling. They are homogenous, with no movement joint, which has caused significant deformations to vertical and horizontal pieces. They are dangerously attacked by corrosion. Balcony and spandrel heights no longer conform to current legislation. The sliding windows sit on lower rollers, meaning they can't be adjusted. This also means the rollers cannot easily move along the runners, which are covered in dust and grime and this makes them difficult to operate. Moreover, the rollers in this location are exposed to the weather and are rusting away. [...] The roller panels need to be replaced. Some of the opening casements are hard to operate. In some cases they are actually dangerous to open"[77]. This blunt appraisal of the state of health—which furthermore called into question the technical expertise of the architect's interwar phase—quickly put an end to the debate over the strategy of restoration versus wholesale replacement of the original parts. In short "since construction in 1933 and as result of age, all of the steel frames, fixed and operable have reached such a point of degradation due to corrosion that, following inspection by qualified technicians, it is clear that replacement of all the frames is necessary, on technical, financial and architectural grounds"[78]. Le Corbusier, added a rider: "There is no point in fragmentary, localised measures: the rust is everywhere. [...] I do kindly request that you accept that all this has been done with a most serious mind and to kindly believe that my solemn advice to you is this: the house is in danger and we face the heaviest of responsibilities. Rust has separated some of the metal components of the facades; it could cause the window glass to shatter and if these were to fall into the street enormous risks and responsibilities will ensue. I have the reputation of a man who knows his trade, and a man of high scruples. So, I urge you, please immediately accept that things are as they are. Whether the expense be great or small is not the point; the point is to do what is necessary"[79].

In spite of the repair techniques proposed by the Swiss engineer Roger Michoud — with whom Le Corbusier maintained a very full correspondance—the Owners' Corporation would have to accept that it had to do an about turn: "For renewal of the facades at Rue Nungesser, we have been obliged, in agreement with Mr Du Plantys and the co-owners, to plan for renovations well beyond the 'de-rusting' of existing metal joinery. This matter has been the subject of discussions and meetings involving all concerned. We are near to a solution on how it will be done which the entire Corporation needs to accept without delay. That solution is to replace all the metal joinery on the two facades, the present solution precluding any other; the deficiency in 'material', the 'deformation' of the frames, edge beams and joints in the exterior face, are all 'too pronounced' and hence 'dangerous'"[80].

50

51

50 Immeuble Molitor: facade in the 1970s (FLC, slide collection).
51 First floor apartment photographed by Véra Cardot and Pierre Joly in 1974. Interior view shows the new Immeuble Molitor envelopes following the 1960s alterations.
52 Immeuble Molitor, east facade, Rue Nungesser-et-Coli, photographed from the stands of the Jean Bouin stadium by René Burri in 1959, before replacement of the envelopes.

81 Handwritten note by Fernand Gardien to Roland Simounet concerning 24, Rue Nungesser-et-Coli, 16 March 1973 (FLC, recent archives).

New envelopes for the apartment

The option for the new facade (and preservation of some of the original fixings) was ratified in autumn 1962, but the approach in terms of construction and materials was still to be defined. Fernand Gardien had finally been nominated Clerk of Works (partially on his own account) and in a note of 1973 to Roland Simounet for the Fondation Le Corbusier Gardien recapped on the principal steps for undertaking the "*rénovation lourde*"—the major refurbishment of the Boulogne block: "The important decision concerning the commencement of work was taken at the meeting at LC's on 16 October 1962. Mr Passédat being a businessman in the metal joinery sector and having been so advised by the managing agent at the time, Mr Du Plantys, and with whom the technical study had been developed in agreement with LC, the tender price of 372,500 francs included for joinery in anodised aluminium. [...] A few days after the meeting of 16 October 1962 the Owners' Corporation initiated a meeting at Mr Guénassiat's [sic.] and the majority decision was to abandon the solution of LC and Passédat on grounds of cost and to adopt instead a version using steel [hot galvanised] (currently executed) and, on the advice of Docteur Delatour, to go with the firm of Legros who it seems had undertaken metalworks for the construction of a clinic for which the Docteur was responsible. [...] I must say that Mr Guénassiat had pushed hard in favour of the steel version. Legros to my mind did not seem quite up to undertaking the renovation of the facades but one had to bow to the majority decision. During the works, there were enormous difficulties both with the scope of work and the funding. Legros actually went into administration while the works were under way at Rue Nungesser, and another contractor proposed by the managing agent had to complete the services as tendered by Legros. [...] I must say the supervision was onerous and these works went on for two years"[81].

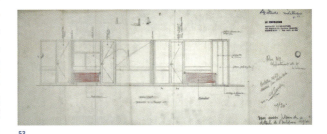
53

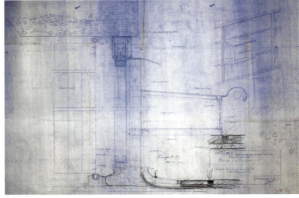
54

As for his own apartment (where the works were slightly different), Le Corbusier, of course had to abide by the decision of the Corporation on the Paris side—the two top floors are visible from the street. But for the glazed wall on the Boulogne side, set back and protected by a concrete balustrade, he had more freedom. Thus, the property after the work—which is broadly as it remains apart from joint strips and of course infill sections—comprised two very different envelopes both in terms of material fabric and construction technology as well as aesthetics.

West facade

On the kitchen-dining-bedroom side, the option envisaged early on was a metal-framed facade along the lines of the timber glazed wall, with polyethylene infill for the bedroom. The plans, drawn by Robert Rebutato and approved by Gardien date from October

55

56

57

58

59

53 West facade of the apartment-studio, variant with metal structure incorporating coloured glass and polyvinyl infill, October 1963 (FLC, 33556).
54 West facade, variant with metal structure by Entreprise Legros & Camillucci, June 1965 (FLC, U1-11-218).
55 West facade, profiles in SCM aluminium, March 1963; as-built variant (FLC, 33561).

56 Portrait of Le Corbusier by René Burri in 1959, in front of timber-framed coloured glass window, re-used in the aluminium glazing.
57-59 Internal and external views of the west wall glazing in 2014.

82 Letter of acceptance dated 7 April 1964: "I confirm our conversation of the 2nd, 35, Rue de Sèvres in the presence of Monsieur Le Corbusier: 1° acceptance by M. Le Corbusier of your proposal for the balcony glazing, Tourelle facade. 2° Execution of glazing in aluminium with anodic protection, natural colour. 3° Commencement from the 6th of the following: a) Execution of glazing in your factory, two weeks, namely by 18 April 1964. b) protection, three weeks, installation to begin 11 May 1964", Letter of Fernand Gardien to Monsieur Legros, 7 April 1964 (FLC, H2-6-720). **83** Report by Fernand Gardien of a meeting held at M. Le Corbusier's home, 13 April 1964, 16 April 1964 (FLC, U1-11-243).

1963. This idea was discarded. Using a totally different approach the architect attempted to go back to the thin profiles and large sliding units of 1934 with a relatively minimal structure in natural matte-finish anodised aluminium with clear glass infill but retaining the 1948 version of the coloured glass niche. This "hybrid", combining the finesse of the 1930s facade with the striking 1950s colour scheme, was also something of a fusion in terms of construction[82]. SCM, a firm that seems to have had an association with Legros (probably because of the latter's specialisation in steel components), proposed some unusual details in terms of assembly methods more reminiscent of structures in pressed steel than extruded aluminium. Fixed to the lower angle piece of 1934 (which survived the vicissitudes of the glazed bay and balcony waterproofing), the sliding transparent frames travelled on "*roulant Hercule*" rollers and as a finishing touch the original Périer blinds were restored in the process and hung back on a new internal rail.

East facade

The studio envelopes (but also those for the door to the balcony of the guest room) were a whole different story: as Gardien's report of April 1964 explains, "the glass wall was rebuilt to match the original including the glass, solid parts and opening frames"[83]. These were therefore steel profiles, the assembly attempting to reproduce the original design in term of thickness and set-out of the elements. On the facade facing Paris, substantial differences are evident, both in the fixed panels (with a much thicker transom in the top) and the opening one, with its rail protruding internally (handle and locking system were re-used). Externally the recessed joint of the middle transom was substituted by a welded flat section. The horizontal pivoting sash under the vault (which has posed endless problems of watertightness over the years) was replaced by a fixed element.

60

While the facade to the street presents some important differences in terms of thicknesses to the nearest millimetre at variance with the original, the horizontal glazing to the courtyard appears to be very close to the original as documented in some of the photos. That could mean that this was the 1934 element redone at various stages, notably the 1950 works of "refurbishment" and replacement glazing. Photographic accounts of the apartment at the time of Le Corbusier's death appear to suggest a different colour to the replacement frames, painted grey. Could the "dark brown" be the remnants of the anti-rust product used for the sliding sashes on rollers, detached from their original paint? By the same token, and in contrast to the contractor's memorandum, the Nevada bricks were not replaced, as photos of the apartment taken after Le Corbusier died show them to be very degraded.

61

84 Report by Fernand Gardien of a meeting of 5 May 1964. Immeuble 24, Rue Nungesser-et-Coli, Paris 16ᵉ (FLC, U1-12-36).

62

Opaque envelopes

For the opaque envelopes, the change of strategy compared with previous renovations was significant. The silicate paints apparently used since the beginning were scrapped in favour of vinyl paints. Thus, "white Silexore on the Tourelle side is replaced on the Nungesser facade by reinforced exterior-grade Cellapol vinyl"[84]. There is very little information on the colour treatment of the "cheeks" either side of the balcony at Le Corbusier's dwelling, which appear in excellent condition in the photos taken at Le Corbusier's death. The red (north, bedroom side) and ultramarine (south, kitchen side) walls may have been done on the occasion of the 1964 works. There are still one or two remnants of colour to this day.

Le Corbusier died in August 1965, but this did not derail the ongoing work of repair to his apartment-studio. His close collaborators André Wogenscky, Robert Rebutato, Roland Simounet, and the "committed Corbusians" grouped around the Fondation Le Corbusier (which inherited the property) became the new guardians. Indeed, long after its designer's passing the apartment-studio would continue to live many lives.

60-61 Immeuble Molitor, east facade. Upper floors photographed by Bernard Hoesli in the 1970s (top) and 2014.
62 Portrait of Le Corbusier in his studio by René Burri, 1960, before replacement of the envelopes by the Owners' Corporation.

103 1934-1965: THE LE CORBUSIER PERIOD

63 Portrait of Le Corbusier on his balcony by the photographer Yousuf Karsh, 1954. The colour scheme for the solid facades, on the west, underwent a remarkable refresh after 1945, including the projecting alcove for the frigidaire in the kitchen, on the south side.
64 Bedroom, captured by Brian Brace Taylor at the time of Le Corbusier's death. The northern cheek of the balcony is painted in very bright red.
65 Traces of blue paint on the southern cheek of the balcony in 2014.
Following pages Portrait of Le Corbusier in the dining room, by Willy Rizzo, 1959.

THE MANY LIVES OF STUDIO-APARTMENT LE CORBUSIER

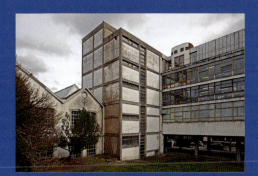

Le Corbusier used his own home as a test bed for new constructional ideas, including west facade timber glazing which follows the Modulor envelope idea used for the Claude & Duval Factory (1946), and wave-form concrete facade units to the main courtyard incorporating vents devised for the Maison du Brésil at Cité Universitaire de Paris (1953).

1965-2014: LE CORBUSIER'S LEGACY
APARTMENT-STUDIO AS HISTORICAL MONUMENT

When Le Corbusier died, on 28 August 1965, the Fondation Le Corbusier became the owner of the apartment-studio and the garage in the basement of the Immeuble Molitor. From that moment on, the property was disused. With all the original furniture (now also including the Salon d'automne lounge chair of 1929), numerous artworks, countless objects and the architect's archives still inside, there was a major security problem to address. During this period the inventory and archiving system used by the Foundation was not quite up to scratch and this collection, including of course a great many personal documents, faced an uncertain future—"On a shelf in full view I found LC's marriage booklet. What are we to make of it? It's all so very sad"[1], lamented Fernand Gardien in 1967. For several months, Noémie Triquoire, the architect's last housekeeper, lived at the apartment to keep an eye on it, despite it being "poorly protected from the elements, with no adequate protection in terms of security and theft."[2] This obviously could not be a permanent solution (Albert Jeanneret, Le Corbusier's brother who at the time was living at the Villa Le Lac, at Corseaux, only stayed for very brief periods). The condition of the rooms continued to decline due to inoccupation, with leaks and water penetration only partially addressed by roof repairs undertaken by the Owners' Corporation in 1967. A radical solution, effective over the medium to long term, was needed.

1 Note from Fernand Gardien to Fondation Le Corbusier, 1967 (FLC, recent archives).
2 Maurice Besset, Notes sur l'appartement Le Corbusier, addressed to Hubert Poyet, Technical Adviser, Ministry of Cultural Affairs, 7 November 1966 (FLC, recent archives).
3 Letter from Jean Petit to Maurice Besset, 18 October 1965 (FLC, recent archives).
4 Letter from André Wogenscky to Jean Prouvé, 5 December 1966 (FLC, recent archives).
5 Letter from Jean-Louis Malet to Jean Kérouault, 13 May 1979 (FLC, K2-18-218).

The idea of selling the property was quickly rejected. The question of how to make use of it was debated at length, not merely to preserve for posterity and add value to Le Le Corbusier's work, but also from the perspective of costs for managing and maintaining it, liability for these now falling to the Foundation, whose own management structure and operation were themselves being discussed at the same time. Thus, after some months of negotiation involving several members of the architect's entourage—Jean Petit, for example "sought reassurance that Le Corbusier's own wishes be respected"[3]—it was decided to rent the apartment to André Wogenscky, right-hand man and later associate of the "Master", who had started up his own design firm in the early 1950s. Despite the critical stance taken by one or two of Le Corbusier's former collaborators (the "rebellion" appears to have been led by Charlotte Perriand[4]), Wogenscky duly moved his office into the Rue Nungesser-et-Coli apartment in 1973.

1969: Repairs following Le Corbusier's death

Meanwhile, in summer 1969, the apartment was cleared of furniture and objects to make way for relatively large-scale renovation. This included overhauling some of the metal joinery (the skylight over the living room was replaced), balcony waterproofing and, internally, electrical rewiring, wall linings (partially replaced and treated with fungicide) and painting works (as we saw, the exterior envelopes had been "renovated" before Le Corbusier's death). These works, preceding the "restoration of external joinery" of the Immeuble Molitor by Jean-Louis Malet, architect for the Owners' Corporation in 1970[5], were not fully documented. Comparing photographs taken at the time of Le Corbusier's death with those taken by Wogenscky's practice, one can assume that the original polychromy was generally respected, albeit with some "simplification" in certain details (for instance the timber strips that frame the painted surfaces and alcoves, which were lighter in 1965).

The bedroom seems to have been a particular focus. From the photographic record commissioned by the Foundation in 1968-69, the black and blue walls respectively to the side of and headbed, an alteration by Le Corbusier from 1951 re-done ten years later, probably disappeared during the architect's lifetime. In the 1969 works the grey shade used for the wall around the pivoting door to the left was deleted, creating a uniform pale, slightly ochre, colour for the wall (the same principle was applied to the wall between the

Previous page Portrait of Le Corbusier on his roof terrace. The wooden sculpture stands on the volume containing the chimney and lift-mechanism (FLC, L4-9-137).
1 View of the studio, by Peter Willi (FLC, L2-10-78).
2-3 Studio in 1965. After the architect died, architectural historian Maurice Besset, one of Le Corbusier's executors, commissioned a photographic record of the apartment from Peter Willi, who in 1977 became the Centre Pompidou photographer (FLC, slide collection).
4 Wall onto the main courtyard; partial view of the dining room in 1965 (FLC, slide collection).
5 Alcove to the en-suite bathroom, 1965 (FLC, slide collection).

1

6 Quotation from Emmanuel Neveu, Bagneux, Peinture, vitrerie, décoration, 8 March 1969 (FLC, K2-17-215).
7 Letter from Fernand Gardien to M. Brue, Peintures Pingère, 30 April 1951 (FLC, K2-17-194).

living room and the vestibule). In the other rooms, the instruction contained in the estimates of the contractor, Emmanuel Neveu, of Bagneux, proposed "polychromy in existing colours"⁶, but we cannot tell if the colours were respected exactly, or if the 1969 "restoration" (which also covered built-in furniture and exteriors) was undertaken with the same care in selecting colours as Le Corbusier had displayed in 1951, when his requirements included "painted areas inside the roof light in the entry hall (between the two sheets of glass), should be painted white with a tinge of blue, not grey as has just been done"⁷.

8 Letter from Jean Jenger, President of the Fondation Le Corbusier, to André Wogenscky, 24 January 1985 (FLC, recent archives).
9 Pierre Lagard, architect, interview, 2 March 2014, conducted by Giulia Marino.
10 The screen for pushchairs, added by Le Corbusier in the lobby in 1950 (cf. FLC, H2-7-159-12), was taken down on this occasion.
11 Due to leaks apparent in the haunches of the vault since 1934 on the Rue de la Tourelle side (as evident in the many repairs in the kitchen), Jean-Louis Malet, architect for the Owners' Corporation, made a major modification during his roof repair works in 1967-1968: "The haunches of the vaults will not be filled with earth as in the past as this is contrary to good rainwater disposal and risks blocking the downpipes yet again"; Letter from Jean-Louis Malet to Fernand Gardien and André Wogenscky, 12 January 1968 (FLC, U1-8-275).
12 Letter from Roger Aujame to Pierre Lagard, 20 January 1987 (FLC, recent archives).

1973-1991: Wogenscky at 24, Nungesser-et-Coli

André Wogenscky and Pierre Lagard, his nephew and associate, took possession in 1973 and remained until 1991 (a clause in the lease required that visitors should be allowed access). During their time the apartment, emptied of all its original furniture and some of the sanitary services, was turned into an architectural studio: the "Director's office" took up the space formerly used for the bed in the bedroom (which explains why the bidet was taken out). Wogenscky's drawing table replaced the marble topped dining table, which also went into the cellar below the Immeuble Molitor. The firm's secretary set up in the living room. The vaulted space of the studio was entirely taken up with drawing tables for Wogenscky's design staff, turning it into a very densely occupied workroom with tables arranged in two rows facing the "constant friend"—the exposed party wall.

Maintenance of the apartment

From the correspondance of Wogenscky "the tenant" with the Fondation Le Corbusier during his stay, we can deduce that modifications carried out were meant to be "respectful", in the knowledge that the "*dernier état Corbu*", the 1965 state, had already been altered. Thus, while visitors often complained about "the current condition, which did not allow 'rediscovery' of what the apartment had once been"[8], internal modifications were designed to be fully reversible (as is the case, for example, with the separation between dining room and living room, achieved with a simple thick curtain), and the alterations very "discreet".

Two programs of repainting, in 1974 and 1986-1987, were carried out with the aim of preserving existing polychromy while adapting the spaces to more utilitarian usage (the painting treatment "Glycerophta, two coats"[9], is in effect more "glossy", i.e. more resistant to wear than the original matte paint). Similarly, a series of localised replacement works were effected on the envelopes, replacing damaged glass (notably wired translucent panels) with new glazing products fixed in grooved galvanised beads now incorporating aluminium flashings. Note that the facade repairs to the Immeuble Molitor date from 1973[10]; when the repairs overseen by André Wogenscky and Pierre Lagarde were carried out the envelopes were simply restored and repainted.

As for the roof garden, which had been modified during the 1967-1968 remedial works by the Owners' Corporation[11], Wogenscky undertook a "reconstruction following the original design", aiming to recreate the 1965 look of the garden, namely drawing on "the diversity that had guided Le Corbusier's choices at the time"[12]: "Irish ivy 150/200, lonicera japonica halliana 150/200.

6

6-7 24, Rue Nungesser-et-Coli in its reincarnation as Wogenscky's studio: the bedroom becomes the architect's personal study; the marble table in the dining room makes room for the drafting table.
8 The architects at work in the studio.
9 André Wogenscky in conversation with a young collaborator in front of the studio wall.

13 (Contractor) Jacques Roussel, Paris, Final breakdown, planting works, 30 June 1988 (FLC, recent archives).
14 Maurice Silvy, Le Corbusier's apartment, 24 rue Nungesser-et-Coli, Paris, repairs to 7th floor terrace access stairway 26 September 1983 (FLC, recent archives).

Climbing rose (sarabande, single flower), lavender, rosa fugosa, hypericum, hedera helix with dentellated leaves, small pots, iris, lily-of-the-valley"[13]. The spectacular yucca planted when the west vault came into being was restored to its place of honour.

Replacement of the pavilion - twice

Among these many repairs, some drastic and some less so in terms of impact on the existing fabric, two major "destructive" interventions stand out: the 1987 replacement of the original Nevada bricks in the spandrels of the kitchen and maid's room, and the replacement of the roof pavilion. Substituting the famous glass bricks, so strongly identified by the round lens-shaped cavity in the internal surface, with more standard models with a vertical grooved face, meant a significant change. But the story of the pavilion and its replacement, not once but twice, is a particularly salutary tale…

In 1983, the Fondation Le Corbusier began their "renovation" of the access to the terrace on the 8th floor, charging Maurice Silvy (known for his collaboration with Jean Prouvé and Joseph Belmont) with the mission. The architect's report, accompanied by a measured survey and taking stock of the transformations that had occurred through the years, did not mince words: "Current condition: it is apparent that the oak joinery with external beads that make up the frames is not original but an alteration made by Le Corbusier himself at an unknown time. The infill comprises panels of either Thermopane-type double glazing or solid elements with sheet aluminium on the outer and oak-faced ply on the inner face. [...] The staircase originally had a steel frame made of simple profiles—tubes and angles—probably with infill similar to the existing. One part remains, where the elements framing the door in sheet steel, giving access to the terrace, are situated. During the alterations he made, Le Corbusier retained the steel door frame, top, bottom and sides, recessed in the concrete frame, and some of the transoms and mullions. The oak frames have been inserted and fixed to the latter. Wooden beads are used externally. But over time these cover-strips, which are thin and nailed in place, have come loose. At that time they had no glues or mastics capable of ensuring a better weathertight joint and more durable workmanship. Water has leaked in and the metal frames have rusted and deformed, widening the gaps in the wood frames, beading, cover strips and metal profiles. As far as one can tell, water penetration below does not come from defects in the lead flashings that provide waterproofing around the edge, but from the failures described above. The joinery is varnished, then painted on the external face. The aluminium panels seem to have been coloured although no trace of this remains. The double glazing is in good condition, apart from two elements which are holed on the outside"[14]. It was a deadly diagnosis; the advanced state of decay of the pavilion, which was not part of the scope of the campaign of replacement of the envelopes in

10-12 After remodelling in the early 1950s, the envelopes of the pavilion are in poor condition. The 1934 steel elements are corroded; the new oak frame and Plymax and plywood infill fatigued (bottom, photo by Arthur Rüegg; next page, FLC, slide collection).

15 *Ibidem*.
16 Letter from Roger Aujame to Jean-Marc Blanchecotte, 16 July 1984 (FLC, recent archives).
17 Letter from Roger Aujame (no addressee, but probably Pierre Lagard), 15 January 1986 (FLC, recent archives).
18 *Ibidem*.

1962-1964, appeared to require total reconstruction, with the exception of the "door and door-case, which are still in fair order and could be conserved"[15]. Based on this verdict, the entire volume of the structure was dismantled including the reinforced concrete awning and its outer posts.

"With degradation getting worse in the apartment due to the poor state of the waterproofing around the pavilion, we had to take the decision to start rebuilding the entire pavilion in replica, glazing included. Once we had the panels taken down, we could see the disastrous state of the slab on top of the pavilion, which extends out over the terrace forming a covered area. There were wide cracks exposing the metal reinforcement, and rust had spalled the concrete in various places. The engineer Hadjidakis, whose advice we sought, recommended building a new slab"[16]. So the idea of reconstructing the pavilion—which was an extreme option—was put to the heritage authorities; it was now a requirement to obtain their advice, the apartment having been listed as an historical monument in a decree of 31 January 1972 (an event which was also noted in the press).

However, when the Fondation Le Corbusier was presented with the works in November 1984 it was not satisfied with the solution adopted, judging that "restored joinery in oak timber is not the same as the previous and taking the decision to reconsider the project in relation to the 1951 works, directed by Corbu"[17]. It was back to square one; and the approach took a radical turn.

The timber-metal joinery, made respectively by two entreprises—Jacques Forlini, at Le Perreux, and Rolandi, at Nogent-sur-Marne—had not been approved by the Fondation Le Corbusier Committee. So it was decided to "go back to the initial solution of 1935: metal frame and glazing using durable, insulating materials like stainless steel and double glazing"[18]. This new version of the pavilion, taking its reference from the original 1934 version, "updated" in terms of the technical approach used, appeared finally to meet with the Foundation's approval: "My dear colleague," wrote Roger Aujame, Secretary General, to Pierre Lagard, commissioned to undertake the work, "here is the result of my investigations among the following architects and administrators of the Fondation Le Corbusier: Madame Charlotte Perriand, Messieurs Roland Simounet, Jean-Louis Véret and André Wogenscky, all of whom, like myself, were former

19 Letter from Roger Aujame to Pierre Lagard, 12 January 1987 (FLC, recent archives).
20 Pierre Lagard, Breakdown of works, undated (FLC, recent archives). The new envelopes are supplied by Ferronerie Chabane, Paris.
21 Letter from Roger Aujame to Pierre Lagard, 12 January 1987 (FLC, recent archives).
22 Letter from Roger Aujame to André Wogenscky, 9 February 1987 (FLC, recent archives).

collaborators of Le Corbusier. The advice I submit to you herewith is the Foundation's official view on this matter. The objective the Foundation established for us was to faithfully respect the proportions the architects intended, but also to create a durable solution, easy to maintain and able to offer superior thermal protection over the original. All are in agreement that the choice of a wood-metal solution used by Le Corbusier during the 1951 renovations of his apartment was one imposed by the financial constraints of the time, and one that has not held up well with the test of time. We have therefore unanimously opted to go back to the original solution (1935), namely: metal joinery and glazing frames, but suggesting light alloy frames, painted throughout, into which we can insert double glazing. It is clear that this would involve frame sections slightly larger than the original, which would preclude a fully accurate replacement '*à l'identique*' of the 1935 version. But there should be no deception. The data we have has changed. The colour shall be strong grey, as low-gloss as possible, approximating the grey used for the original angle pieces of which you have provided a sample"[19].

This "reactivation" of the original envelopes was done using "Technal protimised sections, satin grey 320"[20] incorporating insulating double glazed units. "For all the glazed areas re-using the existing panels, the architect was obliged to use larger frame dimensions than the original, so the work in aluminium does not replicate the original in its proportions"[21]. Using the 1934 construction as its "inspiration", albeit with heavier geometry, the pavilion was completed in the vital year of 1987—the centenary of Le Corbusier's birth. "We think it essential that the apartment be presentable for the centenary"[22], Roger Aujame stipulated. The solution survived until the early 2000s...

13

14

13 The new pavilion in 1987: the plywood infill has been removed, except for the flap on the south side.
14 Plywood ceiling lining from the 1950s reinstated.
15-16 Glazed wall (double-glazing) with very thick powder-coated aluminium frames.

23 Letter from Jean Jenger to Robert Rebutato, 10 January 1990 (Personal Archives of Robert Rebutato). On the same occasion, the Fondation instructed Le Corbusier's erstwhile collaborator to undertake "maintenance of the buildings in its ownership, namely Villas Jeanneret and La Roche and the Rue Nungesser-et-Coli apartment".
24 Atelier Robert Rebutato, Minutes of the Meeting, 17 November 1994 (FLC, recent archives).
25 Fondation Le Corbusier, Dossier for funding application, January 1993 (FLC, recent archives).
26 Atelier Robert Rebutato, Minutes of the Meeting, commencement of construction, 20 November 1994 (FLC, recent archives). This was a *"peinture glycérophtalique aspect mat 1 couche"*; the plywood elements, partially replaced, were treated with *"vernis mat après ponçage"*.
Interview with Robert Rebutato, 20 February 2014, conducted by Franz Graf and Giulia Marino.
27 Work done to the shelving on the left side of the bed was heavily criticised in regard to "placing of the mirror"; letter from Evelyne Trehin, Director of the Fondation Le Corbusier, to Robert Rebutato, 2 November 1999 (FLC, recent archives).
28 Memo of Monteil & Cie, Paris, 7 December 1994; Atelier Robert Rebutato, minutes, 26 October 1995 (FLC, recent archives). See also: interview with Robert Rebutato.

1991-1994 "repairs": to the apartment-studio

André Wogenscky and Pierre Lagard vacated Le Corbusier's apartment in 1991. The Foundation now commenced a new campaign of internal works, aiming to open the place to the public and provide space for researchers for short periods. Alongside the major facade repairs to the Immeuble Molitor (notably renewed works to the balconies, which were now severely decayed), led by Vladimir Jovanovic, architect to the Owners' Corporation, Robert Rebutato, another of Le Corbusier's former collaborators (the plans for the glass wall in the dining room, from 1962, are signed by him) was commissioned initially in January 1990 to manage the maintenance of the apartment-studio[23], then again in 1993, to undertake full "restoration".

17

Interiors

Rebutato's program of works, endorsed by Roger Aujame and Roland Simounet, the Foundation's nominated experts, was framed as "repairs for better or worse"[24] and was monitored (with all discretion) by the *Architecte en Chef des Monuments Historiques*, Hervé Baptiste. The work involved a range of small interventions, not least for "compliance" with building regulations[25] for the spaces and services. It also included repainting "in colours for the walls"—the architect was confident that "colour slides of the period enable us to determine the right shades for each element"[26]—and interior finishes (the option of replacing the ceramic floor tiles was soon discarded for budgetary reasons). Built-in furniture was restored throughout (including the pivoting doors), if not rebuilt as-new (the shelf unit beside the bed[27]). In the kitchen, the tin-sheet bench-top and sink, and the large drawers on the balcony side, were rebuilt.

By the same token, some of the sanitary fixtures were replaced with copies obtained by the technique of resin-casting (the washbasins), or re-enamelled in the workshop and returned to their original form with replacement tap-ware and accessories[28]. Of note also, notwithstanding Rebutato's directions (probably at the behest of Baptiste), joints

18

19

20

29 A sketch in the archives shows the slightly recessed type of joint profile he wanted (Personal Archives of Robert Rebutato).
30 Atelier Robert Rebutato, Minutes of the Meeting, 17 November 1994 (FLC, recent archives).
31 Suggested by Roland Simounet. Atelier Robert Rebutato, record of a visit to the apartment, 2 May 1995 (FLC, recent archives). The idea of "parcloses en rainé de 14 galvanisé" used by Pierre Lagard was retained by Robert Robutato.
32 Atelier Robert Rebutato, Minutes of Meeting, works handover, 21 September 1995 (FLC, recent archives).
33 Record made by Fernand Gardien at a Meeting of 5 May 1964. Immeuble 24, Rue Nungesser-et-Coli, Paris 16° (FLC, U1-12-36).
34 Record of a visit of 9 March 1990, in the presence of Evelyne Trehin and Robert Rebutato (FLC, recent archives).

in the exposed wall were repointed in higher relief than the "rubbed" finish favoured by Le Corbusier (and not in "cement-lime" mortar but in neat cement)[29]. The curved wall of the office in the studio was replaced with new commercially-made Nevada bricks (with a lighter coloured glass body and much thicker joints, which required rows of five blocks rather than six as originally). It is worth noting that, after yet another intervention to the envelopes, the translucent glass wall behind the washbasin in the bedroom was now the last of the Nevada brick elements of the 1934 build.

Envelopes

At the same time as this work was undertaken, an overhaul of the envelopes was also initiated to supplement the work done by Pierre Lagard in 1987. Thus, the "clear glass in the kitchen" and oculus in the apex of the vault were replaced in laminated glass. "All the aluminium sliding doors and French doors", notably the glass facades of the dining and bedroom spaces, were subjected to "checkup and servicing, greasing and adjusting (they work but are not as-new)"[30]. The last non-wired cathedral glass units, which appeared to have been installed during the 1964 renovation by Le Corbusier, were replaced with "wired glass identical to most of the existing"[31], i.e. the 1987 glazing (in reality the "fine-mesh, 710 × 620 cm, panels glazed with pure linseed putty" had a rather less widely spaced mesh than the 1987 versions; the reinforcement was plastic, not metal, and was also considerably more regular). The window over the bathtub in the bathroom of the main bedroom was replaced "with a metal profile in the lower part of the glazed area of the frame"[32], taking care not to make excessive changes to the geometry of the original.

The opaque envelopes seem to have been treated very much in the same vein as the facades of the Immeuble Molitor, which were being overhauled in parallel. "Exterior grade heavy-duty Cellapol vinyl paint"[33] replaced the white Silexore in 1964, and was now replaced in turn with a plastic paint. This overhauling of the courtyard facades was completed up to the top two stories with a finishing treatment of synthetic Pliolite resin on "gutters and lower roof slope in concrete (attic storey)"[34], to protect the exposed reinforced concrete elements and provide improved waterproofing.

17 Condition of the kitchen sink at the time of Le Corbusier' death in 1965. During the 1990s restoration, built-in kitchen furniture underwent extensive rework (FLC, slide collection).
18-19-20 During the 1990-93 intervention, colours were redone 'as existing', while also integrating new services.
21-22 Recent views of the studio east facade: transparent and translucent infill replaced.

21

22

35 Bernard Bauchet, *Étude préalable à la réfection de l'édicule d'accès à la terrasse du logement de Le Corbusier au 24 rue Nungesser-et-Coli*, 20 March 2004 (FLC, recent archives).

2003-2008: reconstructing the pavilion and restoring the bedroom

Pavilion and skylight

Ten years after these "repairs"—perhaps "renovation" is a more apposite description—the Fondation Le Corbusier embarked upon a major new intervention, aiming to replace the 1987 pavilion with a new volume to overcome persistent defects in the waterproofing. In 2003, architect Bernard Bauchet was commissioned to make a "feasibility study for the reconstruction of the entry pavilion on the roof terrace of Le Corbusier's home"; in other words, to comprehensively assess the most suitable strategy. In his preliminary report the architect surveyed the history of this rooftop structure, by then in its fifth incarnation! "After 1984 nothing of the original pavilion survived except the entry door to the terrace and the facade of the guest room. The facades thus existed in two states during Le Corbusier's lifetime: the 1934 version and the 1950 version. It seems more obvious to me to go back to the 1934 version for the reasons below:
– The 1950 rebuild was part of a bigger facade renovation project of the architect's apartment at that time;
– The wood version would be harder to maintain and hence would have a lower life expectancy given the exposure and given that certain essential compositional elements are apparently lost already, namely joinery profiles and assumed colour treatment of the panels;
– The 1934 build with its minimalist steel and glass design was an integral part of the original facade concept and the original facades have not been modified;
– Replicating the 1934 construction does not pose any special difficulty as we can base it on the logic of elements that remain in place and replace the steel with stainless"[35].

The proposal was accepted by the Fondation Le Corbusier which gave its verdict on the set of plans illustrating the two variants. Between the 1965 iteration and the 1934 iteration, it was the latter that won the day. The project was developed out of a fine-grained examination of details in the archival records as well as stratigraphic analysis of elements

23 Detail of pavilion envelopes; still from the film shot by Le Corbusier in July 1937 (FLC, stills 128744).
24 During reconstruction of the pavilion in 2003, attempts were made to reproduce the slim 1934 steel profiles.
25 Pavilion entirely glazed, except for the flap on the south face which has had its metal infill reinstated.
26-29 Details of pavilion envelopes, 2014.

36 Interview with Bernard Bauchet architect, 21 March 2014, conducted by Giulia Marino.
37 Ariel Bertrand, *Rapport de sondages: appartement de Le Corbusier, 24, rue Nungesser-et-Coli*, March 2006 (FLC, recent archives).

still in situ, namely the door and glass wall to the left of the guest room. It concluded that the appearance of the profiles needed to be reconstructed "*à l'identique*". This meant both dimensions and assembly details of the tubes and angles as well as the proportions of the glazed bays (this time with plain safety glass), the glass installed flush with the external face off the corner posts, accents provided only by a horizontal transom in the thickness of the piece and an upright on the side facing the garden bed to the south, which incorporated the flap in sheet metal.

Despite the change of material—stainless steel being preferred for its durability[36]—the need to respect the logic and the geometry of the set-out of these profiles (which were still legible in extant "remnants" of the original pieces) was controlled to the millimetre. To conform to the 1934 scheme, the plywood ceiling linings were also dismantled in favour of a ventilated suspended ceiling, modestly painted.

As for the paint scheme for the new painted stainless steel elements, the colours of the 1934 metalwork were reinstated (natural umber, based on paint analysis of the "remnants" of the 1934 frames[37]). Concrete surfaces, meanwhile, have been simplified somewhat as a result of gaps in the documentation. Period photos seem to suggest a darker shade around the awning, extending down the concrete posts so as to form a kind of "portal" enclosing the glazing frames, while the metal pole and integrated light fitting appear lighter. Also of note, the flashing at the base, added as part of the envelopes' 1950s version, has been retained.

Lastly, the living room skylight, which had been altered several times over the years, was replaced with a new frame in painted stainless steel (in the same natural sienna tone as the pavilion metalwork) with plain safety glass.

25

26

27

28 29

30

31

Bedroom and balcony

With the roof terrace works in full swing, in 2006-2008, Bernard Bauchet was also engaged to restore the bedroom and repair the western balcony, which had been beset by structural problems since the beginning.

The program of works for the bedroom included "restoration" of the furniture, in particular the pivot door and the bed. With input from architect Arthur Rüegg, who was consulted informally, the bed was rebuilt to its original condition, raising it to the correct height and reinstating the two-leg support, by means of a fixing in the western wall on the main courtyard side.

Sanitary fittings in the adjoining bathroom were reinstated along with certain accessories (soap tray, towel rail, mirror, etc.), and detailed analysis was conducted on the colour scheme. Paint research carried out by the restorer Ariel Bertrand, couldn't determine a consistent stratigraphy—as we mentioned the 1934 Salubra wallpapers had been removed by steam and traces of the 1950s colour scheme were lost upon the architect's death. So the preferred option was to reinstate a fairly restrained scheme in greys and ochres. Both masonry surfaces and built-in furniture were treated in this way.

32

33

THE MANY LIVES OF STUDIO-APARTMENT LE CORBUSIER 122

30 Renovations in 2003-2004.
31 Concrete bench and light-well cover in 2014.
32-33 Bedroom during restoration in 2006-2008: paint studies showed a neutral colour treatment for the room. The yellow and blue colours for the recessed cupboard and vent unit to the right of the bed respectively were retained. The bed fixed to the rear wall is raised back to its original height.
34-35 Bedroom in 2014. Built-in furniture elements were carefully restored at this time.

123   1965-2014: LE CORBUSIER'S LEGACY

38 I2E rénovation, for Bernard Bauchet architect, *Vérification de la stabilité de la terrasse, 7ᵉ étage, sur rue de la Tourelle*, February 2008 (Personal Archives of Bernard Bauchet).
39 *Ibidem*.

On this occasion also, substantial works were undertaken on the balcony to correct defects known since 1994, namely "cracks between the rail and the return walls on each side of the terrace"[38], due to "outward movement of the parapet"[39]. Following tests to investigate the nature and condition of the reinforcement, repairs resorted to the principle of "structural consolidation" used in 1958 by Pierre Jeanneret in the same location: the steel section in the cheek to the right of the coping was taken down and replaced with a new stainless steel section, its anchoring to the wall left apparent on the outside.

The natural anodised aluminium glazing frames (kitchen, dining and bedroom) were also dismantled and refurbished and the Périer blinds were diligently restored. Dismantling of the glazing units also allowed for waterproofing treatment around the glazed area where—a recurring pathology—water penetration had gravely impacted the masonry.

39

36-38 Glass wall, west facade: glazing units were taken down and their components restored then returned to their original position. The Périer timber blinds from 1934 were also conserved.
39 West facade, bedroom as it appeared in 2014.
Following pages Portrait of Le Corbusier in his studio (FLC, L4-9-61).

36

37

38

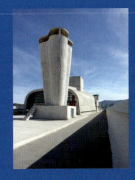

Immeuble Molitor was one of the buildings the integrity of which Le Corbusier defended against the Minister of Culture André Malraux. Unlike Villa Savoye (1931) and the Unité d'habitation de Marseille (1952) for which the process of listing began in 1964, during his lifetime, the Rue Nungesser-et-Coli building only received partial protection (facades, enttrance lobby, courtyards) in 1990. The apartment-studio itself was listed in 1972.

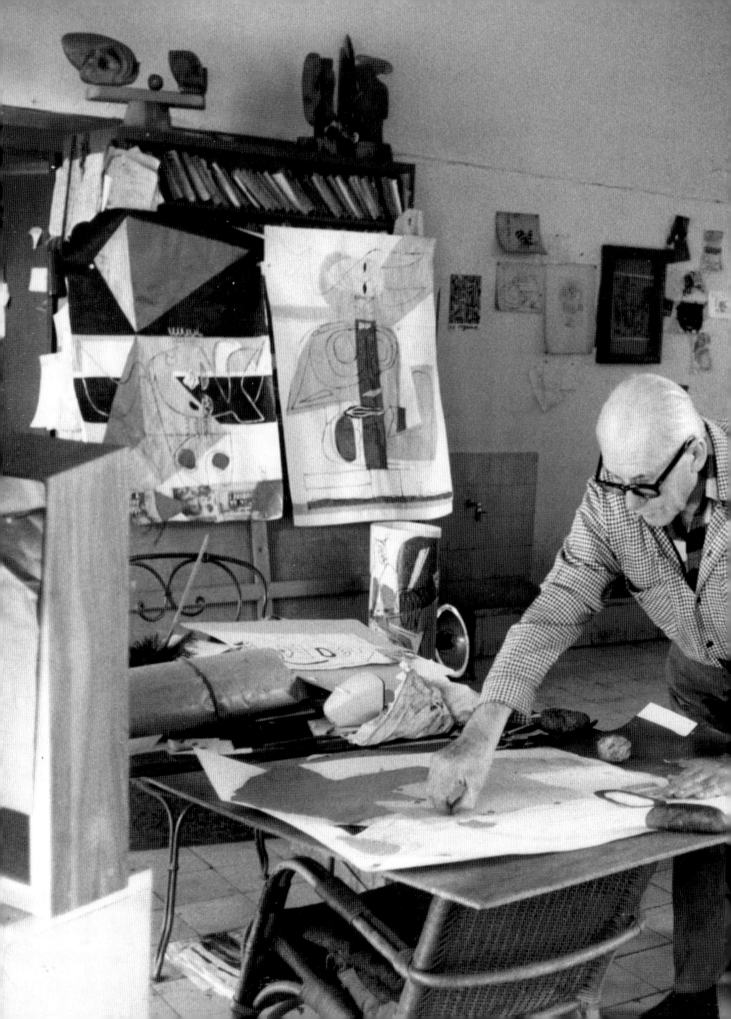

PROJECT

The material history of the apartment-studio at 24, Rue Nungesser-et-Coli comes to a halt, at least in so far as this publication is concerned, in 2014, the year in which preliminary research towards the restoration program was taken in hand. The central story of the numerous transformations brought about through the years now gives way to comprehensive inventorization of this exceptional architectural object, in order that future guidelines for conservation at 24 NC may be established.

This second part of our volume, which looks at the "project" of conservation, is effectively a synthesis of the very challenges faced in pursuit of that end. It looks at the research objectives of the authors, as requested by the Fondation Le Corbusier—which is both the guardian of the architect's memory, the owner of the apartment and the client for the restoration—so that the important job of conserving this emblematic place can be fully informed and supported by detailed research.

These studies are a prelude to any actual works. They approach the subject according to two key themes. First, based on historical analysis and a precise definition of the material fabric, we itemise the "sensitive" aspects by looking at what has been lost and what pathologies have arisen—waterproofing defects, the condition of the metal frames, some of the gaps we see in the phases of colour treatment, etc.—which allows us to devise targeted follow-up analysis. Second, by means of a series of guidelines (in the form of recommendations), we aim to achieve a conservation outcome by preserving the elements and components of the apartment-studio, to lead a broad-ranging yet effective discussion and to agree the best strategic baseline for conserving this iconic work in all its historical complexity, without neglecting subsequent layers, all of which are meaningful in their own right.

The history of construction—a discipline that is changing with the times—has made us accustomed to new ways of reading technology, benefiting from a wider multi-disciplinary approach, and material history, for its part, has taught us that the rigorous analysis of built fabric can inform the conservation project by using diligent, scientific enquiry to help identify its underlying intent. Le Corbusier's apartment-studio is a case in point, a site of prime research importance for the very foundations of conservation of twentieth-century built heritage and for the methods used. Rising above any Manichean points of theoretical discourse, but without reducing the project of conservation to the merely technical, the relationship established between knowledge and practice is close, strong and fruitful. History and the design process feed off one another with unstoppable logic. It is this logic and this alone that guides us, from close involvement with the object, towards the most consistent responses in addressing the big question of modern architecture.

Heritage conservation is a long term process. It requires investigations in full seriousness before construction, it calls for the most rigorous forms of reasoning. These recommendations also incorporate notions proper to the field of museography, as they must be the case of an object of such value where the approach must be carefully considered in regard to presentation and interpretation of the place.

RECOMMEN- DATIONS FOR PREPARATORY INVESTIGATIONS

ANALYSIS AND DIAGNOSTIC ASSESSMENT

The apartment at 24, Rue Nungesser-et-Coli underwent some major alterations during Le Corbusier's lifetime. In addition to some interior linings and radical revision of the internal polychrome scheme, the most substantial changes were those made to the envelopes which very quickly had begun to pose problems and were replaced several times over.

"Rust everywhere. And rust leads to destruction!" Transparent envelopes: stratigraphy and mechanical function

The original steel facades were manufactured by Dubois & Lepeu, openly inspired by the system of sliding sashes on rollers developed by Edmond Wanner for the recently completed Immeuble Clarté in Geneva. The spectacular glazed panels in the dining room, extending to the bedroom in a Nevada glass-brick wall (removed after the war), the studio envelopes, and all the glazed surfaces are huge, with very thin joinery frames made up of a system of flat bar and angle in pressed steel. Although they were treated with projective coating—"frames to be brushed, primed with red-lead, filled and painted with two coats oil finish"—corrosion appeared very quickly in the frames, accentuated by the heating being shut down during Le Corbusier's absence from Paris: he left in 1940 to take refuge in the Pyrenees and did not return until 1942. On his return the verdict was harsh; the architect returned to the issue in a note dated 1948, which is worth quoting at length:

"We need to measure the extent to which the sorry management of this house—which has had no maintenance since 1933—has caused deterioration in a construction that was fairly healthy when it was designed.

– 1° I repeat: the house has not been maintained since 1933.

– 2° Following proceedings that were brought upon me to expel me from my apartment, which I built myself, owing to the real estate agency going under and my ownership rights, represented by the shares I had, being annulled I have, since around 1935, that is to say for 10 years, found it impossible to take action. Powerless, I have watched my own apartment succumb in particular to rust in the window joinery. My proceedings are before the courts, and the agency was bailed out, by the way…

– 3° West facade, Rue de la Tourelle: during my absence in 1941 the Société La Nation, without asking and without my consent, plastered a thick layer of cement on my balcony—they smothered, pure and simple, the sliding windows of my dining room and the thresholds of the bedroom and kitchen in concrete. I sent a bailiff at the time to verify this, when I came back to Paris. As a result the glass gave way under pressure from the rust in 1948, one pane broke entirely and the others cracked diagonally. Besides that with the rust pushing in all directions it was going to cause leaks in the neighbour's house below. I had a glazed wall with oak joinery installed to replace the metal one, which I had to rip out. I begged Seuralite to take advantage of the situation to provide new waterproofing under the old glazed wall that had been pulled out (that was about 9 metres worth of waterproofing). The timber and glass wall was supplied by Maison Sylva at Saint-Dié (Vosges), the glazier was M. Alazard, Rue du Rhin, Paris.

– 4° That was the work I wanted to have checked and which I was obliged to resolve in order to spend the winter there.

– 5° As I was building the apartment at my own expanse I had an understanding with the real estate agency that waterproofing of the roof would be their responsibility, and that was never done. So over the years I undertook the waterproofing of the two barrel vaults (east and west). The roof slabs over my guest room, maid's room and studio were

Previous page Portrait of Le Corbusier by the Hungarian-born photographer Paul Almasy (FLC, L4-9-9).
1 Dining room in the 1930s, pressed steel-framed glazing units, sliding panels (FLC, L2-10-109).
2 Dining room in one of René Burri's photos from 1958; the west facade was replaced in 1948 with an oak-framed timber version designed to the Modulor.
3 Dining room in 2014: the glass wall was replaced again in 1964, during Le Corbusier's lifetime. Anodised aluminium profiles recall the slender 1934 versions; the projecting box with stained glass from 1948 is retained.

1 Note from Le Corbusier to Thintouin, assessor for the Tribunal de Paris in Le Corbusier's proceedings against the Société Immobilière de Paris-Parc des Princes, 19 October 1948 (FLC, recent archives).
2 Letter from Pierre Jeanneret to Le Corbusier, 21 July 1958 (FLC, H2-6-335).
3 See for example, the directions Le Corbusier gave on the wave-form concrete that replaced the envelopes on the main courtyard side of the Molitor in 1959: "Did you think about the small horizontal metal sections in the *'ondulatoires'* at 24 N-C? These should naturally be copper or aluminium (BEWARE of rust!)". Note from Le Corbusier to Gardien, 28 October 1959 (FLC, K2-17-72).
4 Letter from Le Corbusier to Pierre Jeanneret, 16 July 1946 (FLC, K2-17-72).

left unfinished; some were left with only 6 cm of thickness and just a single provisional layer of black bitumen compound on top.
– 6° When I was away in New York in 1946-47, Mr Contesseau's [sic.] architect undertook a repair so extravagant, so risky, the aim of it being to direct all the water from the roof onto the glass window of my guest room (8th floor): what happened as a result? Further spreading of the rust and the recent window cracking.
– 7° The metal framed glazing of the stairwell also had severe rust expansion and this year, 1948, the windows cracked one after the other.
– 8° The vertical glazed area in my painting studio, which is prismatic glass, also cracked due to the rust, and that led to the interior flooding whenever it rained"[1].

The alterations made in 1948 heralded not just a series of changes that would continue almost until the architect's death in 1965, but also attest to his "personal battle against rust", and a radical rethink of his interwar practice of building with steel joinery, an opinion shared by Pierre Jeanneret who was himself at the time faced with the deterioration of the Cité de Refuge curtain walling: "Dear Corbu, [he wrote to his cousin in 1958] for the Armée du Salut, I conclude once again that if the metal is not perfectly protected, it's no use for permanent constructions, it needs too much maintenance. I hope Quillery will find a better solution to avoid any future danger"[2].

"BEWARE of rust!", the architect kept saying in his correspondance during the 1950s[3]. Certainly, early on at least, Le Corbusier "demanded" that Pierre Jeanneret undertake localised repairs to his windows, and took a personal interest in the best methods for repair and protection of steel: "I ask you to please immediately replace the toilet seat in my bedroom [...] I also ask that the west glazing be re-done by a painter, prepped, red-leaded, because the windows are cracking under the effect of rust"[4]. The option of replacing the glazed bay on the west side quickly became the most rational option from the strictly technical point of view, but also an occasion to experiment with a new architectural language, devised to follow the rules of proportion of the Modulor and taking its cue from what would come to be defined, twenty years later, as *brutalist poetics*.

From transparent glazed wall to coloured Modulor

In July 1948, the steel framed glazing was replaced with solid timber framing, incorporating the earliest insulated glazing units made by Saint-Gobain. Replacement of the west glazed bay, which included a fixed projecting light with highly coloured glass, was by no means a trivial development in the evolution of the apartment-studio. This radical change would be quickly followed by replacement of the balcony facade to the guest room on the same pattern—the walls were clad in the meantime with oak ply—and thereafter a major reworking of the pavilion on the roof terrace, where frames in steel supported the solid timber joinery and a new cut-out scheme alternating solid and transparent areas (the ceiling was also clad in plywood at this time). These transformations signalled a profound change in the feel of the apartment, towards something much "warmer" than the initial "purist" version published in *L'Œuvre complète*.

4

4 Glazing to the dining room/bedroom in the 1930s (FLC, L2-10-110).
5 Projecting alcove incorporated into the timber envelopes of 1948. Used to display some of Le Corbusier's collection of objects, this was in due course provided with coloured glass designed to the Modulor (FLC, L2-10-10).
6 Coloured glass installed in the aluminium-framed glazing that Le Corbusier requested in 1964 a few months before his death (FLC, slide collection).

Except for the pavilion envelopes, not replaced until the 1980s (twice!), the timber facades disappeared in the early 1960s. Between 1962 and 1963—at the same time as he renovated the facade of the Immeuble Molitor—Le Corbusier worked on a new strategy for the envelopes. Enthused by the potential of aluminium in terms of durability (no rust!), he opted for a facade that is still there to this day: a large glazed bay, suspended and sliding on rails, the technology of which recalls "traditional" assemblages in folded steel rather than the extruded aluminium which was already widely available at the time. This solution allowed him to reinstate the transparency of the envelopes—without the unavoidable transom in the timber version, which was very much bulkier—but Le Corbusier retained the little projecting, coloured box.

Current condition: a complex stratigraphy

It is difficult now to identify the apartment with a specific historical period. This is especially evident with the envelopes—structural elements as well as transparent infill. Surviving elements dating from the interwar era (e.g. the Nevada-type glass bricks with round lens, in the bathroom of the bedroom) coexist with later alterations—those made during Le Corbusier's lifetime (e.g. anodised aluminium glazing of the west facade, dating from 1964) as well as more recent works (e.g. glass brick spandrels in the rooms facing the small courtyard, replaced in 1986, or the pavilion envelopes reconstructed to the original design in 2005, etc.).

The west facade on Rue de la Tourelle, in its current form, does indeed match that of 1965, the successive alterations being documented only by means of archive sources and a few remnants (e.g. the 1934 steel doorframe profile or the Périer timber shutters, also original). For the studio, where the stratigraphy is much more complex and different phases and remodellings coexist, the challenges for the restoration project are plain to see.

5

6

5 Plan FLC, 13332.
6 Plan Dubois & Lepeu, undated (FLC, 13901).

Daylighting from above, by north-light windows or from a continuous "translucent concrete", were abandoned when the project was in detail design in 1932. The notion of minutely controlled natural light, obtained by defining the material character of the envelopes, effectively guided the design and justified the multiple adaptations that followed. Whether for the street facade or that of the main courtyard, there was a continually evolving idea of expanses of glass characterised by a fine structure of pressed steel. In the exterior view captured on the completion of works (which also corresponds with the construction plans produced by Dubois & Lepeu, dated 22 November 1932[5]), one clearly sees how the first version of the street facade (east) had an entirely translucent surface: reinforced (most likely 'cathedral') glass on the exterior face with fine mesh in the lower part, like the Immeuble Clarté where construction work was completed during

7

8

9

10

7-8 Studio envelopes facing the main courtyard, in 1934 (left, FLC, L2-10-49) and in 2014, including the modifications made in the 1950s.
9-10 East facade of the studio—another feature modified after the war, and replaced in full in the early 1960s.
11-12 Original sliding unit to the east facade, in 1934 (left, FLC, L2-10-63) and in 2014.
13 Glazed walls of the studio, west elevation, main courtyard, including the original hollow profile.
14-15 Glazed walls of the studio, east, Rue Nungesser-et-Coli, replaced in the 1960s, including an exterior flat strip that was absent in the 1934 version.

THE MANY LIVES OF STUDIO-APARTMENT LE CORBUSIER   136

this period, and prismatic glass in a horizontal orientation to direct light and mitigate the effect of glare in the upper part. Only the "Wanner-type sliding sashes"[6] with their plain glass infill allow one to see out. They are also the only ones provided with solar protection in the form of a light-coloured curtain fixed by Ridorail.

Apart from the opaque infills of which no trace now remains (the Plymax panels of the 1950s were replaced in 1995) and the original windows (substituted as needed as revealed in the Robert Doisneau shots of 1945 where we see cathedral glass rather than reinforced), the studio has coexisting elements: the steel structure and sliding panels of the main courtyard, from 1934, including handles; alterations to these same elements by Le Corbusier in the 1950s (hinged casements in the vertical glazed wall facing the courtyard); and new envelopes, designed to the original plan (with a few substantive differences notably depth of horizontal beams) implemented during the "major renovations" of the Immeuble Molitor a few months before Le Corbusier died, and directed by him. To this must be added the more recent modifications to glass infill, from the 1980s-1990s (the differences between glass reinforced with plastic wires on the north east corner are the most blatant), fixed with galvanised steel beads into steel frames.

7 Bernard Bauchet architect, interview, 21 March 2014, Paris, conducted by Giulia Marino; see also: Personal Archives of Bernard Bauchet.

Inventory and mechanical survey

A consistent inventory of the envelopes would be indispensable in order to make the most appropriate choices in moving forward with the strategy for restoration. A detailed study of the facade elements would have to assess the mechanical functioning of the envelopes (resistance of fixings, possibility of repair of the sliding sashes, fixing of handles, fittings, etc.) as well as their surface finish. A detailed survey done in 2005-2006, including taking apart the aluminium elements of the west glazed wall (by architect Bernard Bauchet[7]) yielded an excellent basis for continuing with further analysis (notably the mechanical operation of the opening frames). The studio envelopes, though, seemed to require special attention, as did the upper parts of the facades of the living room and entry hall. This applied to the original elements (main courtyard facing) and the 1960 facade (street facing).

The envelopes needed a minutely detailed condition survey, covering everything from successive paint layers on steel, with testing for the presence of lead in the protective paints and asbestos in the joints, to mechanical tests to check the mechanisms, and the state of preservation of the reinforced glass (where there were diagonal cracks in places). The potential of all these things in terms of conservation needed to be clearly established, independently of the dates.

The original glass bricks in the bathroom of the bedroom became the focus of a special study, aimed at providing a consistent condition survey of both the glass units and the reinforced structure holding them together.

16

16-17 Le Corbusier's study in the southern part of the studio before (above , FLC, L2-10-65) and after the Nevada bricks were replaced in the panel facing Rue Nungesser-et-Coli in the 1990s.
18-19-20 Translucent units in the curved wall behind the washbasin in the bedroom are the last of the original Nevada bricks.
21-22 Nevada brick in the kitchen, in 1934 (FLC slide collection).
23-24 Nevada bricks replaced with more basic commercial glass blocks.

17

18 19 20

21 23

22 24

RECOMMENDATIONS FOR PREPARATORY INVESTIGATIONS

25-26 Pavilion fully glazed in 1934. Plain glass is supported in very slender frames made of pressed steel flat bar and angle.

27-28 Pavilion in the early 1950s: oak timber joinery fixed to the pressed steel structure of 1934; opaque infill alternating with transparent.

29-30 The "all timber" option having been rejected, the pavilion was rebuilt in 1987 in grey powder-coated Technal aluminium profiles.

31-32 In 2004, the pavilion was returned to its former state as a glass box by means of a new painted stainless steel frame, rigorously conforming to the original dimensions.

8 Le Corbusier, *Les maternelles vous parlent*, coll. *Les Cahiers de la recherche patiente*, carnet n° 3, Éditions Gonthier, Paris, 1968, pp. 56-57.
9 *Reportage sur un toit-jardin*, in *Le Corbusier. Œuvre complète 1938-1946*, curated by Willy Boesiger, vol. 4, Birkhäuser, Basel-Boston-Berlin, 14th edition, 2015, [Les éditions d'architecture, Zurich, 1946], pp. 140-141: 140.

"Big problems with the roof". Waterproofing and roof drainage

"All of Paris could be roof gardens! ...
– The objector: No! I am AFRAID it will leak!!!
– The result: slate, tile, zinc... all over Paris, cats wandering the rooftops, with sparrows.

But courtesy of lawn and plants, the apartment up high is shaded from heat and cold by means of the roof garden. The garden grows all by itself. Sun and wind direct and animate, giving it a perfectly delightful form. etc. The roof garden on top of the apartment block near Piscine Molitor in Paris.—20 cm of earth on the concrete, for a lawn (or simply wild grass).—40 cm in places for trees and shrubs.

Between 1932 and 1939 there were flowers too. From 1939 (Hitler), it was forbidden (by L-C) to do any garden work or maintenance. He wanted to try an experiment. Not a single snip of the pruning shears, not one sod turned over: the earth of the garden hardened into a crust never touched for 17 years. Flowers withered and died—except for the lavender and lily-of-the-valley, faithful to the 1st of May tradition. The wind and the birds carried off the seeds: a sycamore started to grow; a laburnum too. The lilacs flowered with abandon. The ivy was splendid. Four rose bushes became very tall eglantines. Gilliflower appeared, then disappeared; orange lilies arrived from somewhere and took over. The proof was found: the reinforced concrete of the roof was sheltered from expansion (waterproofing assured)"[8].

In volume four of *L'Œuvre complète*, Le Corbusier was, if it's possible to imagine, even more explicit: "1940: debacle! Exodus! Paris empty. The eighth floor roof garden is left to its own devices. Heatwave in 1940, heatwave in 1942, winter, rain or snow... The abandoned garden reacted, didn't let itself die. [...] Since that moment, the garden has been left to its fate. No-one does a thing; moss covers the ground, the earth becomes impoverished, but the vegetation thrives... The assumption one makes is this: the roof garden is the ideal protector for the roof; it shields it from negative or positive movement in the concrete, which could be a cause of disruption. [...] There has never been a leak in this roof"[9].

And yet, despite his enthusiasm (and a pinch of bad faith...), defects in the waterproofing and roof drainage of the garden-terrace were among the main pathologies affecting the apartment-studio; over the years they led to severe and repeated degradations. Localised water infiltration, starting from 1934, the year the works were finished, appeared from time to time in the apartment of Le Corbusier and on the sixth floor of the Immeuble Molitor, and were principally defects of design, namely arising from the complexity of the roof shape. The delays, errors and the poor workmanship decried by the designers during the building phase in 1933 also certainly played a part in the dubious level of protection afforded. All of this demanded extensive investigation before restoration could begin.

33

33 Portrait of Le Corbusier on the roof terrace in 1948 (FLC, L4-9-8).
34 Garden in the 1950s.
35 Vegetation at the time of Le Corbusier's death in 1965 (FLC, slide collection).
36 Roof terrace in 2014.

10 Letter from Le Corbusier to Yvonne, around 12 June 1953, in Rémi Baudoui, Arnaud Dercelles (eds.), *Le Corbusier. Correspondance*, vol. III, Lettres à la famille 1947-1965, Infolio, Gollion, 2016, p. 296.
11 *Reportage sur un toit-jardin, op. cit.*, p. 140.
12 Letter from Arsène Cornet to Pierre Jeanneret, 1 December 1932 (FLC, H2-3-58).

13 "With the current state of penetration or wall, one side of which is glass brick, it is not possible for us to get it to bind vertically and hence we are unable to execute the work to the best standard without modifications. Execution on the horizontal part without relief prevents us applying protection (which would be vital to the performance of the waterproof cladding). The ten-year guarantee cannot be applied in this particular case. Letter from E. Ythier Père & Fils to Pierre Jeanneret, 9 March 1950 (FLC, U1-11-156).
14 Letter from Arsène Cornet to Pierre Jeanneret, 15 November 1932 (FLC, H2-3-52).

15 Cost-Sharing for the roof works was vigorously debated between Le Corbusier sand the Société Immobilière de Paris-Parc des Princes and later contributed to delays in execution. Note from Le Corbusier to Thintouin, 19 October 1948 (FLC, recent archives).
16 Report by Le Corbusier and Pierre Jeanneret to

La Société Immobilière de Paris-Parc des Princes, *État des lieux des travaux de maçonnerie, Travaux exécutés par Mr. Cornet, Entrepreneur*, Chapter "Toiture-terrasse", May 1933 (FLC, H2-3-89).
17 Letter from Arsène Cornet to Pierre Jeanneret, July 1934 (FLC, H-2-237).

"I fear this will be trouble". The situation in 1933

The final design of the shape of the top two floors of the Rue Nungesser-et-Coli building—"Corbu's pigeon-house"[10], was, as we have indicated, a long and laborious process owing to the planning constraints. The search for an effective interior spatial idea and perfectly calibrated lighting—the two being inseparable—also seemed to justify the successive remodelling we see in the many variants sketched by the Le Corbusier studio. The eventual solution combined curves—the extrados of the vaults over the main spaces and glass brick at the ends—and flat planes of the central core of the apartment—entry and living room. The situation was complicated further by the eighth-floor guest room as an extension of the pavilion leading to the roof terrace—walkways envisaged in the longitudinal access of the vaults in the August 1932 "concept" were never built; only the balcony of the guest room was retained.

Le Corbusier claimed to have "extended research and experimentation with flat roofs to the point of making the roof garden (left in its natural state)"[11] something of a manifesto. The extremely varied shape of the Immeuble Molitor, however—"the huge difficulties with the roof and the additional beams needed"[12], as the builder put it—posed immediate problems for waterproofing and slopes for drainage. Interpenetrating horizontal, curved and vertical surfaces required particular care in detailing (in 1950, builders would not offer ten-year guarantee on roof repairs for this very reason![13]), but the delay in finalising the plans for the two upper levels, over which the architects hesitated at length, also led to less than perfect outcomes in the execution of the work. In a letter to Pierre Jeanneret, in November 1932, the main contractor Arsène Cornet was clear: "I would remind you that the falls in the central part have only been partly determined and there is no proper drainage from the parts above the walkways at present. We have started on the falls for the 8th, 7th and 6th but I still don't have your confirmation of the price I submitted"[14].

So much for the intrinsic issues with the irregular roof shape and somewhat improvised planning of the works (in the midst of the controversy over approvals[15]). To this one must add the contractor's delays and defects. During the execution phase, as early as May 1933, the architects were already underwhelmed: "The roof terraces have all been rejected as they are at present; the layer of bitumen for the sixth-floor terrace, forming the balcony on Rue de la Tourelle, is not level, with bumps of 0.04 to 0.05, no fall and no protective layer as specified. The upper circular terraces also have some corrugations in the poured bitumen and no fall for water at the base. There is no protection on the bitumen. Water travels along the wall heads on Rue Nungesser-et-Coli, no gutter and no water resistant protection. Some of the water inlets are partly blocked by builders' debris and there's no grille over the top. Ventilation pipes near the lifts have no cap or cage. 0.15 m waterproof cement plinths on the set-back terraces, not done"[16]. In 1934 the question reared again: "At Monsieur Le Corbusier's apartment it's the same thing again, because the fall on the terrace was not correctly done, water collects thereon. Are you not aware of this major work, and who will pay for it?"[17] On the one hand the sloppy work of the contractor was claimed to be at fault; on the other, the product, Hematect (a German synthetic product gauged with asbestos) "forming blisters on the vaults and detaching from

18 "Gentlemen, we point out that the roof covering in Hematec [actually Hematect] done by Cornet on one of our buildings at 24, Rue Nungesser-et-Coli, appears to be substandard. [...] These roofs are over Mr Le Corbusier's personal apartment. We must advise you regretfully that, in regard to your product, this may become a very bad reference, because this apartment, as you can imagine, is very much visited"; Letter from Le Corbusier to Maison Villiger-L'Hematect, 21 June 1934 (FLC, H2-3-292).
19 Letter from Arsène Cornet to Le Corbusier and Pierre Jeanneret, 17 November 1933 (FLC, H2-3-170).
20 Letter from Jean-Louis Malet, architect to the Owners' Corporation, to Fernand Gardien and André Wogenscky, 12 January 1968 (FLC, U1-8-275).
21 Letter from Edouard Barbier architect to Le Corbusier, 2 October 1957 (FLC, K2-17-243).
22 Letter from Le Corbusier to Jean Duclos, Trustee for the Owners' Corporation, 6 June 1950 (FLC, H2-18-20).
23 FLC, K2-17-1 and FLC, H2-6-314.
24 Letter from Le Corbusier to Salvatore Bertocchi, 9 June 1950 (FLC, recent archives); See also: Letter from Le Corbusier to Jean Duclos (Trustee), 6 June 1950 (FLC, H2-18-20).

37

38

39

40

37-40 Immeuble Molitor roofs as they were in the 1960s (FLC, L2-11-25).

the concrete"[18] as Le Corbusier put it in his complaint to Oscar Villiger, distributor for the firm of H. Hegemann, Leipzig, who did not seem to offer the required guarantees in either insulation or waterproofing.

One last crucial point is the presence of vegetation, laid out between the two courtyards and quickly identified as a source of potential degradation, notably from rainwater runoff. Once again, defective execution was to blame: "The 8th-floor gutters have been filled up with earth. Instead of putting in a drain, then loose clinker, then gravel and sand, with earth on top, the way it has been done water transports earth downstream, fatally blocking the downpipes. No precaution has been taken with finishes. I'm afraid I am obliged to make reservations. Water ponding has already caused large water stains on the 6th floor. I fear this will be trouble"[19]. Likewise the decision to extend the shrubbery beyond the containers and planters provided for it up to the webs of the vaults, would be heavily criticised by the Owners' Corporation. The body was "formally opposed" to this option when it undertook the roof repairs (partially at its own expense) in 1967-1968, fearing that "this arrangement is contrary to good rainwater disposal and risks causing more blockage in the downpipes"[20].

"The waterproofing needs total renovation". 1950-2014

In 1957 a condition report determined that the "bitumen film painted onto the cement"[21] of the original form soon proved to be inadequate. The same could be said of the "total lack of maintenance of the gutters and roof drainage much of which was never finished"[22] which Le Corbusier bemoaned in 1950, and defects in the roofing led to substantial degradations demanding continued repairs. Leaks soon appeared in different parts of the apartment; the issue was particularly evident in portions of ceiling associated with the early vault works (and with the kitchen); similarly the curved Nevada brick walls (the alcove for the refrigerator and the office area in the studio) are still somewhat sensitive to this day. There were "call-outs" to Fernand Gardien and Salvatore Bertocchi to help with urgent repairs due to water ingress throughout the 1950s[23]—"you should take advantage of being there to demolish the ceiling over my stairway which has just collapsed due to water penetration"[24], Le Corbusier ordered. It is worth noting that the finish for the painted plywood lining under the studio vault, as well as those in split oak on all the guest room walls, added in 1939, were most certainly retained by the architect as options to camouflage the damage. They would also end up being replaced during the maintenance and restoration work that followed over the years.

25 FLC, U-11-300.
26 Memo from Entreprise Seuralite, Paris, 16 November 1948.
27 Letter from Le Corbusier to Salvatore Bertocchi, 25 July 1963 (FLC, K2-17-251).
28 Memo from Entreprise Soprema, 1963 (FLC, K2-17-251).
29 Unsigned letter to Kérouault, 5 April 1966 (FLC, U1-8-220).

Beginning just after the war, a range of steps were taken to counter the problem (to which were added the frequent leaks in the central heating radiators in the floors below). In 1948, two years before the "complete waterproofing repair works by the Owners' Corporation"[25], Le Corbusier trialled a new waterproofing process involving "torch-on asphaltic fabric in strips under aluminised tape and with hot-applied caulking treatment using a layer of high melting-point Seuralite adhesive"[26] (coupled with Portland cement interior caulk). In 1963, with leaks persisting and threatening the structural elements—"on 12 m long beams from party wall to party wall [...] I found steelwork in the concrete completely rusted practically half way along its length"—the architect turned to Salvatore Bertocchi, his trusted masonry specialist, asking him to review the waterproofing system for the apartment's two vaults"[27]. The "running repairs to the waterproofing to give us 2 to 3 more years"[28] were growing in scope... In spring 1967, after Le Corbusier's death, a "full repair of the multilayer"[29] was undertaken by Jean-Louis Malet, architect to the Owners' Corporation. Again for the Owners' Corporation, architect Vladimir Jovanovic oversaw a new waterproofing treatment in 1987, aimed at completing the localised application of Ruberoïd in 1983 (Maurice Silvy for the Fondation Le Corbusier). A "resin waterproof membrane" replaced the multilayer system of the balcony for the guest room in 1995 (Robert Rebutato, architect to the Fondation Le Corbusier). A multitude of running repairs and patches followed, often done as emergency repairs in response to new leakages, to further complicate an already very complex stratigraphy...

The roof of the Immeuble Molitor today is a spectacular layering of different materials—from latticed aluminium to bituminous membranes, mineral felts and resins—one type here, another there, sometimes incorrectly lapped and often improperly flashed (or with fixing strips attached through the waterproofing layer...).

Ever since works finished in 1930, this has been deeply problematic. Roof protection and roof drainage really need to be seriously—indeed radically—addressed. It is vital that tests be undertaken at points of discontinuity and changes of direction in roof planes. A general inspection of roof gradients and downpipes is essential. "Standard" solutions are not worth considering, a qualified waterproofing expert is needed to conduct an inspection especially in regard to the exposed structural elements (the west exterior beam, balcony to the guest room, etc.) and most vulnerable locations like the curved glass brick walls (study and kitchen, but also the bedroom with the last original Nevada bricks).

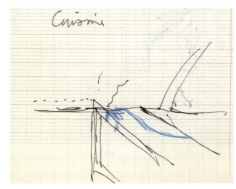

41

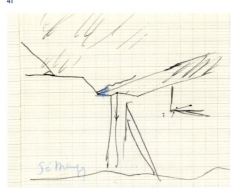

42

43

44

30 Unsent letter written by Le Corbusier to John Voges, Hillegom-Holland, 17 September 1956 (FLC, H2-5-584).

45 46 47 48

"The garden has the effect of protecting the reinforced concrete roof"

In a letter of 1956 (unsent?) to the famous Dutch nurseryman John Voges of Hillegom, a specialist in mail-order bulbs and flowers, Le Corbusier again brought up the alterations to his roof terrace: "My apartment, 24 Rue Nungesser-et-Coli, has a roof garden on the eighth floor with roughly 20 centimetres of earth and 40-50 centimetres in some places. This garden has been in existence for twenty-five years. When war broke out in 1939, it went untended and at that time I decided to leave it unfertilised, unpruned, completely devoid of maintenance of any sort, no leaf sweeping, etc. In recent years I've had it watered on very warm days. The garden has had the effect of protecting the concrete roof very well indeed. During the period 1939-1956, the wind or the birds brought tree seeds: false sycamore now 5 metres high; cythise, 4 metres high, the roses became eglantines, three metres high. The shrubs did especially well, the lavender too, the yucca astoundingly so. The lilas flowered regularly in spring but only for a very short period. Generally the flowers disappeared on account of the weeds (I never let anyone turn over the earth). The ivy just kept growing, etc., etc. The earth had grown extremely poor (lack of fertiliser). The reason for my letter is this: can you suggest some flowers able to survive these conditions? I want to try an experiment. [...] I'm taking this experiment forward with the keenest interest because I believe there is a real solution here to the issue of waterproof, isothermal roofs for reinforced concrete buildings. I was in Ahmedabad at last year's end, luxury villas with the same type of roof, automatically watered with amazing success. Here is my question: do you think that in these conditions of scarcity there are some interesting flowers that could brighten up such roofs in different seasons? (crocus, tulips, maybe hyacinths, snowdrops, buttercups, daffodils, etc., etc.). I am ready to try things out on the two roofs mentioned above"[30].

41-42 The springer line of the vault to the kitchen and dining room was one of the trouble spots identified by Le Corbusier where water was seeping from the roof terrace. Sketches sent by the architect to his collaborators (FLC, H2-7-159).

43-44 Owing to the complex profile of the roof and defective seals, significant problems are still present in these areas.

45-48 Roof coverings in 2014: despite a catalogue of interventions aimed at rectifying the problem, water ingress remains endemic.

31 Letter from Le Corbusier and Yvonne to his mother, 10 September 1951, in *Le Corbusier. Correspondance*, vol. III, cit., p. 199.
32 Letter from Le Corbusier to his brother Albert and his mother, 4 April 1948, *ibidem*, p. 71.
33 See also pp. 143-145 of this report.
34 Unsigned letter to Kérouault, 5 April 1966 (FLC, U1-8-220).

The experiments Le Corbusier had in mind in his correspondence with the nurseryman—suggesting perhaps thoughts of the roof terraces of the Couvent de la Tourette—would not progress. The architect did however work on the rooftop plantings in the 1950s, turning 24, Nungesser-et-Coli into an "admirable garden admired by all"[31]: "Everything comes through—lilacs in flower, yellow gillyflower, lily-of-the-valley. We have a veritable mine of guano to make use of thanks to what Yvonne's thirty sparrows leave behind"[32].

When the rooves were repaired in 1987, André Wogenscky set about reproducing the 'jardin Corbu'[33], to try and reinstate the 1965 appearance using photographic records suggested by Fernand Gardien before the general waterproofing works undertaken by the Owners' Corporation in 1967-1968[34].

The plantings that Le Corbusier wanted are an integral element of the roof works; a study by a botanical specialist would establish if it might be possible to go back and recover the original planting schemes of 1934 and 1965.

49-50 Ivy planted along the fence on the side of the main courtyard was a crucial feature in the layout of the roof garden (FLC, L2-10-148).
51 As with most of the plantings, the ivy has disappeared in recent times. Today the 8th floor garden has a very bare appearance.

49

50

51

Le Corbusier the gardener, 1950, by Willy Rizzo (**52-55**), Lucien Hervé (**54**) and René Burri (**56**). Despite what the architect claims in several texts, the garden seems quite well cared for...

35 *Problèmes d'ensoleillement. Le brise-soleil*, in Le Corbusier. *Œuvre complète 1938-1946, op. cit.*, pp. 103-115;108.
36 Letter from Le Corbusier to his brother Albert and his mother, 1 August 1947, in *Le Corbusier. Correspondance*, vol. III, *op. cit*, p. 45.
37 *Problèmes d'ensoleillement. Le brise-soleil*, *op. cit*, p. 114.
38 Letter from Le Corbusier to Auguste Mione (Bordeaux), 30 May 1950 (FLC, H2-6-265). Several variants were devised for this hood on the dining room side: a three-dimensional, parabolic awning in sheet metal (FLC, K2-17-217, and plans 13534, 13536), a prefabricated reinforced concrete element to fix to the web of the beam (FLC, 13854A), and a cast concrete element lost-formed using corrugated Eternit coffering (FLC, H2-6-265, plan 13745). Although the archives offer only scant images of the sunshade, this last version—similar in construction to the furniture on little wheels made during the same period for the entrance hall of Immeuble Molitor—is probably the one used.
39 Plan FLC, 13855B.

"The heat is unbearable in summer". Condensation and a holistic study of thermal behaviour

"In 1932, the Immeuble Molitor had a facade wholly of glass; we knew it would be hot in a heatwave, but come now! Parisians go on holiday at that time"[35]. In contrast to the 'fatalism' (if not disdain) he showed towards the Immeuble Molitor tenants and their comfort, Le Corbusier often complained of the "dreadful trial"[36] of overheating in his own apartment, a problem that seems to have afflicted it to a chronic degree.

Interior climate control—which was inseparable of course from the control of daylighting—was in fact a central consideration for the project in 1932-1934 as well as its successive evolution. In the original scheme attention was focused on the thermal performance of non-translucent elements as protection against the cold (for instance incorporating fibre-based insulation materials into wall thicknesses). But in successive alterations to the envelopes we see more interest directed towards conditions of comfort in the summertime, or rather the remedying of deficiencies in the design of the fabric.

"In temperate climes, in Paris, I felt the unwelcome effects of the sun in certain seasons (summer) when one is behind a glass panel. This glazing is wonderful for ten months but of course it's the enemy as soon as there is a heatwave. We had to invent something. It was in my private studio in Rue Nungesser-et-Coli where I'd suffered so much in silence (and for good reason) that I began to open my eyes, to imagine this thing that I called the *brise-soleil*, a term that is now is universal"[37]. Le Corbusier had to attempt to tackle the phenomenon of overheating, to the point of turning the constraint and making a creative architectural opportunity of it. From "type of *brise-soleil*, west facade"[38] added in 1950, to the small brise-soleil placed in front of the ribbon windows of the living room in 1951[39], the architect tested a wide variety of passive solar protection devices, many of which later

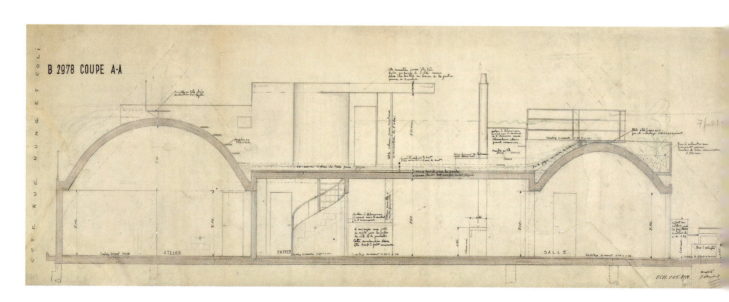

57

40 André Hermant, 'La technique', in *L'Architecture d'aujourd'hui*, n° 2, 1935, pp. 26-29: 27.
41 Section B 2979, 7 July (August) 1932 (plan FLC, 13414).

42 *Archives Robert Doisneau, Atelier Doisneau-Gamma Rapho, Paris.*
43 Note from Le Corbusier for Pierre Jeanneret, 2 May 1946 (FLC, K2-17-185).

reappear in his work (most iconically for the Claude & Duval Factory). The same was true of new products like Plymax spandrel panels incorporated into the existing fabric after the war, or the "plywood with thin metallic sheets on one side or the other"[40], a material first used by the automobile industry, which was making inroads into the building market between the wars (it was distributed in France by the French subsidiary of Luterma) owing to its excellent ability to reflect solar radiation.

From "strong insulation" to "overheating"...

Originally, in the drawing material submitted for the construction permit and in correspondance between the various trades, the architects insisted on "strong insulation" for the solid parts. As with the spandrels facing the courtyard for the Immeuble Molitor, the composition of the upper floor seems to have included a thin sheet of insulation (dry sand or wood fibre, similar to Héraclite[41]) between the structure and the waterproofing layer, with "*dallettes de ciment*" floor tiles on top for the roof terrace hard paving, and plantings for the rest.

The designers at first presented the thermal insulation as a key feature of the scheme and a prominent signal of its modernity. But despite the care applied to its design, it very soon, in Le Corbusier's eyes, became a notorious source of inconvenience for the superstructure which he tried to address with a variety of solutions. The thermal inertia of the solid parts was acknowledged as inadequate given the proportion of "cold glazed wall" surfaces (Robert Doisneau's portraits in winter 1946 make the place look chilly indeed, only partly ameliorated by the electric heater added to the dining room and wood burning stove in the living room![42]). Moreover, the "strong insulation in the floor slabs" was regarded as the principal cause of the decisive problem of summer overheating. Le Corbusier's annoyance comers through in several pieces of correspondance: "You would do me a great favour if you would whitewash the tarred roof of the guest room and the northern part of my studio, also tarred. If we could eventually go over to aluminium for the kitchen, dining room and bedroom that would be good, as the heat is unbearable in summer: the very thick, 'insulating' vaults have the effect of drawing in the heat and radiating it back"[43].

Believing he had identified the principal cause of overheating, Le Corbusier searched for means of alleviating the problem throughout his time at 24, Rue Nungesser-et-Coli. He called upon well-known experts who in turn came up with all manner of new materials and "anti-thermal techniques" they believed would help to control it, not least using the principle of reflection in lightweight alloys (a technique promoted by Aluminium Studal before the war).

In 1950, just as he pulled the plug on certain options for the Cité Radieuse, he undertook a review of the apartment with Pierre Jeanneret: "Mr Arzens, a very knowledgable paint expert said we should not put aluminium sheet up as this oxidises very quickly, turning into a heat sink (metal). One hour later I got a different view in the other ear: an American expert from the US Government saying that aluminium sheet even if it is oxidised has a considerable power to reflect heat, etc., etc. Hard to know. Mr Arzens seems to me to know what he is talking about, it was he who advised me for Marseille. He could

57 Transverse section through the central core, roof terrace vegetation, 7 July 1932, completed 7 August 1932 (FLC, 13413).

44 Letter from Le Corbusier to Pierre Jeanneret, 1950 (FLC, H-2-4-568).
45 Letter from Georges Blanchon—Établissements Barre to Mathieu & Passedat, 22 June 1950 (FLC, U1-11-51).
46 This problem was probably one of provision for air circulation, the ventilated roof having been developed in the execution documents of 2005; Bernard Bauchet, *Restauration de l'édicule en terrasse de l'appartement de Le Corbusier*, FLC, June 2004 (FLC, recent archives).

be useful to you as an adviser on paints at the Armée du Salut as well as Rue Nungesser"[44]. Overwhelmed, in 1950 the architect resorted to adding extra opening lights to the glazed walls of the studio to enable natural cross-ventilation[45]… and in the 1960s he bought an Airwell air conditioner!

From comfort to condensation

Notwithstanding consideration of the physiological comfort of occupants, the nature and assembly of components posed problems of physics for the building. One

58 59 60

finds traces of condensation at the edges of transparent walling with low inertia, at the point of fixing to the masonry support. An indicative case is the condensation inside the pavilion, where the stairwell becomes a heat reservoir for the heated interiors and the glazing was particularly exposed (traces of condensation under the roof covering are explained by poor ventilation in the roof profile itself[46]).

The apartment's infrequent use, lack of natural ventilation and the control of interior climate in winter also exacerbated these forms of degradation, allowing them to progress substantially in some cases. An integral part of the health-check on the roof should be a detailed survey of the apartment's thermal properties by a building physicist. Some theory needs to be applied to the eventual insulation of the opaque envelopes (as a thin layer either internally behind the outer cladding or externally as part of the roof refurbishment) with reference to dynamic modelling. A thermal audit needs to be undertaken alongside an audit of the building services. Individually adjustable, automatic heating and a hygrometric monitoring/control system, to manage mechanical ventilation for instance, need to be given detailed consideration.

47 In September 1932, Arsène Cornet spelled out the composition of the standard slab, with slight differences for the different facades: "Please note our agreement on the conditions for executing the work at Boulogne. On the Rue des Tourelles section, the slab will be poured as follows: laid on the formwork a slab in hollow units and concrete, on which will be laid bricks of cellular concrete. On the cellular concrete there will be a layer of ordinary concrete with small mesh armatures. On the Rue Nungesser-et-Coli part, onto the prepared formwork we will have a layer of Solomite, and onto this layer, cement slab with or without small hollow units. Letter from Arsène Cornet to Le Corbusier, 3 September 1932 (FLC, H2-3-42).
48 Letter from Le Corbusier to Salvatore Bertocchi, 25 July 1963 (FLC, K2-17-253).

"A foolhardy choice". Knowledge and condition of the structural envelopes

There are information gaps concerning the primary structure. The static behaviour of the vaults on their two longitudinal beams, which are simply set into the party wall of the west facade (with the aid of a concrete shear wall to rigidify the system), or held up by an intermediate V-post in the east facade (studio), is clear. Their composition, though, is not something the archives can tell us. The absence of any rust in the west vault, which is simply painted (dining room, bedroom, kitchen) leads us to suppose there is no supporting metal arch (the 'ghosting' referred to earlier is only the stiffening in the reinforced concrete). Similarly, with the generally consistent system of hollow floors in the Immeuble Molitor described by Arsène Cornet[47], we might reasonably claim that what we have is a mixed structure made up of an arc of reinforced concrete and clay block infill.

If we are to confirm the hypothesis, and have confidence in the health of the structure, we need some measurements by a civil engineer. It will be essential to dismantle one or more internal plywood linings; this needs to be done with great care and the state of decay of the elements also assessed, especially the metal fixings to the floor. Likewise, whilst a visual survey has not shown evidence or major structural defects, a series of resistance tests is intended, notably for unprotected external elements like the monumental beam on the west side, which si very exposed and could be affected by concrete carbonatation, as Le Corbusier himself says in a note to Bertocchi in July 1963[48].

58-60 State of the apartment-studio in 2014: condensation issues in the pavilion (left), around the translucent wall of the study (centre) and the guest room.
61 The end of the lateral beam supporting the vault, 1980s.
62 Repair of the wall using concrete under the springer line of the vault, 1990s.
63 The crack that had necessitated repair of the wall during the 1991-94, still visible in 2014.

One place that is especially vulnerable due to its construction type is the west balcony facing Rue de la Tourelle —which has had stability issues since 1950, evident both in the crack through the floor, parallel to the facade, where the overhang begins, and in the partial separation in the parapet. Pierre Jeanneret was warned by Le Corbusier in 1958, and made a plausible attempt to explain the phenomenon which would recur from time to time in the years afterwards: "Dear Corbu, [...] regarding your balcony, on the facade opposite Rue Nungesser-et-Coli. As I recall on the plan, this balcony is partly cantilevered, and since

49 Letter from Pierre Jeanneret to Le Corbusier, 21 July 1958 (FLC, H2-6-335).
50 Letter from Le Corbusier to Robert Guénassia, President of the Owners' Corporation, 19 May 1959 (FLC, H2-6-338).
51 Bernard Bauchet architect, interview, 21 March 2014, Paris, conducted by Giulia Marino.
52 Robert Rebutato architect, interview, 20 March 2014, Paris, conducted by Giulia Marino and Franz Graf.
53 Letter from Fernand Gardien to Salvatore Bertocchi, 5 June 1963 (FLC, U1-8-182).

the cantilever is made of a very thin slab (by Cornet) but has a heavy parapet to support, we should check if there is cracking in the tiles parallel to the facade where cantilever C-D starts, and also if there are any cracks in the parapet at points A and B"[49]. Marginally reassured, Le Corbusier, who was also of the view that "excavations at 18 Rue Nungesser-et-Coli have caused a failure in the wall at 22 which we are built on"[50], had a strut added in the thickness of the right parapet in 1959. With new defects appearing at the same place and in the same manner, this corroded metal element was replaced by a new stainless steel one, fixed by a bolted plate exposed on the exterior face of the balcony during the works carried out by Bernard Bauchet in 2004-2005[51].

Although no cracks are visibly now at this location, a one-off inspection is needed to test the balcony's static behaviour.

In terms of general health, one final aspect should be mentioned: the party wall in exposed rubblestone and brick, on the north side of the studio. The cement joints today are proud of the stone faces, which is not how they were in Le Corbusier's original treatment (photos taken in raking light in the 1930s show it clearly[52]). Similarly, cement was added in the 1990s to dub out under one end of the main beam of the vault on the street side, probably to counter the diagonal cracking caused by the spread of the vault, an issue that had already emerged in Le Corbusier's lifetime (a note from Fernand Gardien dated 1963 states that "Mr Bertocchi is monitoring the crack on the east wall of the studio and has one or two tell-tales in place"[53]). This crack dated from the 1960s and is still visible. It is quite probably associated with "physiological movement" in the volume of the studio. However, and bearing in mind the major works carried out when the Jean Bouin new Stadium was in construction (2010-2013), it requires careful monitoring as part of preliminary investigations for the restoration program.

64 Portrait of Le Corbusier on the balcony seat, west facade, facing Boulogne (FLC, L4-9-27).
65 Le Corbusier on the balcony of the dining room photographed by André Steiner in 1936 (FLC, L4-9-10).
66-67 Cracking in the cheeks of the balcony in the 1950s; sketch with a letter from Pierre Jeanneret to Le Corbusier, 21 July 1958 (FLC, H2-6-335).
68 Plan of the balcony, west facade and partial section of parapet, summer 1932 (FLC, 13647).
69 Repair of consolidation originally carried out by Pierre Jeanneret in 1958, during the 2003-2006 remedial works.
70 Northern end of the balcony in 2014.

64

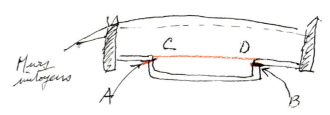

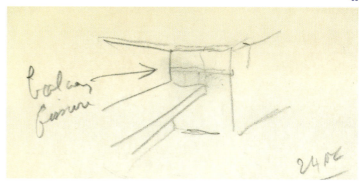

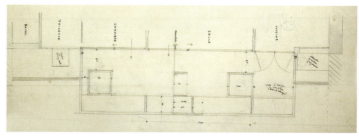

155 RECOMMENDATIONS FOR PREPARATORY INVESTIGATIONS

"Polychromy on the walls helps to create a feeling of space". Colour stratigraphy

Despite some uncertainties on the exact tones used, the archives provide crucial clues on the type of products used in the two great periods of occupation, namely before and after the Second World War (acknowledging the ambiguities of such a simplification). The walls of the living areas in the 1934 scheme "were rubbed down, skimmed, finished, and painted in oil, two coats". The entry lobby and dining room had "Salubra wallpaper on the horizontal" on top of render. Wet areas, being more exposed to humidity, were "brushed, primed, finished with one coat of oil and one of Ripolin". Metal parts (joinery frames, furniture, radiators and exposed pipes) were originally painted with linseed-oil colours. Note that in those days, satin or gloss finishes were saved for built-in furniture and hardware.

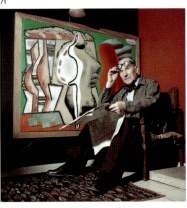

71 Le Corbusier in front of the fireplace, by Robert Doisneau, 1945.
72 Portait of Le Corbusier in the living room, by Felix H. Man, early 1950s: the wall backing onto the small courtyard, retains the light blue-grey paint scheme, with natural timber mouldings. Indirect lighting provided by the so-called Marseille lamp, added in 1939.
73 Portait of Le Corbusier in the living room, by Willy Rizzo, 1958: the north wall is now black, and the fireplace wall a richer shade of red.
74 Living room at the time of the architect's death, 1965 (FLC, slide collection).

54 Letter from Le Corbusier to M. Brue, Peintures Pingère, 26 April 1951 (FLC, K2-17-193).
55 Unsigned note, 29 September 1961 (FLC, U1-8-170).
56 Quote by Raymond Lampens, 18 March 1965 (FLC, U1-8-197).

57 Invoice from Peintures Berger addressed to Mrs Le Corbusier, 27 June 1952 (FLC, K2-17-190).
58 For a description of the supports and samples, see: Ariel Bertrand, *Conservation-restauration de peinture*

Étude de polychromies, chambre de Le Corbusier, immeuble Molitor, Paris, March 2007, p. 11 (FLC, recent archives).
59 Unsigned note, 29 September 1961 (FLC, U1-8-170).

75 76 77 78

75 Alcove between living-room and dining room, late 1930s. Sculpture *Marin à la guitare* by Jacques Lipchitz in the foreground (FLC, L2-10-103).
76 Alcove in a picture from the magazine *DU-Kulturelle Monatsschrift*, June 1961.
77 Alcove at the time of the architect's death, 1965 (FLC, slide collection).
78 Alcove in 2014.

After 1945, numerous adjustments were made to internal polychromy, but it seems the "type" of paint seemed to change radically: Le Corbusier opted for Berger products, which are certainly more matte than the oil paints of the 1930s. Moreover, the architect gave very clear instructions on the finish: "I want colour applied by spray, not by brush on the large green and red surfaces and the small ones as well. I require the work to be done with the most exacting level of technical skill. I am counting on you and I shall be forced to be tough because I was not content with the Matroil applied in the dining room on the seventh floor"[54].

Lastly we can note that two successive deliveries of Salubra were recorded in September 1961[55] and March 1965 (nos. 4320 A and 4320 K)[56], which attest to the usage of this famous wallpaper throughout the time Le Corbusier lived at the apartment-studio.

With the highly complex stratification at 24, Rue Nungesser-et-Coli, there are certain gaps in the information available for research on the internal polychromy, both in regard to the shades, which as we said were changed several times during Le Corbusier's life, and the physical-chemical character of the different products used.

The bedroom is a very good illustration of this. The archives have a reference to a bill in the name of Madame Le Corbusier dated June 1952 for 'Matone' (white, black, natural ochre, yellow ochre), 'Matroil' (interior white, yellow ochre, strong red) as well as 'Bergemail' (light pearl grey and napier green), the latter probably destined for the built-in furniture[57]. Although no instruction was given on where these colours were to be applied, the palette seems consistent with the polychromy stipulated for the bedroom. Studies on the colour selection for this emblematic room in March 2007 (Bernard Bauchet, architect), confirm in a general sense information in the order for Peintures Berger, namely "original decors were painted in shades of ochre, sea green and red ochre"[58]. From the later "retouching" however, there are no traces of the "black wall around the bed, blue at headbed"[59] from the 1950s. This justifies a more detailed analysis of the stratigraphy.

157 RECOMMENDATIONS FOR PREPARATORY INVESTIGATIONS

79 Famous 1958 portrait by René Burri, Le Corbusier standing in front of André Bauchant's painting *Le couronnement de la vierge* (1924) Colours are quite bold, corresponding to the blues and blacks cited in 1961. Ventilator cover to the right of the bed is also painted.
80 Bedroom in the 1930s (FLC, L-10-123, L-10-126).
81 Bedroom at the end of the 1950s (FLC, L2-10-124).
82 Bedroom at the time of the architect's death, 1965 (FLC, slide collection).
83 André Wogenscky's workspace in the bedroom, 1970s.
84 Recent view of the room after restorations in 2007.
85 Portait of Le Corbusier by Felix H. Man, early 1950s.
86 Lobby in the late 1960s (FLC, slide collection).
87 Staircase in a photo by Véra Cardot and Pierre Joly, 1974.
88 Stair and lobby in 2014: the interior colour scheme has become more subtle, notably for the structural members.

79

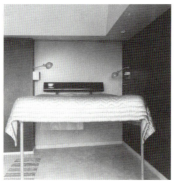
80

81

82

83

84

THE MANY LIVES OF STUDIO-APARTMENT LE CORBUSIER   158

60 Ariel Bertrand, *Étude des polychromies, appartement Le Corbusier, immeuble Molitor*, Paris, March 2006 (FLC, recent archives).

A new campaign of sampling, localised and including research on any fragments of paint or wallpaper that survive behind the plywood linings or in the reveals, should enable all the variations to be mapped and the different "reference states" of the apartment-studio recreated. This would be a sizeable piece of work, looking at all the rooms, so that a certain number of uncertainties can be removed (which, as well as the bedroom, include the north wall of the dining room and the exact shade of the wall facing the entry) through the different phases, so as to be well informed enough to decide on the approach for the restoration.

The exteriors also need to be subject to an equally detailed analysis. Research done in 2006 on the pavilion and the terrace (originally finished in a "cream wash"[60]) should be extended to all the exterior surfaces, including the access walkway leading to the apartment-studio. In particular, the strong colour treatment of the west balcony, which has traces of red and ultramarine respectively on the south and north cheeks and a bright colour on the fridge niche, should be carefully reinstated.

The stratigraphic analysis carried out with the aim of establishing the binders and pigments of the various "layers", in relation to colour charts supplied by producers that Le Corbusier approached, should also integrate notions of preservation. Broadly, this study should recommend procedures for uncovering the reference surface. The technical possibilities for treatment of the original surfaces, namely carefully exposing and conserving them, are incorporated into the restoration project.

85

86

87

88

"Happy and in good health". Built-in furniture and finishes

Designed in association with Charlotte Perriand—the kitchen design is one that can be attributed to her—the built-in furniture can be easily blended with the interior partitions (the wardrobe-door, Le Corbusier's study nook in the glass brick recess of the studio, etc.). This is expressed spatially, but also materially. During analysis, the built-in furniture will be studied in the same way as the interior finishes, by means of its materials and installation.

In this respect there are some major 'families' of materials that can be systematically analysed and explored, independent of their specific uses. This may involve:

- Detailed studies of various manufactured timber products, painted or unpainted (like the different plywood products);
- General stratigraphy of painted manufactured timber products (such as alcoves in the living room, sliding cupboard doors in the studio, Isorel linings, etc.), including their fixing to the main structure and any hardware used;
- General stratigraphy of painted solid timber elements and assessment of their state of conservation (e.g. pivot doors, kitchen drawers, dressing table in the bedroom, etc.);
- Stratigraphic studies of painted metal elements and their state of conservation (e.g. table legs, bed, exposed pipework, heating cylinder in the guest room, etc.);
- Conservation assessment of sheet metal components (e.g. kitchen sink);
- Conservation assessment of ceramic and glass finishes (e.g. floor tiling, kitchen wall tiling, glass mosaic in the bathroom). This analysis also includes the supports, to establish the presence of any hazardous materials;
- Natural stone (e.g. Corentville stone tops, Cipollino marble tabletop, etc.).

There are several furniture items remaining, such as the tubular metal-framed couch, bed (restored during works to the bedroom carried out in 2006), low table in the living room, and the table, the watchmaker's furniture and painter's easel in the studio. The same level of attention is applied to these, aiming to ascertain their state of conservation.

89

90

91

92

"That we might leave our dingy cave in Rue Jacob and start living in more civilised conditions". Comfort: lighting, heating and sanitation

The original central heating could simply be disconnected and replaced with a space-heating system possibly coupled with mechanical ventilation. The original chimney could be a good site for locating new installations. This question needs some exploration, and is linked to the matter of the apartment's overall thermal performance.

An upgrade needs to be looked at for all the installations. Criteria to guide such work (voltage, security, connection to alarms or fire safety controls, etc.) should be dictated by the uses to which the apartment will be put.

Sanitation infrastructure is part of the original scheme devised by Le Corbusier in 1934. In the main bedroom and guest room the plumbing is openly "exposed", consistent with the architect's intent to showcase building services. This needs particular care. While the hand-basins are simple resin reproductions of the original moulds dating from 1994-1995 and the tapware was mostly also replaced at that time, the bathrooms must be regarded as consistent, integral units.

Any upgrade of the plumbing services and equipment to these rooms needs to be focused. Equally, the condition of the metalwork (from the bathtub to the 'accessories') and mirrors (and their supports), will be assessed in considerable detail.

89-92 Dressing table in the bedroom, built-in kitchen furniture, study cupboards, and the watchmaker's cabinet Le Corbusier brought from La Chaux-de-Fonds, etc. The items making up the furniture of the apartment-studio require careful conservation.
93-94-95 Services, some of them replaced over the years (sanitary fixtures, lighting, heating, etc.) are also part of the interior furnishings.

93

94

95

161 RECOMMENDATIONS FOR PREPARATORY INVESTIGATIONS

61 Claude Prélorenzo, 1997 (FLC, recent archives).

"Picturesque disorder".
Use of the apartment and museography

The apartment-studio has been owned by the Fondation Le Corbusier since Le Corbusier died in 1965, and was leased to André Wogenscky, who had his architectural studio there, from 1974 to 1991. Since Wogenscky left, the Fondation Le Corbusier has been grappling with the question of how to re-use the spaces. As the Fondation Le Corbusier Committee remarked in 1997, the question has "cultural, emotional, economic and practical resonances; the issue is invested with significant challenges and is a complex and indeed complicated one"[61], and needs a consistent and thoughtful approach, based on *a priori* investigation, undertaken well ahead of any initial concept for the restoration work.

The options appear wide open: house-museum, open for visitors either regularly or occasionally; research centre; meeting room or base for the Fondation Le Corbusier; exhibition gallery, etc.. As recommended in the course of this study, it is useful to stress how important the 'museographical' aspects are to conserving the place. Whether that means faithfully reinstating the interiors of a given historical phase, or creating looser, pared-down spaces, the question needs to be considered during the planning stages. The constraints—whether in terms of codes and standards for public admission, or security of artworks, objects and furniture—can be very challenging. They need to be evaluated early, and that needs to include consideration of how built objects and fabric might be impacted.

Whatever the chosen outcome, an inventory of furniture, artworks and objects that belonged to Le Corbusier when he lived at the apartment and are still in the Fondation Le Corbusier's possession would be externally useful. It would need to consider everything from light fixtures no longer in situ, to carpets that play a key role in defining the interior spaces.

96 When Le Corbusier died, the painting studio was documented by means of a thorough photographic survey (FLC, slide collection).
Following pages The living room and dining room photographed by René Burri in 1959.

During recent restoration of the Immeuble Clarté in Geneva (1932) the sliding sashes were able to be retained after off-site treatment, by simple repair of the roller mechanism, thus conserving material integrity. The sliding windows of the Weissenhof-Siedlung (1927) semi-detached houses were replaced during renovation in the 1980s. In the 2006 works they were repaired and maintained.

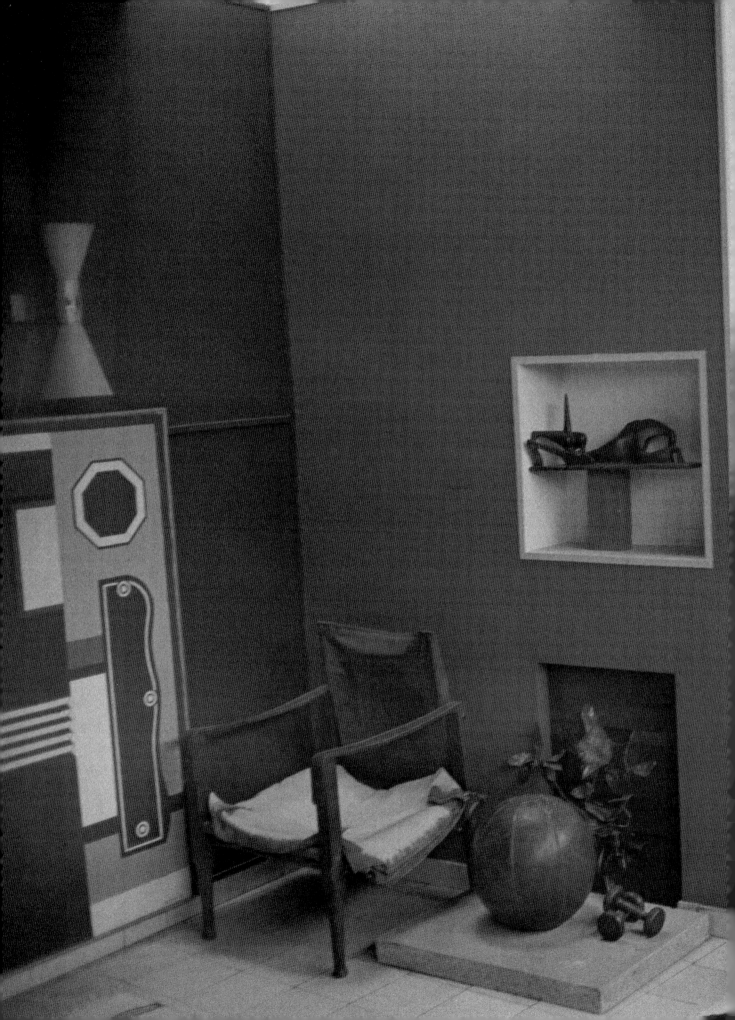

GUIDELINES FOR RESTORATION
CONSERVATION OF A PALIMPSEST

Across the spectrum, from international specialist journals—*L'Architecture d'aujourd'hui*, *The Architectural Review*, *Casabella*, etc.—to the news-stand magazines like *La Décoration intérieure*, *Schöner Wohnen*, even *Paris Match* or the Swiss magazine *DU*—the apartment-studio elicited a major response, stretched out over a relatively long period more or less coinciding with architect's biography. In more recent times, "24 NC" has been the subject of several important historical contributions. Through rigorous research, some have attempted to reconstruct the origins—the work by Jacques Sbriglio and Marie-Jeanne Dumont to name but two. Others have sought to place it within the broader Corbusian catalogue—Henri Bresler, or the university research led by Garcia and Treuttel and Dieter Gyesin. Others, using a more critical approach, have delved into some of the fundamental themes—Rémi Papillault's analysis of "glare", Arthur Rüegg's study of the interiors. Then there are the accounts of Le Corbusier's colleagues and collaborators, from Charlotte Perriand to André Wogenscky. These bear witness to the use of the apartment and, more generally, to the architect's daily life—which he was always happy to share, including in the radio and television media. They are a real key to understanding his œuvre.

These publications have helped to restate the apartment-studio's importance. The present publication, undertaken for the Fondation Le Corbusier, focusing on fabric analysis of the original building and the various transformations it underwent, is intended to complement these other investigations. Methodologically, studying its material history over the long term—from 1934 to 2014—has proven indispensable as a means of acquiring deeper understanding of this emblematic object. Furthermore, investigation focused on the physical data present in the fabric itself has allowed certain crucial questions relating to its conservation, and the special challenges of preservation-restoration, to come to the fore.

Conservation of a palimpsest

Throughout the research, one thing has been apparent: far from the spartan environment captured in photographs of the 1930s—which we know to have been shrewdly staged—the apartment-studio at 24, Rue Nungesser-et-Coli results from a complex layering with multiple meanings. His home was indeed a "permanent building site" during the architect's life, a place of endless experimentation—architectural, plastic, constructional—a place where the paradigms of his œuvre intersected with a very personal idea of domestic life. From its original 1934 character, which was meant to embody interwar theories about the "purist" interior, to a more "brutalist" style drawing on the vocabulary Le Corbusier was developing after 1945, transformation was subtle, but no less radical. Glazed walls, architectural colour, indirect lighting, Modulor, brise-soleil... Here, the grand themes that shaped his output almost appear to have been spelled out with demonstrative intent; probing, borrowing, uneasily self-referential.

The 1934 version in fact survived only until 1939; it mutated again in 1948, heralding the more substantial transformations of the 1950s; replacement of the envelopes—yet again—was still to come, in 1964. When the architect died in 1965, the apartment-studio was already a "palimpsest". Subsequent interventions followed, many of them led by his former collaborators, as the years went by, while a fertile "theoretical" debate rumbled in the background trying to balance pragmatic technical solutions with a certain deference towards the "Master". There were reconstructions "à l'identique"—with all the ambiguity the phrase implies—which tried to reproduce, if not the "original" material at least an impression of it; there were more visible "modernisations", clearly meant to be read as such. All these diverse interventions combined and overlaid one other. The material history of the apartment-studio became one with the material history of its many restorations. If, between 1934 and 1965, the alterations made by Le Corbusier himself attest to an approach to material substance

Previous page Le Corbusier with his dog Pinceau II in the stairwell of the apartment-studio, photographed by Robert Doisneau in 1945.
1 Le Corbusier posing in the dining room for *Glamour Magazine* in 1964.
2 Portrait of the architect at his marble table, by Robert Doisneau, 1945.
3 Le Corbusier with one of his artworks on the west balcony (FLC, L4-9-20).
4 Portait of the artist in the painting studio, by Felix H. Man.
5 Being filmed for an interview in the dining room (FLC, L4-9-16).
6 Portrait of Le Corbusier by René Burri, 1959.
7 Domestic rituals, by Willy Rizzo, late 1950s.

1

GUIDELINES FOR RESTORATION

that was already fluid—take the issue of polychromy for instance, the approach to the 1930s Salubra wallpapers or the Matroil-Berger matte paint of the 1950s—the options chosen during successive restorations were equally varied. In retrospect, they encapsulate the very nub of the question that has been so strongly debated in recent years: what is the proper approach to restoring the built works of Le Corbusier?

Looking at the apartment-studio over the long term, one thing is clear: the timeline of its "many lives" is impossible to untangle. The complex stratigraphy is an integral part of the built object's importance. From this standpoint, two strategies present themselves for the project of conservation: *preservation of the envelopes in their current state* (which, despite some minor interventions here and there, are close to their 1965 condition) and *restoration of the lived interiors*, in other words returning them to their condition of 1965, conserving the alterations he himself made over the years and restoring the interior spaces to how they were at the end of Le Corbusier's occupation.

Conserving the envelopes

The idea of a "complex stratigraphy" is particularly evident in relation to the envelopes, where today we have a coexistence of 1934 elements, the alterations made by Le Corbusier and later interventions—some better than others—dating from after his death. The problem of how to choose a pertinent reference period would be a major one, and certainly is more than an ethical question or a matter of hagiographic temptation.

Reference to the "2014 state" in fact inserts itself as the only strategy for retaining the coherence of the built object as a whole; it therefore comes down to exploring the possibilities for *material preservation of the envelopes in their current state* through exhaustive analysis and detailed recording of the fabric. This naturally means looking for traces of the several "layers", precise dating and in-depth understanding of the built elements, this being a fundamental complement to the analysis of archival sources.

Aside from their scientific value, preliminary studies need to address another objective—condition. Well developed considerations around intervention techniques must come into play early in the piece. Such "operational diagnostics" must be seen as providing a sound basis for whatever *ad hoc* measures must be implemented, in an informed manner, for the strict *preservation of fabric*.

The conservation strategy of course only partly relates to the elements that might interfere with our reading of the built object, as is the case currently with the roof terrace. The roof coverings in effect are sensitive, and appear at present to be of secondary interest. Without any guiding strategy, the process of adding multiple successive layers to the roof terrace over time—it really is a museum of waterproofing treatments!—has only accentuated a defect in performance endemic since the beginning. There is a very high risk of propagating defects due to water penetration and condensation. Similarly, it is illusory to go looking for what Le Corbusier was striving for in the roof garden's "landscape" today. In its current state, not only is the roof terrace an unaesthetic mish-mash, it is also a clear danger to the preservation of the apartment-studio in the short to medium term. As we have recommended, it needs to be looked at comprehensively with the aim

1 Claude Prélorenzo, 1997
(FLC, recent archives).
2 Maurice Besset, Notes sur
l'appartement Le Corbusier,
addressed to Hubert Poyet,
Technical Adviser to the
Ministry of Foreign Affairs,
7 November 1966 (FLC,
recent archives).

of correcting its construction defects while reinstating the remarkable treatment used for the geometry of the eighth-floor (a significant "cleaning-up" exercise avoiding, for example, encasing the free columns or exposed cover flashings).

In this respect the garden, "a real open air room", an indispensable part of the picture in terms of Le Corbusier's work—has a vital role to play in the *restoration* of the roof-scape. In other words, the garden needs to be treated as an interior, faithfully rebuilt to its 1965 form, including furniture and plantings.

In-depth analysis and diagnostics of damp protection for the rooftop-terrace are inseparable from a full study of thermal performance, for interior comfort but also, and above all, for durability—for a major historical monument like Le Corbusier's apartment-studio, the question of energy efficiency may be considered secondary. Any investigation concentrating on thermal properties also, in a general sense, needs to include a survey of the building services. Potential works to heating and mechanical ventilation systems—perhaps even air conditioning—could in fact help to maintain the constant environment that is essential for avoiding major defects due to condensation. This would also allow any alterations to the envelopes, where preservation measures are a higher priority, to be kept to a minimum.

In addition to the electrical installation, which over the past thirty years have been subject to some particularly egregious, not to say damaging changes, that need to be avoided in future—an overall study of the services would also need to look at fire detection and security, depending on the approach to the collections adopted by the Fondation Le Corbusier.

Restoring the interiors

Museography, and more generally the future use of the apartment-studio, is a fundamental issue and to a large extent project options are shaped by these factors. As Fondation Le Corbusier Committee stressed in 1997, this issue "has cultural emotional, economic and practical dimensions, loading it with significant challenges and rendering it a complex, not to say complicated question"[1]. It merits a thoughtful and coherent response. It needs above all to be addressed *a priori*, well before any preliminary design work for the apartment-studio, where a strategy of restoration is applicable, meaning taking it back to the final form it presented during Le Corbusier's time, conserving the various later alterations made by Le Corbusier himself.

These are not new ideas. In fact many of them were already under discussion at the time the Fondation Le Corbusier was created, as a result of the architect's bequest. Maurice Besset, the executor of his will, set the scene: "The apartment can only be used for purposes compatible with the spirit and moral framework of the man who lived and worked there for thirty years, and who created it in his own image. Its re-use must guarantee total respect for the architectural layout and colour scheme determined by Le Corbusier, as well as certain particularly important aspects of the furniture and fixtures"[2]. Explaining the objectives of conservation, Besset introduced a lively exchange of views on the future purpose and use of the place, and especially on the interiors,

3 Undated report (FLC, recent archives).
4 Note by Roger Aujame, 8 March 1997 (FLC, recent archives).

including the personal objects that are indispensable to the "intimate character of a place so closely connected with Le Corbusier, as well as (having) a biographical dimension"[3]. Before clearing out the apartment, Besset commissioned a detailed photographic record, including the roof terrace garden, to make it possible, one day in the future, to recreate the "home of the Master".

André Wogenscky left in 1991 and following the 1994 restorations, prior to the apartment being opened to the public, one critical question arose: "For the moment we acknowledge the apartment is reserved for visits and occasionally for meetings of the Foundation's Management Committee. These will generally be informed visitors, their expectation will be to visit an apartment that is out of the ordinary, given the personality and celebrity of its late proprietor. The artist's workshop in particular should seize one's attention. But in no sense should it be a reconstruction, like the king's chamber at Versailles or Marie-Antoinette at the Bastille like in the Musée Grevin. [...] We want the visitor to partake of an architectural lesson, or more accurately speaking, an architectural experience. Everything else is purely anecdotal. In this experience one thing of capital importance is lacking at present, it no longer exists, and the absence of it destroys the balance that once held. Part of it is the precise placement of paintings, which "marked out" the rhythm over the white walls as opposed to the coloured walls mainly found in the living room and entry hall. Another part of it is the objects so carefully chosen and positioned in alcoves in the living room or on the beams below the web of the vault in the dining room, which lent all the value to the whole"[4]. With this statement in 1997, Roger Aujame was stressing a crucial point: how does one read the apartment-studio in such a condition, empty, devoid of so many objects and movable items which played such a major role in shaping its interior ambiance?

8

9

THE MANY LIVES OF STUDIO-APARTMENT LE CORBUSIER   172

8 Portrait of Le Corbusier in the studio, by Willy Rizzo, 1959.
9 The studio in 2014: the only furniture —the easel, wooden table and the drawer unit from La Chaux-de-Fonds.
10 Portrait of Le Corbusier in the living room, by Willy Rizzo, 1959.
11 Recent view of the living room: a couple of pieces evoke the architect's life: a copy of the 'cow-hide' rug, original low table, one of the earliest of the Grand Confort armchairs, etc.

173 GUIDELINES FOR RESTORATION

5 Le Corbusier, interview with Recteur Mallet, 1951, in Le Corbusier, entretiens avec Georges Charensol (1962) et Robert Mallet (1951), La Librairie sonore, Frémeaux & associés, 1987.

6 Maurice Besset, Notes sur l'appartement Le Corbusier, addressed to Hubert Poyet, Technical Adviser to the Ministry of Foreign Affairs, 7 November 1966 (FLC, recent archives).

'Lived' interiors

The close connection between the architecture and the "personal collection" of Le Corbusier has been subject to various interpretations. The man himself loved to show it and would stress its importance in relation to the internal spatial arrangement and colour scheme. "All these walls, they are bare, but inhabited by a whole crowd of objects. Can you tell us about these things, these curios? We see them all around and they create a deep sense of intimacy." Recteur Mallet's question, in 1951, elicited this response from Le Corbusier: "There are paintings, they are not arranged like a stamp collection but placed in certain spots and lit in certain ways, then there are objects and sculptures by my friends,

12

Henri Laurens, Lipchitz, etc., antiques, modest folk art, Greek objects, they are amazing at actual size, so clear and so moving. There are Byzantine items picked up somewhere in the Balkans, they carry the style of a lost age. There is all sorts. There's what I call my private collection, bits of wood, lumps of stone, pine cones, bricks from buildings that I use as bases for statuettes, there are whole seashells, shells broken by the sea which are really interesting. And yes, let me point out the animal bones, for people who like that sort of thing, animal bones washed up in front of family guest-houses, on the shore [...] To be frank I all this my CP, my "*collection particulière*", and I get so much pleasure from it"[5]. The painting studio, which now is occupied only by the watch-makers drawer cabinets, the La Chaux-de-Fonds table and the trusty painter's easel, was at one time "a picturesque jumble of yellowing papers, books and periodicals piled high, even on the floor [...], empty dried-out paint pots"[6], a far cry from the vast empty space it is today.

13

12 Stone mask (FLC, inventory of objects).
13 Photo taken at the time of Le Corbusier's death: the mask in the alcove; *Marin à la guitare* (formerly *Femme et enfant*) by Jacques Lipchitz (1927) remained its position between living room and dining room throughout Le Corbusier's residency (FLC, slide collection). The sculpture was sold in 1979, and is now at the Centre Georges Pompidou in Paris.
14 Le Corbusier showing his "personal collection" to photographer René Burri.
15 Spanish jugs in grey earthenware, which used to be prominently displayed on the mantelpiece at the Rue Jacob apartment (FLC, inventory of objects).
16-17 A multitude of objects placed around the apartment (photo from 1965) (FLC, slide collection).
18-21 Le Corbusier's collection (FLC, inventory of objects).

14

15

THE MANY LIVES OF STUDIO-APARTMENT LE CORBUSIER   174

16

17

18

19

20

21

175   GUIDELINES FOR RESTORATION

7 *Ibidem.*
8 FLC, Restauration appartement Le Corbusier, minutes of site meeting, 22 November 1994 (FLC, recent archives).
9 *Ibidem.*

Fundamental to our appreciation of the work, the interiors need intelligent thought, incorporating, alongside the conservation of the fabric (or restoration in some cases), traces of the lived experience of the designer and inhabitant. A faithful reconstruction, as Maurice Besset said, "would only turn into a performance, a memory in poor taste, unworthy of Le Corbusier. No-one in the world has the right to parody what he himself referred to as his 'geology', his "stratigraphy" which only has sense in relation to the creative work for which it supplies the primary matter"[7]. All the same, the question remains as to the apartment's current state, and more generally the proper collections management strategy to be adopted. As the Committee stressed in 1994, "the Foundation has to respond to expectations of visitors coming to see an apartment that is manifestly his, not one in a 'recent state' having undergone major modifications"[8]; in its current, bare state it does not really meet that objective. "There are two reasons for these visits: to see the architecture (created by LC) and to see the home (where LC lived)"[9]; owing to a degree of "abstraction" that has now occurred, things are falling short where the second reason

22

23

24

25

22 Ernö Goldfinger House-Museum, 1-3 Willow Road, London (built 1939).
23 Apartment-studio of the artist Nikos Hadjikyriakos-Ghikas, 3, Kriezotou Street, Athens (built 1939 and 1955).
24 Museo Casa Estudio Diego Rivera y Frida Kalho, Juan O'Gorman, Mexico (1929-1931).
25 Casa estudio, Luis Barragàn, Mexico (built 1949).
26 Fondazione Achille Castiglioni, Milan: the 'Studio museo,' formerly the architect-designer's place of business, today hosts a variety of cultural events and is open to the public.
27 Headquarters of the Fondazione Vico Magistretti, in the architect's office, Milan: the old drafting studio still contains some of its furniture and is used as a research room.

26

27

is concerned, all the more so in that the original spaces, as Le Corbusier himself would frequently emphasise, cannot be separated from the objects so artfully arranged within.

Without going to extremes as in the case of the collections management at 1-3 Willow Road, London (the private apartment of architect Ernö Goldfinger, where the original cans of *beans* and bottle of *Ketchup* have been diligently restored and set out in the kitchen!), it seems the idea of using a few choice objects to re-establish the apartment's ambiance of 1965 is workable. This would not have to be done, as in Diego Rivera and Frida Kahlo's house-studio in a building designed by Juan O'Gorman in Mexico, or Nikos Hadjikyriakos-Ghikas apartment-studio in Kriezotou Street, Athens, by recreating interiors down to the "last pot of paint". Instead the collections could follow the model of the Casa Estudio of Luis Barragán: striking a careful balance in the considerate placement of a small number of "evocative" items.

The vast collection held by the Fondation Le Corbusier ranges from objects (Spanish pitchers? An African stone mask? The reassembled berber carpet?), to works of art (still life paintings? the original Léger?), to furniture (prioritising original pieces if possible). Placed in their original setting, these objects can help us interpret the apartment-studio, to sense its architectural character above all. The existing presentation of Villa Savoye, with its completely empty rooms, would be an excellent example of the opposite approach. A detailed museographical study right down to the original lighting concept, which as we know is fundamental to comprehending the work, would guarantee some cogency in the presentation, a philological (scientific) validity that is equally effective in educational terms.

The virtue of this option, we should emphasise, is to enable appreciation of the "spaces", these being inseparable from the ideas of "domesticity" the architect wanted to communicate. It would also be compatible with the apartment's utilitarian function. The Fondazione Achille Castiglioni and the headquarters of the Fondazione Vico Magistretti, both in Milan, are important precedents. In Castiglioni's apartment, exhibitions and conferences take place in the designer's own offices, which have been preserved as-found—furnished with a plethora of small, "poetically charged" industrial objects reminiscent of Le Corbusier's collection. At the Fondazione Magistretti, a "neutral" space for functions coexists beside a room preserved with its original furniture, the architect's office, as-found, adapted simply for use by staff of the Foundation. In both cases, compatibility has been achieved between visits to a historically charged setting and a range of practical uses, not least for planned events that "allow the building to speak".

At the apartment-studio, Rue Nungesser-et-Coli, the vaulted studio space lends itself to such an approach albeit with selected items of furniture, objects and artworks to evoke the original use, whether copies or originals it scarcely matters. In the living areas interpretation panels should be prohibited, so as not to be in conflict with the "house museum" concept (interpretive materials on the history of the place could be "mobile", such as a printed leaflet or multimedia tool). The studio however lends itself to more flexible uses. With furniture and objects displayed for the occasion it would be an excellent events venue. Problems of introducing temporary installations for exhibition purposes, for example, within such a distinctive space, can be avoided—the example of Villa Le Lac, the "Petite Maison" at Corseaux is instructive in this regard. We should note also that the double destination of apartment and studio—a house museum fitted out as such in the living areas and a more multi-purpose studio space for conferences, meetings, exhibitions, or other activities managed by the Fondation Le Corbusier—could complement well the current use of the house museum of Maisons La Roche-Jeanneret.

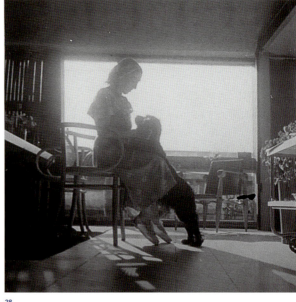

28

The apartment-studio became a *Monument Historique* in 1972, one of the iconic objects of twentieth-century design. Its high degree of material significance as a built object has to be conserved side by side with its non-material values, its "sense of place" as Le Corbusier's home. As a heritage site the two values are deeply intertwined, difficult to separate and rich as a source of meaning and information on the architect's personal world.

The many lives of the apartment-studio pose major problems for conservation ethics both in terms of appropriate technical measures and theoretical approaches to adaptation and use, the two being inseparably linked. A study of the fabric over time, from its original construction phase through its various transformations up to the present day, shows a challenging level of complexity—far outweighing the "endemic" pathologies affecting its condition and the palliative actions that may be needed to address them. Should we return the fabric to a former state, repair it or preserve as found? This is the broader strategic discussion we urgently need to have about twentieth-century architecture, a discussion that lies at the nub of the debate in Europe—and globally—on conservation and restoration of modern and contemporary heritage. We hope this study, in establishing the importance of this palimpsest of exceptional value that is the apartment-studio at 24, rue Nungesser-et-Coli, may contribute substantially to that very discussion.

28 Portrait of Yvonne with Lacky the dog, in silhouette, by Lucien Hervé, 1950s (FLC, L4-9-121).
Following pages Portrait of Le Corbusier in front of the kitchen door, by René Burri, 1959.

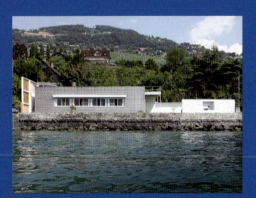

The idea of 'reference state' raises major ethical questions for the restoration of Le Corbusier's works. Each case is different: at Villa Le Lac, Corseaux (1924, top) the Fural cladding added in 1951 to the south wall is conserved; Maisons La Roche-Jeanneret (1925) have recently seen the ochre tone of the original pre-coloured Cimentaline render rediscovered.

SOURCES AND BIBLIOGRAPHY

SOURCES

Fondation Le Corbusier, Paris

GTA Archiv - ETHZ
Institut für Geschichte und Theorie der Architektur, Zurich
– Bernard Hoesli Collection
– Siegfried Giedion Collection
– Alfred Roth Collection

Archives of the Ville de Paris

Archives Municipales of the Commune de Boulogne-Billancourt

Centre Georges Pompidou, Bibliothèque Kandinsky, Paris
– Collection Véra Cardot and Pierre Joly

Historical Archives of the Institut National de l'Audiovisuel, Paris

Médiathèque du Patrimoine, Paris

Musée du Quai Branly, Médiathèque, Paris

Photothèque AGRAM-Saariste photographic library

Private Archives of Bernard Bauchet, Paris

Private Archives of Bertille Chéreau-Benoist, Paris

Private Archives of Studio Willy Rizzo, Paris

Agence Gamma Rapho
– Atelier Robert Doisneau, Paris

Private Archives of Étienne Bertrand Weill, Paris

Private Archives of Robert Rebutato, Paris

Private Archives of Peter Willi, Entrechaux

Musée de l'Elysée, Lausanne
– René Burri Collection

Agence Magnum
– René Burri Collection

Archives d'architecture HES-SO, Geneva
– Bruno Reichlin Collection

Centre d'archives d'architecture du XXᵉ siècle, Paris
– André Wogenscky Collection

Centre Canadien d'Architecture, Montréal
– Pierre Jeanneret Collection

Bibliothèque de la Ville de La Chaux-de-Fonds
– Albert Jeanneret Collection

Institut national d'histoire de l'art, Paris
– Maurice Besset Collection

Réunion des Musées Nationaux, Photographic agency, Paris

Library and Archives Canada, Government of Canada, Ottawa
– Yousuf Karsh Collection

BOOKS

Jacques Sbriglio, *Immeuble 24 N.C. et appartement Le Corbusier*, Birkhäuser, Boston-Basel-Berlin, 1996

Sumet Jumsai, Claude Prélorenzo, Brian Brace Taylor, *24 NC. Appartement de Le Corbusier à Paris*, Li Zenn, 2011

BOOK CHAPTERS

Immeuble locatif à la Porte Molitor, Paris, 1933, in *Le Corbusier et Pierre Jeanneret. Œuvre complète. 1929-1934*, published by Willy Boesiger, vol. 2, Birkhäuser, Basel-Boston-Berlin, 7th series, 1967, [Les éditions d'architecture, Zurich, 1935], pp. 144-153

Immeuble de Rapport à Paris, in *Le Corbusier et Pierre Jeanneret, Encyclopédie de l'architecture. Constructions modernes*, 7th series, Éditions Albert Morancé, Paris, 1937, n.p.

Le Corbusier, *Immeuble 24, rue Nungesser et Coli and Other Buildings and Projects, 1933*, Garland Publishing, New York, 1982

Henri Bresler, *L'immeuble parisien: la théorie mise à l'épreuve*, in *Le Corbusier et Paris, Rencontres de la Fondation Le Corbusier*, Fondation Le Corbusier, March 2001, pp. 113-125

Marie-Jeanne Dumont, "L'immeuble de la porte Molitor" and "L'appartement de Le Corbusier", in *Le Corbusier plans en DVD*, Éditions Échelle 1, Paris, 2005, n. p.

Rémi Papillault, *L'éblouissement et le contre-jour dans l'atelier du 24 N.C.*, in *Le Corbusier et l'œuvre plastique*, XII Rencontres de la Fondation Le Corbusier, Fondation Le Corbusier-Éditions de la Villette, Paris, 2005, pp. 203-215

Juan Antonio Calatrava Escobar, *24NC: la casa de un arquitecto, el lugar de la sintesis*, in Andrés Martínez Medina, María Elia Gutiérrez Mozo, Salvador Guerrero López (eds.), *Foro critica IV. Le Corbusier, Mensaje en una botella*, Colegio Territorial de Arquitectos de Alicante, Alicante, 2011, pp. 51-75

Giulia Marino, *Les multiples vies de l'appartement-atelier du 24NC: histoire, projet, méthode*, in Marc Bédarida (ed.), *Le Corbusier. L'œuvre à l'épreuve de sa restauration*, actes des XIXᵉ Rencontres de la Fondation Le Corbusier, Fondation Le Corbusier-Éditions de la Villette, Paris, 2017, pp. 148-161

ARTICLES AND PRESS

Jean Paul Sabatou, "Un appartement dans le gabarit", in *L'Architecture d'aujourd'hui*, n° 7, September 1934, pp. 47-52

Jean Paul Sabatou, "Immeuble à Paris", in *L'Architecture d'aujourd'hui*, n° 7, September 1934, pp. 41-46

"L'architettura mondiale", in *Casabella*, n° 84, 1934, pp. 46-47

Siegfried Giedion, "Opere di Le Corbusier", in *Quadrante*, n° 19, 1934, pp. 36-40

"Über den Unterschied zwischen anthropomorph und menschlich", in *Schweizerische Bauzeitung*, n° 104, November 1934, p. 14

Philip Morton Shand, "A First Instalment of the Immediate Future. Flat of the Parc des Princes by Le Corbusier and Jeanneret", in *Architectural Review*, n° 77, February 1935, pp. 73-76

A. B. (André Bloc), "Les arts primitifs dans la maison d'aujourd'hui", in *L'Architecture d'aujourd'hui*, n° 7, 1935, pp. 83-85

"L'atelier radieux de Le Corbusier", in *Beaux-Arts. Chronique des arts et de la curiosité,* 9 April 1937, p. 1

"Cordonnier est-il toujours mal chaussé ?", in *Le Décor d'aujourd'hui*, n° 30, 1938, pp. 17-27

Maurice Diricq, "Génial et amer, admiré et injurié, architecte du bonheur, visionnaire de la cité future: Le Corbusier", in *Paris-Match*, vol. 30, n° 253, 1954, pp. 26-33 and 54

Silvia Kugler, "Besuch bei Le Corbusier", in *Du: Kulturelle Monatsschrift*, n° 21, June 1961, pp. 17-31

"Die Wohnung von Le Corbusier. Hier plante ein Genie die Architektur unseres Jahrhunderts", in *Schöner Wohnen*, n° 8, August 1966, pp. 113-122

"Un appartement de Le Corbusier monument classé", in *Le Monde*, 7 April 1973, n.p.

"Porte Molitor Apartment", in *A+U Architecture and Urbanism*, n° 149, February 1983, pp. 11-18

Peter Carl, "Le Corbusier Penthouse in Paris, 24 Rue Nungesser-et-Coli", in *Daidalos*, n° 28, June 1988, pp. 65-75

Philippe Rouault, "Le Corbusier Calendar", in *Kenchiku Bunka*, vol. 52, n° 606, April 1997, pp. 1-8

Mara Partida, "Sobre algunos dibujos para el 24, Nungesser-et-Coli", in *Massilia 2003. Annuario de Estudios Lecorbuierianos*, Fundacion Caja de Arquitectos, Barcelona, 2003, pp. 118-129

Alfred Escot, "Dans l'appartement de… Le Corbusier", in *L'Express Styles,* 4 December 2008, n.p.

L. M., "Musées. Appartement-atelier de Le Corbusier", in *16 Le journal de votre député maire*, September 2008, n.p.

"L'appartamento ideale per Le Corbusier", in *La Stampa Casa*, 6 September 2010, n.p.

AUDIOVISUAL REFERENCES

Jean Epstein, *Les bâtisseurs*, 1937

Les architectes s'emploient à créer les villes de demain, television program, Radio Télévision Française *L'Art retrouvé*, 1 January 1945

Le Corbusier, radio interview with Robert Mallet, 1951, in *Le Corbusier, entretiens avec Georges Charensol (1962) et Robert Mallet (1951)*, La Librairie sonore, Frémeaux & associés, 1987

Jean-Marie Drot (producer), *Le Corbusier expose son plan d'urbanisme pour Paris*, television program, Radio Télévision Française *L'Art et les hommes-Paris peut-être*, 28 March 1956

Michel Mitrani, Jean Prat (producers), *Le Corbusier à propos de la ville de Chandigarh en Inde*, television program, Radio Télévision Française *Plaisir des Arts*, 18 January 1959

Le Corbusier in his Paris home and studio, television documentary, BBC, 1960s

Max Favalelli, Pierre Gillon, *Ce soir on cambriole… Le Corbusier*, radio program, Radio Télévision Française, 31 July 1960

Adam Saulnier, *Le Corbusier à Chandigarh*, television program, Radio Télévision Française, 15 April 1962

Jacques Manlay, *Le Corbusier à Pessac et l'habitat social aujourd'hui*, television documentary, Radio Télévision Française (footage of the apartment, taken from *L'Art retrouvé* 1945)

Christian Archambeaud, Jacques Barsac, *Le Corbusier*, Co-production Cine Service Technique, INA, Gaumont, Fondation Le Corbusier, La Sept, Antenne 2, Mission Cable, Channel Four, RTSR, Thomson Technique de Communication, 1987 (footage from the 1960s)

ACADEMIC PUBLICATIONS AND REFERENCES

Dieter Gysin, *Immeuble à la Porte-Molitor: Analyse eines Miethauses von Le Corbusier im Vergleich mit traditionellen Pariser Miethäusern*, typescript, no date, 198 pages

Francois-Xavier Créteaux, Patrick Céleste, *Le Corbusier: 24 rue Nungesser-et-Coli*, École d'architecture de Versailles, Versailles, 1988

Le Corbusier, "La ville radieuse", in *American Architect*, n° 147, November 1935, pp. 16-18

Henri Clouzot, "La ville radieuse", in *Beaux-Arts. Chronique des arts et de la curiosité*, 22 November 1935, p. 3

Jean Alazard, "L'exposition de la cité moderne", in *Travaux publics & bâtiment*, 3 April 1936, pp. 1-2

Raymond Mc Grath, A. C. Frost, H. E. Beckett, *Glass in Architecture and Decoration*, Architectural Press, London, 1937, p. 199

Frederick Gibberd, *The Modern Flat*, Architectural Press, London, 1948 [2nd edition], pp. 102-103

Le Corbusier, *New World of Space*, Reynal & Hitchcock, New York, 1948, p. 117

Le Corbusier, *Creation is a Patient Search*, Praeger, New York, 1960, pp. 107 et 118-119

Marc Emery, *Un siècle d'architecture moderne en France 1850-1950*, Éditions Horizons de France, Paris, 1971, pp. 92-93

Roger Sherwood, *Modern Housing Prototypes*, Harvard University Press, Cambridge-Massachusetts, London, 1978, pp. 83-86

Arthur Rüegg, *Équipement de la maison 1927-1937. Le Corbusier, Pierre Jeanneret, Charlotte Perriand*, personal work records, Fondation Le Corbusier, 1980

Jean-Claude Delorme, Philippe Chair, *L'école de Paris. 10 architectes et leurs immeubles*, Éditions du Moniteur, Paris, 1981, pp. 130-152

Arthur Rüegg, "Le charme discret des objets indiscrets", in *Archithèse*, n° 1, 1985, pp. 41-45

Tim Benton, "Le Corbusier y la promenade architecturale", in *Arquitectura*, nos 264-265, January-April 1987, pp. 38-101 [98-101]

Vittorio Prina, "Itinerario Domus 28: Le Corbusier e Parigi", in *Domus*, n° 687, October 1987

Le Corbusier, *Corbu vu par*, Pierre Mardaga éditeur, Liège, 1987, pp. 49-50

Bertrand Lemoine, Philippe Rivoirard, *L'architecture des années 30*, Délégation à l'Action artistique de la Ville de Paris, Éditions La Manufacture, Paris, 1987, pp. 182-183

Pierre Joly, *Le Corbusier à Paris*, Éditions La Manufacture, Paris, 1987

Robert Doisneau, Jean Petit, *Bonjour Monsieur Le Corbusier*, Hans Grieshaber, Zurich, 1988

Henri Robert-Charrue, "Voyage à Paris", in *Habitation: revue trimestrielle de la section romande de l'Association suisse pour l'habitat*, 61ᵉ année, nos 1-2, January-February 1988, pp. 11-16

Bruno Marchand, "Le Corbusier: les typologies du logement collectif entre les deux guerres. Une études de cas", in *Habitation: revue trimestrielle de la section romande de l'Association suisse pour l'habitat*, 61ᵉ année, n° 4, April 1988, pp. 12-17

Hervé Martin, *Guide de l'architecture moderne à Paris—Guide to Modern Architecture in Paris*, Éditeur Syros-Alternatives, Paris, 1990, p. 227

Maurice Culot, Bruno Foucart, *Boulogne-Billancourt. Ville des temps modernes*, Pierre Mardaga, Liège, 1994, pp. 274-285

Jacques Sbriglio, *Construire dans la ville existante*, in *Le Corbusier: La ville, L'urbanisme. Rencontres des 9 et 10 juin 1995*, Fondation Le Corbusier, Paris, 1995, pp. 73-79

John McKean, "Key Buildings that Continue to Refresh", in *Architects' journal*, vol. 205, n° 23, June 1997, p. 68

Gilles Ragot, Mathilde Dion, *Le Corbusier en France: projets et réalisations*, Le Moniteur, Paris, 1997 [2nd edition], pp. 171-178

Charlotte Perriand, *Une vie de création*, Éditions Odile Jacob, Paris, 1998, pp. 55-56

Arthur Rüegg, *Le Corbusier Moments in the Life of a Great Architect*, Birkhäuser, Boston-Basel-Berlin, 1999

Dominique Lyon, Anriet Denis, Olivier Boissière, *Le Corbusier vivant*, Telleri, Paris, 1999, pp. 88-96

Michael Webb, "Le Corbusier in Paris: Restoring the Legendary Modernist's Private Penthouse", in *Architectural digest*, vol. 56, n° 7, July 1999, pp. 50-58

George H. Marcus, *Le Corbusier. Im inneren der Wohnmaschine*, Schirmer-Mosel, Munich, 2000, pp. 8-17

Eric Lapierre, *Identification d'une ville, architectures de Paris*, Éditions du Pavillons de l'Arsenal-Picard éditeur, Paris, 2002, pp. 100-113

Jacques Barsac, *Charlotte Perriand, un art d'habiter 1903-1959*, Éditions Norma, Paris, 2005, pp. 119-123

Françoise Ducros, *Le Corbusier, l'œuvre plastique*, Édition de la Villette, Paris, 2005, pp. 202-215

Lara Nachtingal, Didier Herman, "Le Corbusier en Île-de-France", in *Connaissance des arts*, n° 632, November 2005, pp. 88-96

Deborah Gans, *The Le Corbusier Guide*, Princeton Architectural Press, New York, 2006, pp. 60-63

André Wogenscky, *Les mains de Le Corbusier*, Éditions du Moniteur, Paris, 2006, pp. 31 and 62

Jacques Sbriglio, *Le Corbusier. Habiter: de la villa Savoye à l'Unité d'habitation de Marseille*, Cité de l'architecture et du Patrimoine, Paris, 2009, pp. 50-51

Eric Lapierre, *Guide d'architecture Paris Pavillon de l'Arsenal 1900-2008*, Éditions du Pavillon de l'Arsenal, Paris, 2009, p. 405

Patrick Moser (ed.), *René Burri. Le Corbusier intime*, exhibition catalogue (Corseaux, Villa Le Lac Le Corbusier, May-October 2011), éd. Castagniééé, Lausanne, 2011

Béatrice Andrieux, Quentin Bajac, Michel Richard, Jacques Sbriglio, *Le Corbusier. Lucien Hervé: contacts*, Éditions du Seuil, Paris, 2011, pp. 27-45

Arthur Rüegg, *Le Corbusier: meubles et intérieurs 1905-1965*, Scheidegger & Spiess, Zurich, 2012, pp. 129-135, 160 and 305-309

Tim Benton, *Le Corbusier. Secret Photographer*, Lars Müller, Zurich, 2013

Jacques Barsac, *Charlotte Perriand: L'œuvre complète*, vol. 1, 1903-1940, Éditions Norma, Paris, 2015, pp. 220-229

ACKNOWLEDGMENTS

The authors wish to thank the FONDATION LE CORBUSIER, who commissioned the research that gave rise to this publication. We thank first and foremost the President of the Foundation, ANTOINE PICON, former Director, MICHEL RICHARD, and Director BRIGITTE BOUVIER for the confidence they placed in us during the project in 2013-2014 and their support for the publishing of this study. We express our sincere thanks also to BÉNÉDICTE GANDINI, architect to the Fondation Le Corbusier, who shared with us her knowledge of the background to restoration of the apartment-studio. Thanks also to ARNAUD DERCELLES and ISABELLE GODINOT for their priceless assistance during archival and iconographic research.

We acknowledge with thanks the many individuals who replied to our questions, shared their accounts and gave us access to their archives:

NATHANAËL ARNOULD Institut National de l'Audiovisuel, Paris, NICOLE BAJOLET-STEINER, BERNARD BAUCHET, FRANÇOISE BÉDOUSSAC Archives de Boulogne-Billancourt, TIM BENTON, SILVIA BERSELLI, MÉLANIE BÉTRISEY Musée de l'Élysée, Lausanne, ANNE-CATHÉRINE BIEDERMANN and ISABELLE ARTAUD Agence photographique de la Réunion des Musées Nationaux et du Grand Palais, Paris, CATHÉRINE BIGOT Saint-Gobain Archives, Blois, PATRICK BONGERS Galerie Louis Carré, Paris, VÉRONIQUE BOONE, BRIAN BRACE TAYLOR (†), CLOTILDE BURRI, GIOVANNA CASTIGLIONI and ANTONELLA GORNATI Fondazione Achille Castiglioni, Milan, JENNIFER CESA, SARAH CHAPALAY Centre d'iconographie, BGE, Genève, SÉBASTIEN CHAUFFOUR, BERTILLE CHEREAU-BENOIST, GIULIA CHIARIOTTI, CATHÉRINE COLEY, MÉLANIE DELAUNE PERRIN, SARAH FRIOUX-SALGAS Musée du quai Branly, Médiathèque, Département Patrimoine et Collections, Paris, FRANÇOIS GOVEN, JACQUES GUBLER, RENATA GUTTMAN Centre Canadien d'Architecture, Montréal, JUDITH HERVÉ NAÏMA KADDOUR Magnum Photos, Paris, YANNICK LACROIX Library and Archives Canada, Ottawa, PIERRE LAGARD (†), CARLOS LOPEZ Bibliothèque de la Ville, La Chaux-de-Fonds, BERNADETTE ODONI and CATHÉRINE MAUDET Archives d'architecture, HES-SO (ex Université de Genève), Genève, GÉRARD MONNIER (†), JUTTA NIEMANN Association Willy Maywald, NICOLAS PATIOU Bridgeman Images, MARGHERITA PELLINO Fondazione Vico Magistretti, Milan, ALEXANDRE RAGOIS Cité de l'architecture & du patrimoine, Archives d'architecture du XXe siècle, Paris, GILLES RAGOT, ROBERT REBUTATO (†), DOMINIQUE RIZZO and LAETITIA BRAQUENIÉ-VIOT Studio Willy Rizzo, Paris, ARTHUR RÜEGG, BRUNO REICHLIN, ISABELLE SADYS Gamma Rapho, Paris, JACQUES SBRIGLIO, JENNY SCHNEIDER Mairie de Boulogne-Billancourt, PHILIPPE SZPIRGLAS and LAURE WEILL Archives Étienne Bertrand Weill, AURÉLIEN VERNANT Frac Centre, Orléans, BRIGITTE VINCENS Bibliothèque Kandinsky, Centre Georges Pompidou, Paris, PETER WILLI, FILINE WAGNER GTA Archiv, ETH, Zurich.

PHOTOGRAPH CREDITS

Numbers refer to pages in the publication, letters to the order of images on the page, from top to bottom and from left to right.

|| RECENT PHOTOGRAPHS || **Franz Graf**: 69b, 69c | **Giulia Marino**: 1st and 4th (top) cover pages, 35a, 38a-b, 39a, 39a-d, 49a-b, 51b, 51d, 68b-c, 69b-c, 73b, 73c, 80, 81b, 81d, 81f-g, 95b, 97b, 99b, 101b-d, 102b, 104c, 105b-d, 118b-d, 119a-b, 120b, 121a-e, 122b, 123a-b, 124a, 125a-d, 133c, 136b, 136d, 137b-e, 138b, 139c, 139e, 139g, 141b, 141d, 143c, 146b, 146d, 147a-d, 148c, 152a-c, 153b, 155f, 157d, 158f, 159d, 160a-d, 161a-c, 163a, 163c-d, 172b, 173b, 176b-c, 177b, 179b, 179d | **Claudio Merlini**: 163b | **Patrick Moser**: 179a | **Stephan Rutishauser**: 105a || ARCHIVES OF SPECIFIC INSTITUTIONS || **Fondation Le Corbusier**, Paris: 14, 15a-b, 16a, 18a-f, 19a-g, 20a-c, 21a-d, 22b-e, 23a-f, 24, 25a-c, 27a-c, 28, 29a-b, 33a, 33c-f, 34a-f, 35b, 36a-b, 37a-b, 40, 41a-c, 42, 43b-c, 44a-b, 46a-b, 47a-c, 48, 51c, 52a, 54a-b, 55a, 55d, 56, 57a, 57c, 58a, 59a, 61a, 64a, 65a-b, 66a-e, 69a, 78a-b, 79, 81a, 81c, 81e, 82, 86c, 87, 88a-c, 90a-c, 92a-b, 93a, 93c, 93f-g, 94, 95a, 96, 98, 100a-c, 108-109, 111a-d, 114, 115a-b, 118a, 120a, 126-127, 133a, 134, 135a-b, 136a, 137a, 139a, 139d, 139f, 140a, 140d, 142, 143b, 145a-d, 146a, 146c, 148a-b, 149b, 150, 154, 155b-d, 156d, 157a-c, 158b-d, 159b, 162, 168, 169b, 169d, 174a-b, 174d, 175a-f, 194, 198; **Paul Almasy**: 130-131; **Lucien Hervé**: 26b, 45a-b, 72b, 88d,

89a, 91a, 93b, 93d, 97a, 149c, 178; **Willy Maywald**: 85; **Olivier Martin Gambier**: 69d, 139b, 179c; **Albin Salaün**: 22a, 27d, 28, 29-a-b, 62, 63b, 65c; **Paul Almasy, Keystone ATS**: cover, 193; **André Steiner**: 155a; **André Villers**: 90d; **Peter Willi**: 52b, 71a-b, 110, 138a | **Archives de l'Institut gta, ETH, Zurich; fonds Alfred Roth**: 26a; **fonds Bernard Hoesli**: 102a | **Archives d'architecture HES-SO, Genève, fonds Bruno Reichlin**: 153a | **Centre Georges Pompidou, MNAM-CCI Bibliothèque Kandinsky, Dist. RMN-Grand Palais, Fonds Cardot et Joly**: 98b, 159c; **André Steiner**: 63c, **Gisèle Freund**: 196-197 | **Fondazione Achille Castiglioni, Milan**: 177a **|| PRIVATE ARCHIVES ||** **Archives René Burri, Magnum, Paris**: 99, 101a, 103, 133b, 149e, 158a, 164-165, 169e, 174c, 179-180, 191, 200 | **Atelier Robert Doisneau, Gamma Rapho, Paris**: 12-13, 45, 61c, 64c, 74-75, 84a-b, 156a, 166-167, 169a, 186 | **Gamma Rapho, Paris**: 17b, 187; **Yousuf Karsh**: 104a | **Archives Étienne Bertrand Weill, Paris**: 72a | **Archives Michel Sima, Rue-des-Archives, Bridgemann Images, Paris**: 31, 195 | **Studio Willy Rizzo, Paris**: 51a, 53, 76-77, 83b, 89b-c, 91b, 93e, 106-107, 149a, 149d, 156c, 169f, 172a, 173a, 188-189, 190a, 190b (photographs on permanent display at Studio Willy Rizzo) | **Archives Michael Ochs**: 192 | **Arthur Rüegg**: 55b-c, 68a, 113c, 140b, 153c | **Bernard Bauchet**: 116a-b, 117a, 122a, 122c-d, 124b-d, 141a, 141c, 155e | Brian Brace Taylor: 104b | **Bertille Chereau-Benoist**: 113b **|| EXTRACTS FROM PUBLICATIONS ||** *L'Architecture d'aujourd'hui*, n° 6, 1933: 16b | *L'Architecture d'aujourd'hui*, n° 5, 1934: 16c | *Le Corbusier et Pierre Jeanneret. Œuvre complète. 1929-1934*, 1967, [1935]: 21, 43a, 55e, 57b, 58b, 61b, 63a, 64b, 70, 72a, 73a, 140c | *Le Corbusier et Pierre Jeanneret. Œuvre complète. 1934-1938*, 2015, [1946]: 33b | *Le Corbusier et Pierre Jeanneret, Encyclopédie de l'architecture. Constructions modernes*, 7e série, Éditions Albert Morancé, 1937, n.p.: 17, 27e, 30a-b, 32, 136c | *Le Corbusier, Clavier Salubra*, Bâle, 1931: 59b | Felix H. Man, *Eight European Artists*, William Heinemann, 1953: 67, 156b, 159a, 169c | Ivan Zaknic, *Le Corbusier. Pavillon suisse*, Birkhäuser, 2004: 73d | María Isabel Navarro Segura, Enrique Gramell, Sophie Bernard, *Le Corbusier expose*, Silvana editoriale, 2011: 83a | *Le Corbusier, Le Modulor*, Éditions L'Architecture d'aujourd'hui, 1950: 86a-b | A+U Architecture and Urbanism, n° 149, 1983: 112, 113a, 158e | Dominique Lyon, *Le Corbusier vivant*, Telleri, 1999: 117b | Danièle Pauly (ed.), *Le Corbusier et la Méditerranée*, Parenthèses, 1987: 143a |

For the work of Le Corbusier © 2017, FLC ProLitteris, Zurich.

The authors have given the names of photographs as far possible from the information in their possession. They would be pleased to hear from persons concerned of any error or omission.

10 nov 48.

C'était une très belle lettre, mais cette sacrée petite chienne a tout gâté :

on a pu la réinspirer ! Mais on a eu chaud !

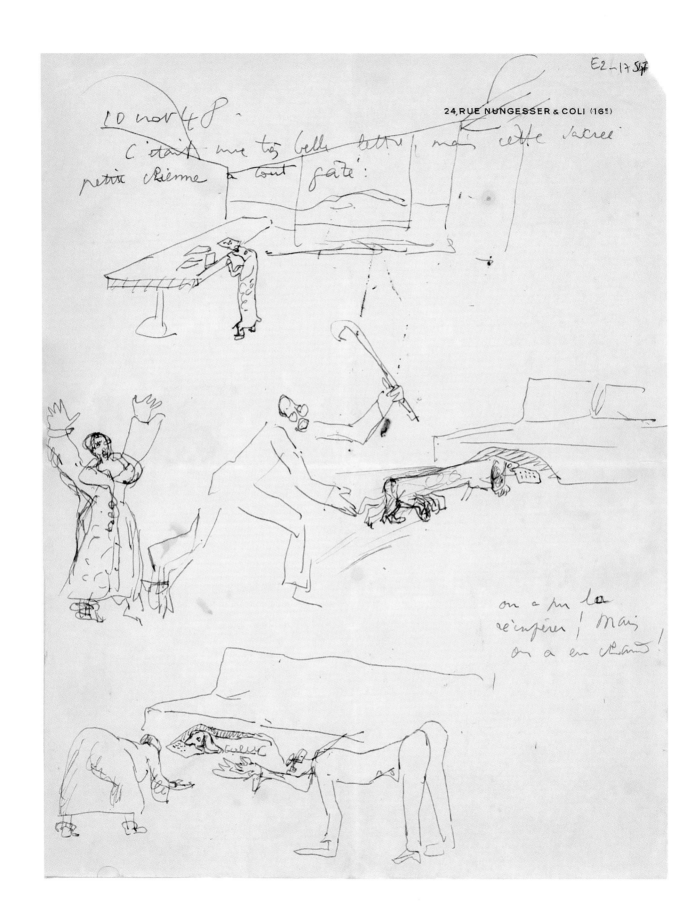